Debra's Natural Gourmet Cookbook

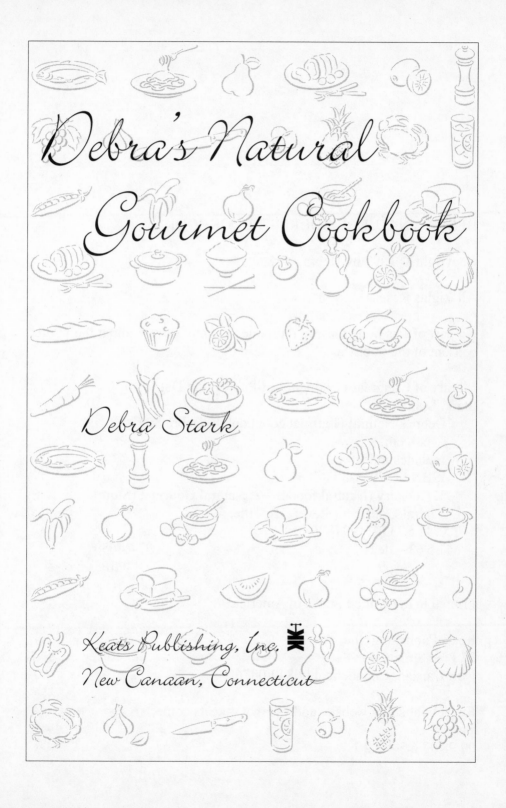

Debra's Natural Gourmet Cookbook

Debra Stark

Keats Publishing, Inc.
New Canaan, Connecticut

DEBRA'S NATURAL GOURMET COOKBOOK

Library of Congress Cataloging-in-Publication Data
Stark, Debra.
    Debra's Natural Gourmet cookbook / Debra Stark.
        p.   cm.
    Includes index.
    ISBN 0-87983-803-5
    1. Cookery (Natural foods)   2. Natural Gourmet (Store)
    I. Natural Gourmet (Store)   II. Title.
    TX741.S733   1997
    641.5'63—dc21   97-24650
                                                         CIP

Printed in the United States of America

Keats Publishing, Inc.
27 Pine Street (Box 876)
New Canaan, Connecticut 06840-0876

Keats Publishing website address: www.keats.com

99 98 97 6 5 4 3 2 1

Acknowledgments

A special thanks to Mary Kadlik, who remained calm and reined me in when I suggested turnips and radishes might make a good soup! To all the kitchen crew at Debra's Natural Gourmet, who didn't fuss when handed new recipes to try. And to our customers, who gladly ate everything.

Thanks to the rest of the staff, who put up with me when I left them stranded so I could work on the book. Thanks especially to Hannah Bitterman, Kathleen Larkin, Page Loeser, Audrey Nolan, Grace Pintabona, Cynthia Price and Susanne Russo.

Thanks to Claudia Vestal for typing, editing, sticking her two cents in and keeping me on track. Thanks to Lynn Zipf, who came in at the last minute and pointed out I needed to tell people how to use strawberry cream once it was made!

To Susan E. Davis, my editor at Keats Publishing, who made me laugh and makes me sound better than I do, thank you, thank you. To everyone at Keats, thanks for your support along the way.

My love, again, to my family, who keep telling me to slow down and stop taking on so many projects. I tell them it's all to do with food. They roll their eyes.

Contents

Introduction

Balance and harmony are key in nature and critical to *our* health and happiness. We need balance and harmony not only in our lives, but in the food we eat. Food has to satisfy all the senses—to taste great, please the eye and smell wonderful. Great food has to nourish body and soul! If it doesn't, we're depriving ourselves of the pleasure of food, and we're not feeding our bodies so they can regenerate, heal and reach optimal health.

Most cookbooks address body or soul, but not both. Remember the cookbook with the killer chocolate cake or the one with the string bean "meatloaf"? Is it possible to combine pleasure with health? Of course, it is!

In my first cookbook, *'Round-the-World-Cooking at The Natural Gourmet* (Keats, 1994), I did combine body and soul, although not explicitly. I didn't state that foods that fight fatigue are potassium- and magnesium-rich foods like beans, potatoes and leafy green vegetables. Nor did I say iron-rich foods like blackstrap molasses, dried apricots or seaweed should be eaten if you're feeling run down and tired.

People who bought *'Round-the-World-Cooking at The Natural Gourmet* call or write letters letting me know they love the recipes and that the results are delicious. They rave about how easy the recipes are to follow. What they don't say is how hard it may have been for them to start to use whole foods. Nor do they tell me what motivated them to eat differently.

Customers in our store, Debra's Natural Gourmet in Concord, Massachusetts, talk about these things all the time. They ask questions such as "Why is whole wheat flour better than white flour?" "How should I store it?" "How can I use it?" "Will my family hate it?" "What is quinoa?"

They tell us they felt compelled to learn about natural foods because of a health problem in the family or because they are concerned about environmental toxins and stress and their effects on our immune systems.

We have a love-hate relationship with food in this country. Although we know natural is better, we load our shopping carts with junk food because we're afraid of and don't know how to use natural foods. We believe if something is good for us it must taste awful! To most people, natural means a plateful of beans topped with sprouts! When we do turn to natural foods, it's often as a last resort because someone is ill. We know what we put into our mouths can make a difference in our health, but we don't know how to make dietary changes. We often feel insecure or defensive about our food choices. Half the time we're afraid we're doing things wrong; the other half we're afraid that should tofu touch our lips, we'll never again eat chocolate mousse!

I decided to take a new tack with this book. Not only are recipes yummy, easy to prepare and nourishing for the soul and bod, but I've included bits of information like brown rice is high in B vitamins and tofu contains plant estrogens which may help prevent breast and prostate cancer. The type of information I had fun learning together with customers at Debra's Natural Gourmet!

May you find these "tidbits" as interesting as we all do, and may you and yours enjoy what you eat and achieve balance and harmony. May our motto "Eat Well, Be Happy!" become a part of your lives.

About the Tidbits

I opened Debra's Natural Gourmet in October 1989 because I wanted to cook and be able to sell what I made! A funny thing happened along the way. People bought our terrific food but kept asking how we were able to make soups without fat, were almonds *really* okay to eat, were they getting enough protein and how could they make beans more digestible. Learning became an adventure for us all and "tidbits" were born!

I'm not a doctor and have no formal training in food or nutrition. I was lucky to have been brought up on natural foods and natural medicines by a mother who thought for herself. She taught me that each of us can take charge of our own health and make a difference.

Some of the books we use as general reference in our store and which you might enjoy reading are listed here:

Cooking for Healthy Healing by Linda Rector-Page
Food: Your Miracle Medicine by Jean Carper
4001 Food Facts by Myles H. Bader
Healing with Whole Foods by Paul Pitchford
Healthy Healing by Linda Rector-Page
The Neal's Yard Bakery Wholefood Cookbook by Rachel Haigh
Prescription for Nutritional Healing by Phyllis & James Balch
Rx Prescription for Cooking and Dietary Wellness by Phyllis & James Balch
The Whole Food Bible by Christopher Kilham

Of course, there are zillions of other great books out there. And there are wonderful magazines like *Natural Health* and *Vegetarian Health,* which offer a wealth of knowledge. *Read. Learn. Be empowered!*

Plea for Organic

Simply put: organic food means higher nutrient values, no poisons and less harm to our planet.

The use of chemical fertilizers has resulted in a decrease in nutrients found in foods. Commercially grown carrots tested from all over the country were found to be almost devoid of nutrients. And the protein content of commercially grown grains has declined 11 percent over a 10-year period. The U.S. Department of Agriculture is looking into deficiencies of trace minerals in the food needed to sustain life because farmers replace only those minerals necessary for crop growth. As an example, overuse of potash is creating magnesium deficiencies. We need magnesium to utilize calcium and to relax our muscles.

Many pesticides approved for use by the Environmental Protection Agency (EPA) were registered before research linking these chemicals to cancer and other diseases had been established. Now the EPA considers 60 percent of all herbicides, 90 percent of all fungicides and 30 percent of all insecticides carcinogenic. These are poisons designed to kill living organisms. Aren't we living organisms, too? Because of our size, pesticides don't kill us outright or immediately. I believe they do affect us long-term and are responsible in part for skyrocketing increases in cancers and other modern illnesses.

Although organic food many seem more expensive, conventional food prices don't reflect hidden costs borne by all taxpayers (that's you and me), including the more than $74 million in federal subsidies, pesticide regulation and testing, hazardous waste disposal and cleanup, environmental damage, increased medical health care costs due to exposure to carcinogens and the harm done to farm workers exposed to those chemicals. If you add these real costs up, a head of commercially grown lettuce costs us over $3.

Buy organic when you can. Apart from economic and environmental reasons to eat organic, none of us want anyone else we know to get cancer. Nor do we want to use pesticides and herbicides as a means of birth control; studies show that pesticides and herbicides affect sperm counts and sperm motility in men. Someone said, "Real men eat organic!"

What You Need to Know

In this section I discuss various basic things about cooking with foods found in natural food stores—substances like tahini and tamari or brands like Fakin' Bacon or Nayonnaise—which may be new or strange to you. I hope the sentence or two here about each and the recipes in the book will make you eager to try them until they become part of your repertoire in the kitchen! At the end of the book in Miscellaneous, you'll find a listing of twelve favorite superfoods.

Bragg's Liquid Aminos and Dr. Bronner's Mineral Boullion: These liquid concoctions have been around since I was a little girl. They both taste salty and can be used to season food. Although they're not low in sodium, they do contain less than salt and are rich in minerals and protein. One spa I went to put out Bragg's and hot water to sip as an afternoon pick-me-up. Bragg's is made from soybeans and water only. Dr. Bronner's contains everything but the kitchen sink: ingredients like soy beans, molasses, peppermint and dulse.

Brewer's Yeast: Also called nutritional yeast, it's an excellent source of protein and B vitamins. It's one of the best ways to boost my immune system and energy when I am stressed. My favorite brand is Lewis Laboratories (as I've said elsewhere in the book). The taste is nice because it's the only nutritional yeast grown on sugar beets.

Brewer's yeast is not the same as candida albicans yeast. Theories differ on whether or not you can use it if you have candida.

Fakin' Bacon: This tempeh (soy) vegetarian version of bacon tastes amazingly like the real thing!

Flax Seed Oil: It's the richest source of omega-3 essential fatty acids and has good amounts of omega-6 essential fatty acids, too. Flax seed oil is not good to bake or cook with, but it's excellent as part of a salad dressing or to blend with cottage cheese, yogurt or tofu. If you suffer from flaky skin in the winter, try a tablespoonful or two of flax seed oil daily!

Grains: Except for bulgur and couscous, grains are cooked by bringing the correct amount of cooking liquid to a boil in a pot large enough to accommodate the increase in volume of the grain after cooking. (Don't forget to use up that vegetable stock!) Add grain to boiling liquid, stir once, allow liquid to return to boiling, turn heat down low, cover pot and simmer grain until soft. Don't stir grains after they come to a boil because too much stirring makes them gummy. For fluffier grains, stir with a fork after grain is cooked and let sit, covered, for an additional 10 minutes.

Grain	Amount of Boiling Water to Grain	Cooking Time (minutes)
Amaranth	3 to 1	20–25
Barley, hulled	3 to 1	60–90
Barley, pearled	2 to 1	45
Buckwheat	2 to 1	15–20
Bulgur	1 to 1	Pour boiling water over, let sit 15–20, until all water absorbed
Cornmeal	3 to 1	20–25
Couscous	1 to 1	Pour boiling water over, let sit 15–20, until all water absorbed
Millet	2½ to 1	25–30
Oats, rolled	2 to 1	20–30
Oats, steel cut	3 to 1	30
Quinoa	2 to 1	10
Rice, brown	2 to 1	45
Rice, wild	2 to 1	45–60

An easy way to cook rice is to put it into a pot with the appropriate amount of water, bring water to a boil, lower heat, cover pot and simmer until rice is done. Again, don't stir during cooking process. Should your rice be sticky, stir in several spoonfuls of soy granules. Let pot stand covered for 10 minutes. Not only will the granules absorb excess moisture, but they'll give rice a nutty flavor and gourmet look.

Add salt to grains at the end so as not to retard the cooking process.

Grating Pecorino Romano Cheese: This flavorful sheep's milk cheese can be tolerated well by many people who can't have dairy products. To grate, use the steel blade of a food processor, and place Romano cut into 1- to 2-inch cubes in the workbowl. Grate about 2 cups at a time. Turn machine on and off several times and then let it run until cheese is grated. Grate more than you need for a particular recipe. Store extra in the refrigerator or freezer.

Greasing: Use a thin film of half soya liquid lecithin and half vegetable oil or butter. Liquid lecithin alone is too thick to spread easily. Diluting with oil works like magic. Always keep a jar of the lecithin/oil mixture on hand in the cupboard to grease with.

To grease, use a pastry brush to spread mixture. Natural flours tend to stick to pans, but they won't if you grease with this mixture. Baked goods turn out of pans in a snap!

Legumes (peas and beans): Always sort and rinse before use to eliminate stones and debris. The amount of water needed for cooking legumes is generally 3 to 4 times their volume, or 2 inches above beans, with more boiling water added as necessary during cooking. Refer to the chart below for cooking. Usually 1 pound dry beans = 2 cups dry = 4–5 cups cooked. You can substitute canned beans in any recipe. Drain and rinse first.

Don't soak beans when using a pressure cooker. *Nor is it necessary when cooking beans in a standard pot.* A lazy way to cook beans is to simply bring them to a boil uncovered and boil vigorously for 10 minutes to release the gases. Then cover and simmer until soft.

Legumes (dried)	Soaking Time (hours)	Regular Cooking Time (hours)	Pressure Cooking Time (minutes)
Adzuki beans	3–4	1	15
Black-eyed peas	8–12	1½	10–15
Black turtle beans	3–4	1	10–15
Cannellini beans	8–12	1½	20
Chick-peas	8–12	3	25
Kidney beans	8–12	1½–2	20
Lentils, brown	None	⅓	(Not applicable)
Lentils, red	None	¼	(Not applicable)
Lima beans	4–8	1½	20

Mung beans	4–8	¾	10
Navy beans	8–12	1½	20
Pinto beans	8–12	1½	20
Soy beans	8–12	3	50
Split peas, green	None	1–1½	(Not applicable)
Split peas, yellow	None	1½	(Not applicable)

Add a piece of seaweed called "kombu" to the beans while they cook. It helps break down the part of the bean which is hard for us to digest and which causes gas. Add salt or acidic ingredients, such as tomatoes, when legumes are almost finished cooking. Adding them during cooking toughens the beans.

Once cooked and cooled, legumes may be kept for several days in the refrigerator or frozen. To freeze, cool, pack into jars and leave ½ inch at the top for expansion during freezing.

Dried legumes, stored away from sunlight and moisture, last for years. Beans excavated from Incan temples were capable of germination!

Milks: You can use cow's milk or rice, soy or oat milk interchangeably in recipes. Although rice, soy and oat milks can be made at home, for the sake of convenience, all are available on the shelves of natural food stores and some supermarkets are beginning to stock them. For soups, always use fresh sweet milk. In baked goods where there is baking powder or baking soda, soured milk (what most people call spoiled and pour down the drain) works best. It makes baked goods lighter. There is no health danger from using sour milks, nor will you taste the sourness in the finished product.

Nayonnaise: This brand of mayo is made from soy beans and has no eggs. Not only do you get more of those phyto (plant) estrogens which are said to be so good at helping prevent breast and prostate cancer, but you get less calories, much less fat and great taste, too. Nayonnaise was the only soy mayo on the market for years, but that has changed and there are now other similar products. Just read the ingredients to make sure you're getting nothing artificial and no sugar!

Oils: Olive, sesame and canola oils are flavorful. Because they are digested more slowly than other foods, oils help create a feeling of satiety. Olive and sesame are the least processed of oils and are said not to require refrigeration. However, refrigerate if you don't use them quickly after opening. Refrigerate all other oils.

Organic Produce and Ingredients: Use organic products whenever possible, even though individual recipes in this cookbook do not specify their use. Nutrient levels in food grown organically, without pesticides and herbicides, are greater than in commercially grown foods.

Salt: Always use sea salt.

Seeds: Sesame seeds are always brown and unhulled. Sunflower and pumpkin seeds are hulled.

Sucanat: This is a brand name for organically grown sugar cane which is pressed and the juice sun-dried. No refinement whatsoever—nothing removed, nothing heated, nothing added. Sucanat does not give me the shakes the way honey sometimes does. By the time this book is printed, it's likely other companies will be producing sweeteners like Sucanat. It's also possible Sucanat will not always be organically grown sugar cane.

Sweeteners: No sweetener can be eaten with impunity, and their use is often debated. We rely primarily upon honey or maple syrup for sweetening. Other options are fruit juice concentrate, rice syrup, barley malt and date sugar (made from pulverized dates). The Food and Drug Administration has let back into this country a South American herb called Stevia, which is much sweeter than sugar. It's noncaloric and is used in other countries in diet soft drinks.

Tahini: This sesame paste is made from hulled toasted sesame seeds. Sesame butter is made from unhulled sesame seeds. Use interchangeably. Both are wonderful sources of calcium and protein.

Tamari and Shoyu Soy Sauces: These fermented soy bean liquids rise to the top when miso is made. Tamari and shoyu are processed without chemicals, unlike other soy sauces, and are rich in flavor. Tamari used to be wheat free, while shoyu was not. This is no longer the case, so if you are allergic to wheat, be sure to read labels.

Appetizers

Appetizers are those little things you feed people while waiting for everyone to arrive or while everyone waits for the main event! Appetizers whet the appetite. They make us say "yummm."

Appetizers have grown up. They're more than pigs-in-a-blanket and cheese balls. I still love simple appetizers like Humous and Babaganoush. But those recipes are in my first book. Use them along with Caponata Tempeh and Garlicky Potato Almond Dip that you'll find on the following pages.

Stuffed Baguettes

This sauce makes a great stuffing for baguettes, which are filled ahead of time and sliced for serving. It also works well in pita bread or as a topping for goat cheese, rice, beans, poultry or fish.

Not only do I love olives, but I'm convinced the reason Americans aren't passionate about olives is that we have mostly been exposed to the awful, treated, tasteless things that sit in cans on supermarket shelves or languish on salad bars. Like olive oils, there's a world of wonderful olives out there waiting to be tasted!

Makes about 6 cups

1 or 2 whole-grain baguettes
1 7-ounce jar roasted red bell
   peppers, drained and coarsely
   chopped
8 cloves garlic, minced
¼ cup capers, drained
½ cup pitted French green olives,
   coarsely chopped

½ cup pitted kalamata olives,
   coarsely chopped
1 small zucchini, minced
1 small yellow squash, minced
2 cups tomatoes, diced
pepper to taste

Combine all ingredients, except baguette, in a mixing bowl.

Cut baguette in half. (I like Baldwin Hills or The Baker because they are whole grain.) Scoop out some of the insides to make indentation for vegetable mixture. Fill and push bread together. Wrap tightly with plastic wrap. Vegetable juices will soak into bread as it sits, so let it sit a few hours.

Unwrap and slice to serve.

Caponata Tempeh

Tempeh is fermented soybeans which are soaked, boiled, treated with a fungus, wrapped in banana leaves and left to ferment. Unsavory sounding, tempeh has a rich flavor and is a strong antibiotic. Eating it is another way to introduce soy into your diet.

Serves 4   *Bake at 425°*

1 eggplant, about 1¼ pounds
2 zucchini
¼ cup olive oil
2 tablespoons olive oil
1 red onion, minced
4 cloves garlic, minced
1 red bell pepper, diced
1 green bell pepper, diced
1 yellow bell pepper, diced

5.5-ounce package barbecue
   flavor tempeh
1 cup tomato sauce
2 tablespoons rice vinegar or red
   wine vinegar
salt and pepper to taste
4 scallions, trimmed and sliced
   to garnish

Preheat oven to 425°.

Quarter eggplant with skin on and slice ½ inch thick. Quarter and slice zucchini the same thickness. Brush both with ¼ cup olive oil and spread on cookie sheets. Bake for 30 minutes. Take trays out of oven and let cool slightly.

Meanwhile, in a pot, saute onion, garlic and peppers with remaining olive oil. When vegetables are soft and slightly browned, about 7 minutes, add tempeh, tomato sauce and vinegar. Simmer another 5 minutes or so until tempeh is heated through.

In a large mixing bowl, toss together eggplant, zucchini and pepper tempeh sauce gently with a rubber spatula. Adjust seasoning to taste.

Garnish with scallions and serve.

Note: *Use other flavors of tempeh if you prefer.*

Middle Eastern Zucchini Pancakes

This makes a delectable, savory appetizer! Walnuts are native to the Middle East and, like many other nuts, contain linoleic acid which helps lower cholesterol. Recent studies indicate the fat in walnuts and almonds may prevent cancer.

Makes about 18

1 pound zucchini, coarsely
   grated
2 bunches scallions, minced
4 eggs
½ cup whole wheat pastry flour
1 teaspoon oregano
1 teaspoon basil
1 teaspoon tarragon

½ teaspoon thyme
½ teaspoon dill weed
½ teaspoon pepper
½ cup crumbled feta or
   goat cheese
1 cup chopped walnuts
olive oil for sauteing

Combine all ingredients, except olive oil. (You can use a food processor to grate the zucchini or grate the old-fashioned way by hand.) Gently warm olive oil in a large skillet. Drop batter by heaping tablespoonfuls into skillet. Saute until pancakes are golden brown, about 3 minutes per side.

As each batch is done, transfer to cookie sheet in a 300° oven. Keep warm until ready to serve and serve hot!

Variations: You can substitute pine nuts for walnuts, but I like walnuts because they are a wonderful source of essential fatty acids as well as being yummy. You can also use spelt flour if you are allergic to wheat.

Stuffed Mushrooms
with Walnuts

The nice thing about this appetizer is that it can be prepared early in the day to serve that evening. Mushrooms are edible fungi! They contain small amounts of valuable nutrients and add a subtle flavor to any dish. According to Chinese medicine, common mushrooms are also said to reduce "heat toxins" that come from eating meat.

Makes about 30 mushrooms

1½ pounds large mushrooms, cleaned	¼ cup ricotta cheese
4 cloves garlic, minced	¼ cup feta cheese
½ cup lemon juice	⅓ cup fresh basil
2 cups water	2 tablespoons olive oil
1 teaspoon salt	½ cup walnuts, chopped
	salt and pepper to taste

Remove stalks of mushrooms. Place garlic, lemon juice, water and salt in a large saucepan. Bring liquid to a boil. Add mushrooms and simmer over low heat for 5 minutes. Drain, but save liquid for soup or freeze for future poaching.

Using the steel blade of a food processor and quick on/off turns, combine ricotta, feta, basil and olive oil. Add walnuts and process so they are chopped, but not pureed. Spoon stuffing into small bowl and add salt and pepper to taste.

Stuff mushroom caps with filling so the stuffing is level rather than heaped, or mushrooms will be overwhelmed by flavors of the filling.

Serve at room temperature drizzled with a little olive oil or heat in 350° oven for 5–10 minutes and serve warm.

Potato Tamales with Black Beans and Chard

This makes a great summer appetizer when you can save those corn husks. It's simple to make but gives the impression you took time to fuss. You'll be serving up plenty of protein, fiber and complex carbs, too, with the combination of potatoes, cornmeal and beans.

Makes 8

1 pound unpeeled boiling
   potatoes, steamed until tender
1 cup olive oil
1 cup masa harina or fine
   cornmeal
½ teaspoon salt
½ teaspoon cinnamon
½ teaspoon cloves

1 teaspoon chili powder
1 teaspoon salt
1 small onion, minced
8 cloves garlic, minced
2 small chiles, minced
2 cups cooked black beans
1 large bunch chard, chopped
8 corn husks, softened in water

When potatoes are soft, mash, skins and all. Add remaining ingredients, except husks, and stir until well-mixed and fairly smooth. You can mash beans or leave them whole, whichever you prefer. Personally, I like the difference in texture when the beans are left whole.

Place ½ cup mixture in center of each husk. Fold in long sides, then ends. Tie with a piece of string or corn husk torn into a ribbon. Arrange seam side down on rack in steamer. Cover and steam over high heat until filling is solid, about 30 minutes.

Serve with salsa on the side.

Note: *Of course, you can add cheese to this appetizer if you choose!*

Garlicky Potato Almond Dip

Don't we all love to dip and nibble? Here's a dip that is a change from humus or other bean dips.

Almonds have the highest calcium content of all nuts and are also high in protein and vitamin B2. They are said to relieve lung conditions like coughs and asthma.

Makes 2 cups

1 large unpeeled potato
½ cup almonds, toasted
6 garlic cloves
¼ cup lemon juice, *optional*

¼ cup olive oil
salt and pepper to taste
pinch nutmeg

Steam potato in a little water until tender, about 10 minutes. Drain and cool. (Always steam vegetables in a cup or two of water, no more. Drink the liquid or save it for soups or for cooking rice. It's too nutritious to pour down the sink!)

Using the steel blade of a food processor, blend ingredients. Don't puree, as you want some texture from almonds. Adjust seasoning to taste.

Serve at room temperature with vegetables like carrot and celery sticks or pitas for dipping.

Note: *Potato is considered a nourishing food if eaten with its skin. Just scrub potatoes—never peel!*

Sweet and Spicy Vegetable Sauce

Sweet potatoes are rich in beta carotene and high in fiber. The Center for Science in the Public Interest rates them second of all vegetables in terms of overall nutrient content. Don't peel them so you won't lose any nutrients!

Garlic was used in Ancient Egypt to build strength. Today we know it lowers serum cholesterol and blood pressure and helps prevent heart attacks and stroke. I use a lot of garlic.

Makes about 6–8 cups sauce

2 medium sweet potatoes, cubed
1 cup water
2 tablespoons olive oil
1 onion, minced
2 green peppers, minced
2 celery ribs, chopped

6 cloves garlic, minced
2-inch piece of ginger, minced
¼ teaspoon allspice
4 cups diced tomatoes
salt and pepper to taste

Steam sweet potato cubes in a cup of water until tender, about 5 minutes. Drain and puree using the steel blade of a food processor and quick on/off turns. Or mash like you would white potatoes using a potato masher.

Gently warm olive oil in a skillet. Add onion, pepper, celery, garlic, ginger and allspice to skillet. Stir to coat and saute until fragrant and vegetables begin to brown, about 5 minutes.

Add tomatoes and bring mixture to a boil. Reduce heat to low and simmer for 5 minutes. Stir in sweet potatoes and season to taste. Spoon into bowl and serve sauce with vegetable dippers or corn chips.

Note: *This sauce makes a terrific topping for couscous or beans, too!*

Red Bean Puree and Wilted Spinach

Spinach is thought to have originated in Persia. It is high in iron, calcium and magnesium and builds good blood. It won't constipate you like iron tablets doctors prescribe!

Serves 6

1 cup red beans
6 tablespoons olive oil
6 cloves garlic
salt and pepper to taste
2 tablespoons olive oil
2 cloves garlic

6 slices whole grain sourdough bread
8 cups spinach, coarsely chopped
2 tablespoons olive oil
2 tablespoons lemon juice

Sort beans, checking carefully for stones. Wash and cook until soft (review directions for cooking beans in What You Need to Know in front of cookbook). Drain beans and using the steel blade of a food processor, puree together with 6 tablespoons olive oil, 6 cloves garlic and salt and pepper to taste. Spoon puree into a bowl.

In same processor, blend 2 tablespoons olive oil and 2 cloves garlic. Brush mixture on bread slices. Grill or broil until bread is lightly browned on both sides, a few minutes per side.

While bread is in oven or on grill, wash spinach. Gently warm remaining 2 tablespoons olive oil in a large skillet. Add greens and cook for a few minutes. Sprinkle lemon over spinach and cook until wilted. Drain.

To serve, spread bean mixture over bread and top with greens. This is messy to eat but worth every bite.

Chick-Peas Masala

Ghee is clarified butter, or butter with milk solids removed. Unlike butter, ghee can be heated to a high temperature without burning, which makes it suitable for sauteing. Ghee is used a lot in Indian cooking and leaves food crispy, dry and light. It is said to heal gastrointestinal inflammations such as ulcers and colitis.

Serves 8 as an appetizer

2 cups chick-peas
½ cup ghee
1 onion, minced
8 cloves garlic, minced
1 tablespoon fresh ginger, grated
1 cup tomatoes, diced
½ teaspoon ground coriander
½ teaspoon chili powder

½ teaspoon ground cumin
1 teaspoon garam masala
1 tablespoon fresh cilantro, minced
½ cup mango juice
salt and pepper to taste
cilantro to garnish

Sort chick-peas, checking carefully for any stones. Wash and cook until tender (review directions for cooking beans in What You Need to Know in front of cookbook).

Gently warm ghee in skillet and saute onion, garlic and ginger until onion is translucent, about 5 minutes.

Add remaining ingredients and simmer, stirring from time to time, until liquid is mostly gone, about 15 minutes. Add cooked chick-peas. Cover and simmer over low heat for about 10 minutes to give chick-peas the chance to absorb flavors. If necessary, drain off liquid. Add salt and pepper to taste.

To serve, spoon into bowl and garnish with cilantro. Serve with pappadums, pita or endive leaves firm enough to scoop some up.

Tofu Guacamole

I love avocadoes because they taste good and contain the good fat (essential fatty acids needed for the health of every cell in our bodies) that makes hair and skin sleek, silky smooth and healthy. By adding tofu, we're adding protein to guacamole as well as cancer-preventing plant estrogens. Also, garlic appears to lift the mood and is a good cold medication.

Makes 5–6 cups

1–2 pounds soft tofu
4 ripe avocadoes, peeled, pitted
and mashed
6 cloves garlic, minced or
pressed with garlic press

2–4 tablespoons lemon juice
2 cups tomatoes, diced
salt and pepper to taste

Mash all ingredients together. Taste and adjust seasoning. (If you like a smoother guacamole, blend using the steel blade of a food processor.)

Serve with vegetable dippers or corn chips. Makes a pretty combination with blue corn chips.

Serving Suggestion: *This makes a terrific filling for pita bread sandwiches, with some sprouts thrown in for lively interest and texture. If you like your guacamole spicy, add a pinch of cayenne or mince a jalapeno pepper and toss in.*

Split Pea Puree

Split peas, both yellow and green, cook quickly and lose their shape when cooked. They're full of fiber and have more zinc than any other bean or pea. Without zinc, wounds won't heal.

More studies have been done on garlic than on any other food. Mice exposed to chemical pollutants and then fed garlic developed 75 percent fewer tumors than mice exposed to the same pollutants and fed no garlic.

Makes 4–5 cups

¼ cup olive oil
6 cloves garlic, minced
7 cups water

2 cups split peas
salt and pepper to taste
2 tablespoons capers

Gently warm oil in a large pan. Add garlic and saute for a minute or two. Add water and split peas. Bring to a boil. Reduce heat, cover and simmer for about 50 minutes. Stir occasionally. Peas should be very soft.

Uncover and simmer until thick, creamy and reduced to about 4½ cups, about an hour. Stir often. Season with salt and pepper.

Cool to room temperature and stir in capers. Serve with vegetable dippers, pitas or crisp crackers.

Spicy Dilly Beans

You can use this mixture to pickle almost any vegetable. The beauty of it is that you don't have to sterilize or seal. And whatever you pickle will stay fresh in your frig for at least a month and still be crunchy and delicious.

Green beans have been found to promote normal function of liver and pancreas.

Makes 3 quart jars

12 cups green beans, untrimmed
2 cups water
1¾ cups apple cider vinegar
8 garlic cloves
1½ tablespoons coarse salt

1 tablespoon pickling spice
1½ teaspoons dill seeds
½ teaspoon crushed red pepper
1½ cups fresh dill sprigs,
** coarsely chopped**

Combine pickling ingredients, except dill sprigs, in a large bowl. Stir and let stand at room temperature for 2 hours until salt dissolves.

Put 4 cups beans into each of three wide-mouth quart jars. Pour pickling mixture to cover. Place a few dill sprigs in each jar and close lids tightly. Refrigerate at least 10 days.

Spiced Nuts

Don't worry about the fat in nuts. It's essential fatty acids needed for good health, and it helps prevent heart attacks and lowers cholesterol. Studies show that people who include nuts in their diet have less problems with obesity because essential fatty acids stimulate the body's burning of saturated fats. Pumpkin seeds are an old-time remedy for killing intestinal worms. Appetizing thought!

Makes about 5 cups   *Bake at 300°*

2 tablespoons tamari soy sauce   **¼ teaspoon cayenne pepper**
4 teaspoons chili powder   **5 cups mixed nuts (almonds,**
2 teaspoons cumin   **walnuts, pumpkin seeds,**
2 teaspoons curry powder   **peanuts and so on)**
2 teaspoons garlic powder

Preheat oven to 300°.

In a large bowl, toss nuts with tamari. Combine spices and sprinkle over nuts. Mix well. Transfer to a baking sheet.

Bake until nuts are golden and almost dry, about 15 minutes. Shake pan once or twice to stir nuts. Cool. Store in air-tight jars in the frig or freezer.

Special Company Nut Mix

Sunflower seeds belong to the daisy family and probably originated in or around Mexico. They were cultivated and worshipped by the Incas. Rich in protein, the vitamin B group and minerals, sunflower seeds are particularly high in potassium. Like most nuts, they contain linoleic acid, thought to help counteract the possible build-up of cholesterol from saturated fats and oils. They may also be sprouted.

Makes 2 cups   *Bake at 375°*

½ cup sunflower seeds   1 teaspoon sea salt
½ cup pumpkin seeds   1 tablespoon poppy seeds
½ cup unsalted soy splits   1 teaspoon vanilla extract
½ cup pine nuts   ¼ teaspoon ground ginger
1 tablespoon sesame oil   ¼ teaspoon ground nutmeg
1 tablespoon honey or rice syrup   ½ teaspoon cinnamon

Preheat oven to 375°.

Combine the first 4 ingredients in a large bowl. Mix the remaining ingredients thoroughly in a smaller bowl, then add to nuts and toss to coat. Spread in a shallow baking pan or cookie sheet with sides and bake for 25 minutes. Stir from time to time. Serve this mix warm or cold.

Note: *Make sure you refrigerate or freeze nuts so that their natural oils don't become rancid. Also, make sure that the nuts you buy are not commercially treated with preservatives or dyes.*

Maple Toasted Seaweed

Nutritionally, seaweed ranks high. There's a long tradition of seaweed use as both food and medicine in Japan, but we in the West are still largely afraid of it. However, I bet you'll love this sweet, crunchy appetizer or snack!

Kelp is said to kill the herpes virus. Researchers have found sea vegetables remove radiation from the body and act as decontaminators.

Makes about 2–4 cups   *Bake at 300°*

½ cup kelp or kombu   **½ cup water**
¼ cup maple syrup   **1 cup unhulled sesame seeds**

Soak dried kelp or kombu in water to cover until soft. Drain and snip into bite-sized pieces. Bring maple syrup and water to a boil. Reduce heat and add seaweed. Simmer until liquid is evaporated, about 2 hours. Mix in sesame seeds and place seaweed on a baking sheet.

Bake in a 300° oven for 25 minutes. Turn over halfway through baking. Remove tray from oven. When chips cool, they will be nice and crisp.

Marinated Tofu

We became so enamored of the smoked tofu for sale in the store that we wanted to try marinating our own at home. It's a snap. Tofu soaks up whatever flavor you give it—peanut butter sauce, teriyaki or salad dressing. Here's a marinade for horseradish lovers. Horseradish is a warming and cleansing protective food which helps get things moving and working properly, particularly in lungs and colon.

Serves 4

1 pound firm or extra firm tofu
2 large garlic cloves, minced
2 tablespoons ginger, minced
2 tablespoons prepared horse-
    radish or wasabi (Japanese
    horseradish)

2 tablespoons tamari soy sauce
½ teaspoon hot oil or sauce or ¼
    teaspoon cayenne
2 tablespoons toasted sesame oil
2 tablespoons rice wine vinegar
1 tablespoon prepared mustard

Drain tofu. Put a heavy pot or bowl on top of it for 30 minutes to press excess moisture out. Alternately, wrap tofu in a kitchen towel. If you've no time, skip this step—it's not the end of the world! Cube or slice tofu into ¼-inch slices.

Combine marinade ingredients in a mixing bowl or use a food processor to blend. Lay tofu in a shallow pan and pour the marinade over it. Cover tightly and refrigerate 2–3 days for best flavor. If you prefer after two hours, you can saute tofu in marinade for a few minutes until golden.

Serving Suggestions: *Serve with stir-fried vegetables and rice, in a sandwich with sprouts and avocado or with steamed veggies and baked potato. It even goes well cubed in a tossed salad.*

Curried Tofu

Chilled marinated tofu is refreshing and light—great in summer. Tofu, like soy milk, contains protein, iron, calcium and B vitamins (the nerve and stress vitamins). Tofu is easy to digest and easy on our planet. It's a food one can become very fond of. Do not laugh.

Garlic again! Garlic is said not only to slow the growth of tumors but in some cases to actually make them disappear.

Serves 4

1 pound firm or extra firm tofu	**1 teaspoon curry powder**
6 tablespoons olive oil	**¼ teaspoon red pepper**
⅓ cup rice vinegar	**2 cloves garlic, minced**
1 tablespoon lemon juice	**salt and pepper to taste**

Drain tofu. Press out excess moisture as described in previous recipe. Cut into cubes or ¼-inch slices.

Combine marinade ingredients in a mixing bowl or use a food processor to blend. Put tofu in a shallow dish and pour marinade over it. Cover tightly and refrigerate overnight or longer.

Serving Suggestion: *Great tossed with green onions and about 2 cups cooked brown rice.*

Scallops Marinated with Citrus and Chiles

An appetizer that's a snap to prepare. Also good over tender spring lettuce as a salad. Papayas or mango provide digestive enzymes which not only act as digestive aids, but tonify the stomach and help counter indigestion and the pain of rheumatism.

Serves 8

1 pound scallops
2 teaspoons grated orange rind
1 red onion, halved and sliced
   thinly
1 jalapeno pepper, finely minced
½ cup lemon juice

½ cup orange juice
1 teaspoon salt
2 cups papaya or mango, cubed
2 avocadoes, cubed
parsley or watercress to garnish

Wash and place scallops in glass, ceramic or stainless steel dish. Combine together with orange rind, onion, pepper, citrus juice and salt. Toss so scallops are well coated. Cover and refrigerate for 24 hours.

To serve, toss gently with papayas or mango and avocado. Garnish with parsley or watercress.

Note: If you are uncomfortable "cooking" scallops in the dressing, feel free to saute them for a few minutes in a skillet with a little olive oil.

Tomatillo Chile Vinaigrette

Make this vinaigrette chunky by cutting veggies into small dice. Serve over tofu, beans, fish or use as a dip!

Tomatillos, not true tomatoes but gooseberry relatives, are paper-husked green tomatoes native to Mexico. They grow just as easily in home gardens as do regular tomatoes and can be found in many super-markets these days. If you can't find them, you can substitute green toma-toes, about the size of cherry tomatoes.

Makes about 3½ cups

6 tomatillos, husked, rinsed and diced
½ cup jicama,* peeled and diced
2 tablespoons red pepper, diced
2 tablespoons yellow pepper, diced
1 papaya, peeled, seeded and diced

1 jalapeno, seeded and finely diced
2 tablespoons lemon juice
1 tablespoon balsamic vinegar
2 tablespoons olive oil
2 cloves garlic, minced
minced fresh coriander, *optional*

Combine all ingredients. Salt to taste.

*Jicama is another Mexican vegetable widely found in supermarkets. You have to peel it, and it's crunchy, juicy and a little sweet. Cut into thin strips, it makes a wonderful vegetable to serve with dips.

Turkey Keftas

The combination of spices transforms this dish into something exotic and mouth-watering. The bran keeps keftas moist and adds fiber, something most of us need more of in our daily diets.

Serves 8 as an appetizer

½ cup bran
½ cup tomato or mango juice
6 cloves garlic, minced
½ teaspoon cayenne pepper
1 teaspoon ground cloves
1 teaspoon ground allspice
1 teaspoon ground ginger

1 teaspoon ground cardamom
½ teaspoon ground nutmeg
½ teaspoon ground cumin
½ teaspoon salt
½ teaspoon pepper
1 pound ground turkey
½ cup olive oil, *optional*

Mix bran together with tomato or mango juice, garlic, herbs and spices. Let stand for 10 minutes, or until bran has absorbed juice.

Add ground turkey and mix well. Cover and refrigerate at least an hour to give flavors a chance to mix.

Shape into 2-inch meatballs. Broil or grill for a minute or two on all sides, or gently warm olive oil in a skillet and saute until meatballs are lightly browned.

To serve, try yogurt as a dipping sauce or with fresh tomatoes, cucumbers and olives.

Note: Bran needs to be eaten with fluids because it absorbs liquid and you want it to be able to move gently through your system!

Creamy Yogurt Dip with Garlic and Herbs

The nutritional and medicinal uses of naturally fermented yogurt have been known for hundreds of years in the Middle East. Because yogurt bacteria break down milk sugar to produce lactic acid, yogurt is easier to digest than cow's milk and has a beneficial effect on the digestive system.

Makes about 2 cups

2 cups plain yogurt
4 cloves garlic, minced or
    pressed with garlic press
1 tablespoon dried dill weed

1 tablespoon dried basil
1 tablespoon dried parsley
salt and pepper to taste

This is simple. Just mix the ingredients together, refrigerate for an hour, and put out with vegetable dippers or whole grain crackers.

Variation: Use soy yogurt or silken or soft tofu instead of yogurt. If using tofu, blend using the steel blade of a food processor or blender until smooth.

Variation: Combine 2 cups yogurt with half a small minced red onion, 1 teaspoon dijon mustard, 1 teaspoon tamari soy sauce, some dill and garlic. Add lemon juice to taste instead of salt and pepper.

Variation: To yogurt, add some minced garlic, 2 tablespoons olive oil, a few minced scallions, 1 small minced cucumber, salt and pepper to taste.

Variation: To yogurt, add 2 tablespoons sesame seeds, some minced garlic, 4 tablespoons tamari soy sauce, 4 tablespoons tahini, 2 tablespoons lemon juice and salt and pepper to taste. If you like ginger, add 1 teaspoon ground ginger. Garnish with sliced scallions.

Note: This can be made up to 48 hours ahead of use, but may get a little watery. However, you can also throw it together as company is walking in the door.

Soups

Here are guidelines I hand out in soup classes I teach at the store. It's impossible to make bad soup if you follow simple rules. The recipes here and in my first book are a snap to prepare and taste great! Try them and you'll get rave reviews. (Speaking of rave reviews, Lise Stern, a writer for *The Boston Globe,* touted our soups as the best in the Boston area in her book *The Boston Food Lover.* She also mentions our cookies and granola!)

1. You don't have to use bouillon cubes or canned soup broth to make good soup. Chopped onions and garlic makes great soup base together with vegetables, beans, grains and herbs. You save money, feel virtuous and infuse your soup with the therapeutic properties attributed to onions and garlic.
2. Save the liquid from steaming vegetables in glass jars and store in the frig to use in soups. (Or you can freeze it for another time.) Using vegetable stock is a great way to add nutrient-value to soups.
3. Cut vegetables into pieces which fit easily onto a spoon and into a mouth.
4. Add salt (or miso and tamari soy sauce) when soup is done. Add seaweed to soup when you start cooking. Use a piece of seaweed called "kombu" (kelp) in soup whenever it contains beans, because kombu

is said to break down the part of beans that we have difficulty digesting and which causes gas. Kombu is also rich in minerals.

5. Add herbs to soups when they're almost done. That way you get their full flavor.

6. Add tomatoes and acidic foods after beans and grain are soft. Otherwise, the acidity will prevent beans and grains from cooking fully. They'll stay tough! The same applies to salt. Taste and add just before serving.

7. Save cream, butter and flour for desserts. Cream and butter soups are too heavy and rich. Thicken soups instead with pureed vegetables. Potatoes work wonderfully. If you want your soup to taste decadent, try sauteing onions and garlic in a spoonful of olive oil before adding remaining ingredients to kettle.

8. Remember that many soups taste better the second day when flavors have had a chance to marry. Never throw away leftover soup. You can freeze it in glass jars—just leave room at the top of the jar for expansion. Or invite a crowd over for a soup party!

9. Russian soup recipe: "Take what you like. Wash, chop and put in pot."

10. Studies show people who eat soups have less difficulty controlling weight because no matter how thick a soup and how filling it is, it's still largely water and vegetables, which are lower in calories. And hot soup makes us eat slower, which gives time for the brain to signal we've had enough to eat!

11. Want more fiber in your diet? Throw a handful of bran into hot soup 5 minutes before serving. It won't change the taste of the soup, and bran in hot liquid works like magic to regulate the body. (Works much better than sprinkled on cold cereal or mixed into juice.) Bran will give your soup a gourmet appearance with flecks of brown. Just like the old-fashioned potato onion soup in my first book!

12. Don't peel vegetables like carrots, potatoes, parsnips or yams. Scrub with a vegetable brush under running water, dice or slice and add to pot. Save yourself time, aggravation and nutrients which lie just under the skin!

Carrot Parsnip Soup

Steamed vegetables, pureed, taste creamy. Adding olive oil makes them luscious. Parsnips, native to Eastern Europe, have a sweet, floury taste. They're said to help cleanse the liver and to be mildly diuretic.

Serves 6

2 parsnips, unpeeled, sliced	**2 cups soy or rice milk**
2 carrots, unpeeled, sliced	**2 tablespoons olive oil,** *optional*
1 large onion, chunked	**½ teaspoon nutmeg**
2 cups water	**salt and black pepper to taste**

Place parsnips, carrots, onion and water in a soup pot. (Vegetables can be cut into large pieces because you're going to blend them later.) Cover pot and simmer for 15 minutes.

Blend soup in a blender or food processor until smooth. Depending on the size of your machine, you may need to blend soup in more than one batch. Transfer each batch to a second pot. Use just enough liquid from the pot and milk of your choice so vegetables flow under blades. Once all vegetables have been pureed and put into second pot, stir remaining liquid into soup. Add olive oil if you want. Add nutmeg, salt and pepper to taste.

Heat soup to just below boiling and serve piping hot with warm crusty rolls or hearty whole grain bread. A green salad serves as a colorful counterpoint.

Note: *You can make this soup skinny by using nonfat soy or rice milk and leaving out the olive oil. Introducing soy products this way to your family is terrific. They'll never know by the taste, believe me!*

Cream of Spinach Soup

This soup gets its creamy consistency from potatoes and onions. Lo-cal, it leaves room for dessert! Interestingly, nutmeg, with its aromatic and warm flavor, is reputed to relieve abdominal swelling and indigestion.

Serves 4–6

1 onion, chopped
4 potatoes, diced
6 cups water or vegetable stock
2 pounds fresh spinach

¼ teaspoon nutmeg
½ teaspoon black pepper
½ teaspoon salt
1 tablespoon olive oil, *optional*

Scrub potatoes, but don't peel. Wash spinach.

In a soup kettle, simmer onion and potatoes in water or vegetable stock until tender, about 10 minutes. Add spinach and cook until spinach wilts and is soft, about 2–3 minutes.

Using the steel blade of a food processor or a blender, blend until coarsely ground but not pureed.

Put back in soup kettle together with spices. Adjust seasoning to taste. Add the olive oil for a richer soup.

Miso Vegetable Soup

Miso is made by fermenting soybeans, rice, barley or wheat under pressure for a year or two. Salt is added, and the resulting paste is extremely nutritious, a complete protein, high in minerals and some B vitamins.

Serves 4

6 cups water
2 tablespoons seaweed, like
   kombu
2 large carrots, cut into 1-inch
   matchsticks
1 leek, cut into matchsticks

4 shiitake mushrooms, sliced
2 tablespoons miso
1 tablespoon tamari soy sauce
1 pound tofu, diced
4 scallions, thinly sliced

Combine all but last 4 ingredients. Bring soup to a boil, reduce heat and cover pot. Simmer soup for 5 minutes.

Blend miso with tamari soy sauce in a small bowl. Stir into soup. Add tofu and scallions, and simmer another minute.

Taste and adjust seasoning. Serve.

Note: Miso is added at the end of cooking because it contains living bacteria and enzymes from fermentation which are destroyed by boiling. The bacteria and enzymes not only promote good digestion but are said to enhance the immune system and be good for someone who is feeling under the weather. But miso is high in sodium, so if you are on a sodium-restricted diet, miso is not for you.

Mushroom and Hazelnut Soup

Hazelnuts, or filberts as they are also called, have a mild flavor and are high in potassium, calcium and sulphur. They complement cooked vegetables and grains. You'll be surprised at the rich, wonderful taste of this soup.

Serves 8

1 cup hazelnuts
4 tablespoons olive oil
3 large onions, chopped
16 cups mushrooms, chunked if large

5 cups water or vegetable
  stock
pinch nutmeg
salt and pepper to taste

Toast hazelnuts on a pan in a 350° oven for 10 minutes. Set aside to cool.

Gently warm olive oil in a soup kettle and saute onions until soft, about 5 minutes. Add mushrooms and cover pot. Cook on low heat, covered, for another 5 minutes. Add water or vegetable stock and bring soup to a boil. Add pinch nutmeg and simmer soup for 10 minutes.

Puree soup together with hazelnuts in batches in a blender or food processor (using the steel blade and on/off turns). Transfer each blended batch to a second soup pot. Adjust seasoning with salt and pepper and re-heat gently, if desired.

Note: *Some people prefer chicken stock, which is fine—just make sure you're using homemade chicken stock or chicken stock without preservatives, sugars, MSG and the like. No point ruining a good soup!*

Island Coconut Soup

Coconut has gotten a bad rap for years. But coconut is rich in lauric acid (50 percent of fatty acids in coconut are lauric acid), a medium-chain fatty acid like that found in human milk, known to have unique antimicrobial properties. Lauric acid is one of the best virus-inactivating fatty acids. Besides, coconut oil is one of the most stable oils known to humanity. It's been used for cooking, baking and frying for thousands of years in other parts of the world because it doesn't become rancid. So coconut every once in a while is okay. And coconut has a unique taste.

Serves 6

1 onion, minced
6 cloves garlic, minced
7 cups water or vegetable stock
3 potatoes, scrubbed and diced
3 sweet potatoes, scrubbed and diced
½ cup brown rice
2 carrots, diced
2 stalks celery, diced

½ teaspoon thyme
½ teaspoon cinnamon
½ teaspoon ginger
½ teaspoon cayenne pepper
1 small can coconut milk
1 large bunch greens, chopped, washed and stemmed
1 teaspoon salt
1 teaspoon black pepper

In a soup kettle, place all ingredients except coconut milk and greens. Simmer until rice is tender, about 40 minutes.

If you want soup to appear thicker, puree half. Otherwise, leave chunky. Add coconut milk and a large bunch of greens such as spinach or chard. Add salt and pepper to taste.

Potato Soup with Dill Pesto

Dill is a member of the parsley family and is said to aid digestion and circulation and to help lower blood pressure. It's widely used in Scandinavia as a condiment and often paired with salmon, cucumber and potatoes.

Serves 4

4 large potatoes, diced   **salt and pepper to taste**
1 large onion, chopped   **1 cup fresh dill**
1 parsnip or rutabaga, diced   **2 tablespoons pine nuts**
1¼ teaspoons dill seeds   **2 tablespoons olive oil**
4 cups water or vegetable broth

In a soup kettle, simmer potatoes, onion, parsnip or rutabaga and dill seeds together with water or vegetable broth until potatoes are tender, about 15 minutes.

Puree soup in batches in a blender or food processor (using the steel blade and on/off turns). Transfer each blended batch to a second soup pot. Add salt and pepper to taste.

To make pesto, blend dill and pine nuts with olive oil.

Ladle soup into bowls. Place a dollop of pesto in each and swirl with a knife.

Suggestion: *Short on time? Use any prepared pesto instead of making your own.*

Vegetable Soup with a Kick

This soup has a little kick because of cayenne, which gets the circulation going, helps ward off vampires and bugs and separates the men from the boys. Don't like heat? Can't take the challenge? Leave out the cayenne, and you've a delicious soup that won't put hair on your chest.

Potatoes are said to be "expansive" and improve one's nurturing and compassionate nature. They are comfort food.

Serves 10

4 potatoes, diced
2 large onions, diced
4 cloves garlic, minced
2 stalks celery, diced
2 carrots, diced
2 parsnips or small rutabagas,
   diced
2 cups corn

1 cup peas
½ cup red lentils
½ teaspoon thyme
½ teaspoon marjoram
½ teaspoon basil
½ teaspoon dill
¼ teaspoon cayenne, *optional*
salt and pepper to taste

Place all ingredients in a soup kettle. Bring to a boil. Lower heat, cover pot and simmer until vegetables and lentils are soft, about 30 minutes.

Hot and Sour Soup

This is a lighter soup because it has no beans (tofu doesn't seem like a bean) and no grain, but it still makes a complete meal. Make this when you want something nourishing but not so filling in your tummy.

Mushrooms contain germanium, an element said to improve cellular oxygenation and strengthen immunity.

Serves 4–6

¼ cup dried shiitake mushrooms, chopped
8 cups vegetable stock or water
1 cup assorted fresh mushrooms,
sliced
½ cup bamboo shoots
½ cup water chestnuts
1 cup bok choy, diced to fit easily
onto a spoon
2 teaspoons fresh ginger, minced

4 cloves garlic, minced
2 eggs, beaten
8 ounces firm tofu, cubed
3 tablespoons tamari soy sauce
3 tablespoons rice wine vinegar
3 tablespoons honey or rice syrup
1 tablespoon toasted sesame oil
salt and pepper to taste
pinch cayenne pepper
sliced scallions to garnish

Place dried mushrooms into soup pot together with water or vegetable stock. Bring to a boil and turn off heat. Let mushrooms sit in hot water about 30 minutes.

Add fresh mushrooms, bamboo shoots, water chestnuts, bok choy, ginger and garlic. Bring soup to a boil and then reduce heat. Simmer covered for 10 minutes.

Beat egg with fork and add to soup in a steady stream while stirring. Stir in tofu, tamari, vinegar, sweetener and toasted sesame oil. Warm soup thoroughly and season to taste. Serve garnished with scallions.

Quinoa Corn Chowder

Quinoa, referred to as the lost grain of the Incas, is farmed today in Peru, Bolivia, and the high mesas in Colorado. Quinoa is one of the few grains said to be a complete protein. It sprouts when it cooks, too! Mild and buttery tasting, quinoa takes on whatever personality you choose to give it. It thickens this soup, or any soup, beautifully.

Serves 4

2 cups water or vegetable stock
½ cup quinoa
1 potato, cubed
1 carrot, diced
1 onion, chopped

1½ cups corn
4 cups milk, or soy or rice
   milk
salt and pepper to taste
dry parsley to garnish

Simmer quinoa, potato, carrot and onion in water or vegetable stock until tender, about 15 minutes.

Add corn. Simmer another 5 minutes.

Add milk. Bring almost to boiling. Season to taste and serve garnished with dry parsley.

Tomato Rice Soup with Tofu

This soup is thick, more like a stew. It's an easy way to introduce people to tofu; you might even try smoked or flavored tofu. So give folks phyto (plant) estrogens in that tofu! Of course, you can substitute any leftover grain or bean for the rice.

Serves 10

1 large onion, chopped
4 cloves garlic, minced
½ teaspoon orange peel
1 tablespoon basil
1 teaspoon marjoram
pinch cayenne
4 cups diced tomatoes

1 cup tomato puree
2 tablespoons tomato paste
2–3 cups water or vegetable broth
2 cups cooked brown rice
1 pound tofu
salt and pepper to taste
parsley to garnish, *optional*

Place all ingredients except tofu into soup kettle. Bring soup to a boil and then turn down heat to low, cover pot and simmer for 10 minutes.

Stir in tofu and let pot sit covered for 5 minutes to heat tofu through. Taste and adjust seasoning. Serve garnished with parsley if you like.

Variation: You could use 2 quarts tomato juice instead of tomato products and water.

Deluxe Mushroom Barley Soup

Soup is throw-it-in-a-pot kind of cooking and real comfort food. It's especially wonderful on a cold, blustery day. Wrap your hands around a steaming bowl. Serve it to your best friend, your loved ones. Know you're doing them good. To me, the mere thought of soup releases inhibitions!

Serves 6

7 cups water or vegetable stock
1 onion, diced
1 potato, diced
2 stalks celery, diced
6 cloves garlic, minced
2 carrots, diced
1 parsnip or turnip, diced
¼ cup dried lima beans

¼ cup yellow split peas
¼ cup barley
¼ cup brown rice
¼ cup dried shiitakes, broken up
1 tablespoon dried dill
salt and pepper to taste (or use Bragg's Liquid Aminos)

Combine ingredients in a soup kettle. Bring soup to a boil, cover and simmer over low heat until tender, about 1½ hours.

Season to taste and serve. If you want a thinner soup, add more water or tomato juice.

Variations: Feel free to add any vegetables you want to take out of the refrigerator or for which you have a yen. Add more of one bean, less of another or only barley instead of barley and brown rice. Experiment!

Lentil and Mushroom Soup

Wonderfully hearty is this nonfattening soup. Great on a cold, blustery day! Lentils, a member of the pea family, are a good source of calcium and magnesium, protein and vitamin A. They don't need long cooking, so they make soups a snap. They're easy on the budget, too.

Serves 8–10

1 tablespoon olive oil	**2 cups mushrooms, sliced**
2 onions, chopped	**2 stalks celery, sliced**
2 cloves garlic, minced	**1 bay leaf**
16 cups water or vegetable stock	**1 teaspoon rosemary**
2 cups lentils	**salt and pepper to taste**
2 carrots, diced	**parsley or watercress to garnish**

Gently warm olive oil in a soup kettle. Saute onions and garlic until golden, about 10 minutes.

Add remaining ingredients. Simmer for 45 minutes. Add more water if soup is too thick.

Season to taste. Garnish with parsley or watercress.

Revitalizing Soup

One health spa I visited encouraged us to put Bragg's Liquid Aminos in hot water midmorning and midafternoon as a quick pick-me-upper. Made from soy beans, Bragg's has been around since I was a little girl. It tastes salty and looks a little like soy sauce.

People who claim to hate brown rice never mind it in soups. Use whatever kind of brown rice you prefer. Short grain brown rice is said to be higher in nutritional value and lower in calories than long grain. Both, however, are nutritious and high in B vitamins

Serves 4

⅔ cup lentils
⅔ cup split peas
⅔ cup brown rice
6 cloves garlic, minced
1 onion, chopped
2 stalks celery, diced
2 carrots, diced

½ teaspoon ginger powder
½ teaspoon pepper
2 teaspoons Bragg's liquid
  aminos
pinch cayenne
8 cups water or vegetable
  broth

Place all ingredients in soup kettle and simmer for 1 hour, stirring occasionally.

Curried Red Lentil Soup

Red lentils are richly flavored and fast to cook. You'll love them combined with chick-peas and curry. Like lentils and lots of other beans, chick-peas have calcium, magnesium, vitamin A, iron and potassium. Not bad for "lowly" beans. This makes a pretty soup to serve!

Serves 4

1 large onion, chopped
4 cloves garlic, minced
½ teaspoon dried thyme
1 tablespoon curry powder
2 cups red lentils
6 cups water

2 cups cooked chick-peas
salt and pepper to taste
cayenne pepper to taste
2 tablespoons minced parsley
**   to garnish**

Combine first 7 ingredients in a soup kettle. Bring to a boil. Lower heat, cover pot and simmer for 20 minutes, or until lentils are tender. Season to taste, garnish and serve.

Split Pea and Yam Curry Soup

Yams are a variety of sweet potato. We all know how de-lish they are and how healthy. Lots of beta carotene that fights cancer. They're also rich in protease inhibitors which protect us against viruses.

Serves 4

1 tablespoon olive oil	2 teaspoons curry powder
8 cloves garlic, minced	8 cups water
½ teaspoon turmeric	2½ cups yellow split peas,
½ teaspoon chili powder	washed
1 teaspoon cumin seeds	2 yams, scrubbed and cubed
1 teaspoon mustard seeds	salt and pepper to taste

Gently warm olive oil in soup kettle. Add spices and stir to coat kettle. Warm in pot until aromatic, about 2 minutes. Add water, peas and yams. Bring soup to a boil. Lower heat, cover pot and simmer until peas are soft, about 30 minutes.

Remove soup from heat. Puree half the soup and add back to kettle. Let stand for a few minutes, season to taste and serve.

Lima Bean
and Split Pea Soup

This is as easy as the split pea soup from our first cookbook, one of our all-time favorites. Although lima beans originated in South America, they are now grown mainly in Madagascar and are sometimes called "butter beans." They are particularly high in potassium and sodium and starchier but less fatty than other beans. You may not want to add any salt to taste because limas are naturally salty.

Serves 8

2 cups dried lima beans
1 cup green split peas
2 onions, chopped
8 cloves garlic, minced
3 large carrots, halved and
  sliced
3 stalks celery, sliced
2 medium potatoes, diced
8–10 cups water or vegetable
  broth
salt and pepper to taste
parsley to garnish

Put all ingredients into a soup kettle and bring to a boil. Turn down heat, cover pot and simmer until beans and peas are cooked, about 2 hours. Season to taste with salt and pepper and garnish with parsley.

Russian Yellow Split Pea with Chestnuts and Dried Plums

This wonderful winter soup is a frequently requested recipe in our store. Chestnuts have almost no fat and are high in protein. They're hearty, filling and by nature have a slightly sweet flavor. Ever try chestnut flour in baking? We have and it's yummy!

Serves 6–8

10 cups water or vegetable stock
1¼ cups yellow split peas
½ pound dried chestnuts
2 onions, diced
4 cloves garlic, minced
½ teaspoon turmeric
pinch cinnamon
1 apple, cored and cubed

6 pitted prunes, diced
2 cups diced canned tomatoes
½ teaspoon dried mint
1½ tablespoons lemon juice
½ teaspoon cayenne pepper
salt and black pepper
½ minced red onion, *optional*
¼ cup dried parsley, *optional*

In a soup pot, place 10 cups water or vegetable stock together with peas. Bring to a boil, reduce heat to low and simmer, covered, until peas are tender, about 40 minutes.

Coarsely chop chestnuts. Add to soup pot together with onion, garlic, turmeric, cinnamon, apple, prunes, tomatoes, mint, lemon juice and cayenne pepper. Simmer for another 20 minutes. Add salt and pepper to taste. Sprinkle with minced red onion or parsley to serve.

Sopa de Arroz Mexicana

Dish out big bowls of this soup, sit by the fire and enjoy someone's company and good conversation. Your waistline will love you, too. There is no fat in this soup! Like most of the soups in this chapter, this combines grain and bean, so you'll be eating complete protein. Zucchini needs almost no cooking. It's best slightly crisp and pretty, bright green. Add it at the last minute, always.

Serves 6–8

2 cups yellow split peas
⅓ cup raw brown rice
1 large onion, chopped
6 cloves garlic, minced
4 carrots, diced
4 stalks celery, sliced

12 cups water
2 zucchini, diced
8 ounces salsa
salt and pepper to taste
2 tablespoons dried parsley to garnish

Wash split peas and rice in a mesh colander. (If you like soup so thick the spoon stands up, add ½ cup more split peas and increase rice to ½ cup.)

In a large soup kettle, place peas, rice, onion, garlic, carrots and celery, together with water. Bring soup to a boil. Cover, lower heat and simmer until peas are tender, about 1½–2 hours.

Add zucchini and salsa. Salt and pepper to taste. Stir in parsley for color. Serve with a green salad and enjoy.

Mexican Rice and Garbanzo Soup

Wonderful, homey and satisfying. Share this soup with people you love. Using brown rice gives you a whole food. White rice has had the bran and germ removed, and all you're left with is starch.

Serves 8

1 onion, chopped
4 cloves garlic, minced
1 cup raw brown rice
1 cup cooked garbanzos (chick-peas, canned is fine)
2 cups diced vegetables: carrots, parsnips, celery, pepper, kale

1 bay leaf
1 cup diced canned tomatoes
6 cups water or vegetable broth
pinch thyme
salt and pepper to taste

Place all ingredients in a pot. Gently bring soup to a boil. Lower flame, cover pot and simmer until rice is tender and soup is ready, about 1 hour. What could be easier? Of course, you could throw the soup into a crock-pot in the morning and come home to dinner.

Note: *My favorite brown rice is organic brown basmati which smells like popcorn when it cooks.*

Portuguese White Bean and Kale Soup

Make this soup when kale is plentiful. I like kale in soup because you don't have to worry about overcooking it like you do spinach or chard. And kale, rich in carotenoids, is said to be one of the best cancer-fighting vegetables. It's rated as the healthiest of all veggies by the Center for Science in the Public Interest. Yes, you too can learn to love kale!

Serves 8

1½ cups white beans
2 tablespoons olive oil
1 large onion, diced
4 cloves garlic, minced
½ package Fakin' Bacon, diced
1 tablespoon marjoram

1 tablespoon basil
8 cups water
1 large bunch kale (5 stems), chopped
umeboshi paste or lemon juice to taste
salt and pepper to taste

Sort beans, checking carefully for stones, rinse and cover with water 2 inches above beans; add more water as necessary during cooking. Bring beans to a boil uncovered. Boil vigorously for 10 minutes to release gases, then cover and simmer until soft, about 1½ hours. (Review directions for cooking beans in What You Need to Know in front of cookbook.) Alternately, pressure-cook beans for 20 minutes.

Gently warm olive oil in a soup kettle and saute onions, garlic and Fakin' Bacon until onions are translucent. Add cooked beans, herbs, water and kale and bring soup to a boil. Turn down to a simmer, cover and cook for 10 minutes.

To serve, add seasonings to taste, starting with 1 teaspoon lemon juice or umeboshi paste, and ladle into soup bowls.

Note: *Fakin' Bacon is a great soy product which gives everything a wonderful smoky flavor.*

Shiitake, Bean and Berry Soup

What kind of grain berries to use? How about spelt or kamut? Both are ancient relatives of wheat, with a higher protein content. If you like rye or barley berries, use those in the soup. Just try a new combination!

Serves 6

1 cup navy beans	1 large potato, diced
½ cup grain berries	1 large parsnip, diced
3–4 quarts water or vegetable stock	2 carrots, sliced
	2 stalks celery, sliced
8 cloves garlic, minced	¾ ounce dried shiitakes
1 bay leaf	1 tablespoon dried parsley
pinch thyme and oregano	salt and pepper to taste

In a large soup kettle, place beans and berries with water or veggie broth. Bring to a boil and boil uncovered for 10 minutes to release gases. Then put remaining ingredients into the pot, with the exception of the last two. Bring soup to a gentle boil. Reduce heat to low, cover pot and simmer for an hour and a half.

Sprinkle dried parsley in soup, add salt and pepper to taste and serve piping hot with a loaf of crusty bread.

Suggestion: *If you like, put soup up in the morning in a crockpot and eat it for dinner that night. You can also put this soup up on a lazy Sunday while you're reading the paper. You can then refrigerate, warm and serve for dinner during the week.*

Mom's Chicken Barley Soup

Barley is especially good in soups. Just like chicken soup, it is reputed to be good for those who are feeling underpar. Barley is said to be good for those with heart problems and to stimulate the liver and lymphatic system which moves toxic waste from the body.

Serves 8

1 cup raw barley
12 cups water or vegetable stock
4 cups cooked chicken, diced
2 large onions, chopped
3 stalks celery, diced (leaves and all)

1 pound carrots, diced
2 parsnips, diced
1 bay leaf
2 tablespoons dried parsley
1 tablespoon dried dill weed
salt and pepper to taste

Place barley in a large soup kettle with water or vegetable stock. Bring to a boil and then turn down heat to lowest setting. Simmer for about an hour. (Barley loves to bubble over, so use the largest pot you have to save cleaning your stove!)

Add remaining ingredients and simmer soup for 30–45 minutes, or until carrots are tender.

Taste and adjust seasoning. I like a lot of black pepper in this one.

Variation: You can make this soup vegetarian by leaving out the chicken. Just add more of some seasonings to compensate for the richness of the chicken.

Variation: Use turkey instead of chicken. This is a great soup to make with leftovers after Thanksgiving.

South-of-the-Border Chicken and Black Bean Soup

The black beans discolor the chicken, but who cares, because they taste great! Black beans are considered very south-of-the-border and very gourmet. Black beans are also said to be warming and beneficial to kidneys and the reproductive system.

Serves 10

4 tablespoons olive oil
1 pound boneless chicken, diced for soup
2 green peppers, diced
2 tomatoes, diced
1 large onion, minced
4 cloves garlic, minced
¼ teaspoon cinnamon
½ teaspoon cloves

1 teaspoon chili powder
1 teaspoon oregano
½ teaspoon black pepper
5 cups cooked black beans, mashed
2 cups corn
6 cups water
1½ teaspoon salt

Gently warm olive oil in a soup kettle. Add all ingredients except beans, corn, water and salt. Stir until aromatic and onions and peppers begin to soften, about 5 minutes.

Add beans, corn, water and salt. Bring to a boil over medium heat. Cover pot and simmer for 20 minutes. Taste and adjust seasoning.

Variation: *To make this soup vegetarian, just leave out the chicken. Black beans and corn make a complete protein.*

Chicken, Potato and Root Vegetable Soup

Great for when you have leftover chicken or turkey. We don't use root vegetables in this country as much as we ought. They're satisfying, inexpensive and good keepers. Potatoes are said to balance alkalinity and acidity in the body. Rutabagas, members of the turnip family, are said to help clear congestion. You just might grow to love them!

Serves 4–6

4 potatoes, cubed (about 1 pound)
4 parsnips or rutabagas, cubed (about 1 pound)
1 sweet potato, cubed
1 carrot, cubed
6 cups water or vegetable stock
1 bay leaf
½ teaspoon thyme
2 cups cooked chicken or turkey, diced
salt and pepper to taste

Place vegetables in a soup kettle together with water or vegetable stock and bay leaf. Simmer until vegetables are very tender, about 15 minutes. Remove bay leaf.

Using the steel blade of a food processor or a blender, puree soup in batches until smooth. Place the batches into a second soup pot. Stir in thyme and cooked chicken or turkey. Bring to simmer. Season to taste with salt and pepper, ladle into bowls and serve.

Note: *I've read that rutabagas shouldn't be eaten by anyone who has kidney problems.*

New England Fish Chowder

I grew up with Manhattan fish chowder—no milk or cream. Living in New England, I've come to love New England chowder, but I prefer soy or rice milk in mine and no flour.

Serves 6–8

¼ cup olive oil
1 onion, diced
1 green pepper, diced
4 stalks celery, diced
1½ pounds red or yellow
   potatoes, cubed
1 cup fish or vegetable stock or
   water

5 cups soy, rice or regular milk
1 pound cod, cut into 2-inch
   pieces
½ pound haddock, cut into
   2-inch pieces
1 package Fakin' Bacon, diced
salt and pepper to taste
parsley to garnish

In a soup kettle, gently warm olive oil. Saute onion, green pepper and celery over low heat for 5–10 minutes, or until vegetables are soft. Stir in potatoes (which have been scrubbed, but not peeled) and fish stock. Increase heat to medium, cover and simmer soup until potatoes are tender, about 10 minutes.

Add milk, fish and Fakin' Bacon. Remove pot from heat and let sit, covered, for 30 minutes. Season to taste with salt and pepper. Heat briefly for a minute or two, stir and serve garnished with parsley.

Variation: You can leave out the Fakin' Bacon if you don't like a smoky bacon taste. Sometimes I've added a few tablespoons nutritional yeast instead, which imparts a little smokiness and doesn't spoil the soup for me. Don't try this experiment on company until you've tried it on yourself!

Hot or Cold Carrot Pea Soup with Tarragon

Like many European dishes intended for pureeing, this soup includes a handful of rice for body instead of milk or cream. I like my soup with some texture, so I cook the rice separately and leave it whole. But you can cook the rice with the soup and puree it, too. Doing so saves an extra step and washing an extra pot.

Serves 4–6

1 tablespoon olive oil
1 onion, chopped
2 cloves garlic, minced
2 pounds carrots, coarsely
   chopped
1 teaspoon tarragon

7 cups water
½ cup brown rice
1 cup water
2 cups peas (frozen work fine)
salt and pepper to taste
tarragon to garnish

In a large soup kettle, gently warm olive oil. Add onion and garlic and stir to coat. Saute until onion is soft, about 5 minutes. Add carrots, tarragon, 7 cups water and bring to a boil. Lower heat, cover pot and simmer for 45 minutes, or until carrots are very soft.

At the same time, put rice and 1 cup water in a small pot. Bring to a boil, lower heat, cover pot and simmer rice for 45 minutes.

Remove carrots from soup with a slotted spoon and puree them with the steel blade of a food processor or a blender, adding cooking liquid as needed. Stir puree back into soup. Add rice, peas and salt and pepper to taste. Simmer soup for 5 minutes.

Refrigerate until well chilled. Ladle into bowls to serve. Garnish with tarragon.

Serving Suggestion: *This soup is good served hot, too.*

Carrot Beet Soup

This pretty soup is great for summertime and hot evenings. Make ahead and serve to company with dark bread, corn on the cob and herbed goat cheese. Cleansing and high in iron, beets are good to eat once a week. They are said to improve circulation and strengthen the heart. Together with carrots, beets are said to regulate hormones during menopause.

Serves 4

1 tablespoon olive oil
1 onion, diced
3 carrots, sliced
4 small beets, cubed
2 cups water

2 cups milk, soy or rice milk
2 tablespoons balsamic vinegar
¼ teaspoon fennel seeds
pinch allspice
salt and pepper to taste

Gently warm olive oil in a soup kettle. Saute onions until soft, about 5 minutes. Add carrots, beets and water. Bring to a boil. Lower heat, cover pot and simmer soup for 15 minutes, or until carrots are soft.

Remove pot from stove. Puree using the steel blade of a food processor. Put puree back in soup pot and add remaining ingredients. Warm through and serve.

Cold Cucumber Soup

When the weather is hot, this cooling soup hits the spot. Not only do cucumbers cool us down, but they are said to quench thirst, relieve swelling in hands and feet, cleanse the blood and purify the skin. Be sure to use the whole cucumber because many of its therapeutic benefits are enhanced by nutrients in the skin, which is also rich in silicon (good for joints, skin and nails) and chlorophyll (the essential green stuff which rejuvenates and renews).

Serves 6

2 cucumbers, grated
4 cups yogurt
2 teaspoons salt
1 teaspoon black pepper

2 tablespoons dill weed
3 cups cold water
1 teaspoon garlic powder

Mix all ingredients. Refrigerate until cold, at least three hours.

Variations: You can also prepare this soup with chopped walnuts, raisins, chopped green onions and celery.

Cucumber Miso Soup

Miso contains enzymes which are helpful for digestion, as you already know. And cucumbers contain a digestive enzyme that breaks down protein and cleanses the intestines.

Serves 4

1 tablespoon olive oil
4 cucumbers, diced
2 cloves garlic
1 tablespoon miso

1¼ cups water
salt and pepper to taste
yogurt to garnish, *optional*

Gently warm oil in a soup pot. Add cucumbers and garlic and saute gently for 5 minutes.

Using the steel blade of a food processor, blend cucumbers and garlic with miso and water. Season to taste.

Pour into serving bowls and chill until very cold, at least two hours. Serve with warm rolls and topped with a dollop of yogurt.

Summer Tomato and Ginger Soup

Pickled ginger is used extensively in Japanese and other Asian cooking. It warms the body and is said to aid digestion. You can find it in a natural food store or an Asian store. I like Eden and Great Eastern Sun pickled gingers best.

Even though tomatoes are acidic, after they are digested, they are said to alkalize the blood and be helpful in cases of rheumatism and gout.

Serves 4

8 cups tomatoes, diced
1 small cucumber, chunked but
   not peeled
8 ruffles pickled ginger

2 tablespoons rice wine vinegar
1 teaspoon salt
½ teaspoon pepper
pickled ginger to garnish

Using the steel blade of a food processor, blend all the ingredients. Taste and adjust seasoning. Chill and serve very cold.

Garnish with a piece of ruffled ginger.

Summer Fruit Soup

Not only is this soup beautiful to look at and light to eat, but it takes advantage of the fruits of summer. I like to add the cranberries for tartness and always have some in my freezer. If you wish, just leave them out!

A little cinnamon in the diet of ulcer sufferers and adult-onset diabetics may soon be seen as medicinally prudent. The active ingredient in cinnamon appears to fight ulcers and helps boost the effectiveness of insulin.

Serves 8–10

**4 cups cherry, apple, mango or
fruit juice mixture of your
choice
1 cup fresh orange juice
1 cup all-fruit jam
1 tablespoon orange zest
1 pound nectarines, peaches or
apricots, halved, pitted and
sliced
1 pound cherries, pitted, or
blueberries**

**1 pound seedless red grapes
1 pound seedless green grapes
1 pound strawberries, hulled
and quartered
½ pound cranberries, *optional*
1 teaspoon almond extract,
optional
pinch cinnamon, *optional*
mint or yogurt to garnish**

In a saucepan, combine the juices, jam and zest. Bring to a boil over moderate heat and boil for a minute or two to dissolve the jam.

Add fruit and boil for no more than a minute. Taste and adjust flavorings. Depending upon the fruit used, you may want to add the almond extract or a pinch of cinnamon.

Chill and serve very cold. Garnish with mint or a swirl of yogurt.

Note: *If you prefer, you can puree half for a less chunky soup.*

Salads

To make salads, toss together any fresh vegetables with a little olive oil, lemon juice or vinegar and salt and pepper. Add garlic. You've got a great salad.

Use only extra-virgin olive oil of the highest grade and quality available. It's cold-pressed from olives at room temperature and not extracted with solvents. Be sure to read labels. By definition, "pure olive oil" or "olive oil" are oils extracted with solvents and then blended with "virgin olive oil" (cold-pressed but with a higher level of free oleic acid than "extra-virgin olive oil." Oleic acid can change the taste of the oil or impart a bitterness.)

Olive and sesame oils are said to be the least processed and healthiest oils to use. Some sources say they don't require refrigeration, unlike canola and safflower oils. Nonetheless, do refrigerate both sesame and olive oil if you don't plan to use them quickly—within a few weeks after opening.

This is the perfect place to discuss flax seed oil, which is a terrific source of essential fatty acids. If you suffer from dry skin in winter or cracks around your fingernails and mouth, you're lacking in essential fatty acids and would benefit from a couple of tablespoonfuls of flax seed oil daily. Flax seed oil on salads is the way to go. Always refrigerate flax seed oil as it is very perishable.

To dress a salad using flax seed oil, spoon two tablespoons over your salad together with the juice of half a lemon or some vinegar. I also like to sprinkle a teaspoon brewer's yeast and some dulse flakes on my salad. Voila! Nutritional nirvana that tastes good. (Of course, you can leave out the brewer's yeast and dulse flakes and have a normal tasting salad, but try it both ways. You might be surprised and find you like the superfood way best!)

If you dry salad greens after washing by using a salad spinner (well worth the $10), your greens will be crisper and require less dressing for terrific taste.

You don't have to wash or dry greens at all if you use mesclun, a mix of baby greens available in most supermarkets across the country. Mesclun usually has some bitter greens in the mix, too, which are cleansing, good for the skin and high in iron. Mesclun used to be only for gourmets. Not any more. I love romaine, but use lots of mesclun for salads because I've little time to wash romaine.

The greener your salad, the higher the vitamin and mineral content. Romaine and mesclun are some of the best greens, while iceberg is the worst.

Spinach and Mesclun with Raspberry Dressing

Doesn't everyone love raspberries? They impart a lusciousness to greens that is unexpected! Among other attributes, spinach cleanses the blood of toxins that cause skin inflammation and redness.

Serves 8

Dressing:
½ cup fresh raspberries
3 tablespoons raspberry vinegar
¼ cup olive oil

½ pound fresh spinach, washed
 and torn into bite-sized pieces
½ pound fresh mesclun
salt and pepper to taste
½ cup fresh raspberries to
 garnish

In a blender or using the steel blade of a food processor, combine the raspberries, vinegar and olive oil.

In a large bowl, toss the greens with the dressing to coat. Season to taste with salt and pepper. Garnish with raspberries.

Variation: You can substitute romaine or leaf lettuce for mesclun (baby greens). You can substitute strawberries or peaches for raspberries. Just try to match the vinegar to the fruit. For instance, we have a peach vinegar in our store, but you could use any fruity vinegar or even a balsamic vinegar.

Spinach and Endive Caesar Salad

A simple variation on Caesar salad from our first cookbook. Spinach is rich in iron and chlorophyll and builds blood. High in vitamin A, it's used in the treatment of night blindness. However, if you are prone to kidney stones, eat spinach sparingly.

Serves 4

2–3 cloves garlic
1 teaspoon ground mustard
1 tablespoon lemon juice
3 tablespoons olive oil
3.5-ounce can anchovies
1 pound spinach, washed, spun
   dry and torn into pieces

2–3 heads endive, washed and
   torn into bite-sized pieces
¼ cup freshly grated pecorino
   Romano cheese
whole wheat croutons, *optional*

Crush garlic with press into a salad bowl. Add mustard, lemon and olive oil. Mash anchovies into dressing with fork until they form paste.

Add spinach and endive to the bowl. Toss until leaves are well-coated with dressing. Sprinkle salad with cheese and toss again. Add croutons (try our recipe below or make your own), if desired. Serve at once.

Variation: *For a vegetarian version, substitute Bragg's liquid aminos or Dr. Bronner's mineral bouillon for anchovies (see What You Need to Know in the front of the book for a more complete description).*

Croutons:
¼ cup olive oil
2 cloves garlic, mashed

2 cups diced whole wheat bread
   (½-inch cubes)

Gently warm olive oil in skillet. Add garlic and bread. Saute over medium heat. Shake pan until croutons are browned on all sides.

Alternately, mix bread with olive oil and garlic in a bowl and place on cookie sheet in oven. Bake at 350° until croutons are brown and crisp. Turn from time to time.

Black Bean Salad with Sun-Dried Tomatoes and Green Onions

This makes a wonderful company salad—colorful, hearty, with a complex taste. There are great oil-packed sun-dried tomatoes on the shelves of stores these days, but our favorite is still our own. You'll find it in Miscellaneous at the end of the book.

Serves 4

½ cup oil-packed sun-dried tomatoes, chopped
3 tablespoons balsamic or red wine vinegar
¼ cup olive oil
4 cups cooked black beans
1 red bell pepper, diced
1 bunch scallions, sliced

1 cup feta cheese, crumbled or 4 hard-boiled eggs, chopped
8 cups mesclun or romaine lettuce, torn into bite-sized pieces
1 teaspoon chili powder
1 teaspoon cumin
salt and pepper to taste

Toss all ingredients together in a large mixing bowl. Taste and adjust seasoning.

Note: Review notes for cooking beans in What You Need to Know at the front of the book or buy canned, organic beans. It is said that black beans help ease low back and knee pain.

Red Kidney Bean Salad with Curry

Tomato is said to encourage a healthy appetite and digestion and help the body deal with symptoms like high blood pressure and red eyes.

Serves 4

¼ cup olive oil
2 bay leaves
1 teaspoon cinnamon
½ teaspoon cardamom
1 teaspoon ginger
1 teaspoon turmeric
½ teaspoon chili powder
4 cloves garlic, minced
1 onion, minced

2 cups diced tomatoes
1 carrot, diced
1 turnip, diced
1 yellow pepper, diced
2 cups cooked kidney beans
salt and pepper to taste
8 cups salad greens, torn into
   bite-sized pieces

In a skillet, gently warm olive oil. Add herbs and spices and let sizzle for a few seconds. Add vegetables and saute gently until onions are brown and carrots and turnip are almost tender, about 5 minutes. Add beans and simmer another 10 minutes to give them time to absorb flavoring. Season to taste.

To serve, bed each plate with mixed greens, spinach or romaine lettuce, and spoon bean mixture over greens.

Variation: You could turn this dish into a simple entree by serving it hot without the salad greens. Substitute steamed greens or serve a green vegetable alongside.

Avocado Pineapple Salad

Don't be afraid to try this. The enzymes in the pineapple are great for digestion and for reducing inflammation, and they are said to balance the essential fatty acids in avocado.

Avocadoes contain lecithin, a brain food, and they're a protein source often recommended for nursing moms. People who experience difficulty digesting fatty foods often thrive on avocadoes. Beautiful skin loves avocadoes.

Serves 4

2 avocadoes, cubed
½ fresh pineapple, diced
2 oranges, diced
¼ cup celery, diced

1 tablespoon lemon juice
½ cup papaya or mango juice
½ teaspoon salt
½ cup parsley, minced

In a large bowl, combine everything. Toss gently with a rubber spatula. Refrigerate 30 minutes to an hour and serve.

Note: *Make sure the papaya or mango juice is natural and not sugared.*

Broccoli and Carrot Salad

Broccoli, a variety of cauliflower, has been grown in Europe for 3,000 years. In addition to being an anticancer vegetable, broccoli is said to brighten eyes and help reduce eye inflammation.

Serves 6

4 cups broccoli florets
2 cups diced carrot
2 teaspoons dijon mustard
3 tablespoons rice vinegar

1 tablespoon olive oil
2 teaspoons dried oregano
salt and pepper to taste

Steam broccoli and carrots until just crisp and tender, about 3 minutes. Transfer to a large bowl and cool. Combine rest of ingredients to make dressing, pour over vegetables, toss to coat and season to taste.

Note: It's important not to overcook broccoli. You want that bright green color which means the rich chlorophyll content is still intact and will do you some good! Chlorophyll has virtually the same molecular structure as hemoglobin—red blood cells. So chlorophyll is often referred to as "the blood of plant life." While iron forms the basis of hemoglobin, magnesium forms the basis of chlorophyll.

Colorful Cabbage Salad

This is based on a salad I used to eat at Brownie's Restaurant in New York's Greenwich Village when I worked there as a college student. Brownie's was the first natural food restaurant in the country. I remember Sam Brown fondly. Not only is this salad colorful and nutritious, but I've read that if you eat cabbage regularly, you won't get cold feet!

Serves 8–12

½ head green cabbage, finely shredded
½ head red cabbage, finely shredded
2 carrots, grated
small bunch flat parsley, minced

3 tablespoons lemon juice
½ teaspoon salt
½ teaspoon black pepper
½ teaspoon garlic powder
¼ teaspoon allspice
¼ teaspoon turmeric

Shred cabbage by quartering and slicing thinly with a sharp blade.

Place all ingredients in a salad bowl and toss. If you want a richer taste, mix in a spoonful of olive oil.

Refrigerate at least 30 minutes before serving. It lasts well for several days.

Note: You really want the cabbage sliced finely. It's hard to chew when it's not.

Double Tomato Salad

This salad is perfect in summer when tomatoes are ripe. For variety, feel free to throw in cooked white beans, parsley, endive or some fresh spinach. Tomatoes are said to relieve dryness and thirst and to detoxify the body in general. However, as a member of the nightshade family (tomatoes, peppers, potatoes, eggplants), they may be aggravating to arthritics because they upset calcium metabolism. (Our favorite recipe for sun-dried tomatoes is in Miscellaneous at the end of the book.)

Serves 4

2 pounds tomatoes, sliced
¼ cup chopped oil-packed sun-dried tomatoes (use oil in salad, too)
2 tablespoons balsamic vinegar
½ cup green olives, halved
½ cup black olives, halved
1 teaspoon marjoram
1 cucumber, diced
½ cup feta, crumbled, *optional*

Toss all ingredients together. Taste and adjust seasoning.

Summer Cucumbers with Yogurt, Garlic and Dill

In Eastern Europe, heavy sour cream is used. There's no substitute, that's for sure, but using full-fat yogurt tastes good, too. I've used a kefir cheese that tastes almost as good as sour cream when I'm not counting calories. You can make your own yogurt cheese by spooning yogurt into cheesecloth, tying it and letting it drain over the faucet in the kitchen sink for 2 hours. However, authentic yogurt cheese needs to be drained for 24 hours. Many of the calories drain away in the process, especially if you use fat-free yogurt.

Yogurt is more digestible than milk and is said to boost the immune system and kill off harmful bacteria. Use yogurt with live cultures to replenish friendly flora after a bout of illness or use of antibiotics.

Serves 4

2 large cucumbers	**6 cloves garlic, minced**
2 small, tender yellow summer squash	**32 ounces thick yogurt**
	1 teaspoon dill weed
handful of radishes	**1 teaspoon salt**
½ small red onion, minced	**¼ teaspoon black pepper**

Scrub vegetables using a vegetable brush under running water. Trim, but do not peel.

Using the shredding disk of a food processor, grate cucumbers, summer squash and radishes. Place in a salad bowl with rest of ingredients. Mix together using a rubber spatula. Chill, covered, in the refrigerator for about an hour.

Serve cold.

Serving Suggestion: *This salad makes a wonderful, refreshing lunch or dinner during the summer. Serve with black bread.*

Grated Beets in Thick Yogurt Sauce

Remember the "Glowing Salad" from our first cookbook? If you have a food processor, this salad also takes 5 minutes to make. In addition to being cleansing and high in iron, beets are used to treat nervousness. Eat them raw once a week for beautiful skin. Because beets are also a laxative, have a small portion of this salad if you are not used to them.

Serves 6

1 pint full-fat plain yogurt or
  yogurt cheese
6 cups grated raw beets
2 cloves garlic, crushed with
  garlic press

2 tablespoons lemon juice
pinch salt, *optional*
chopped parsley to garnish,
  optional

To grate beets, cut off greens, trim top and bottom and scrub well with a vegetable brush. Don't peel. Simply grate using the shredding disk of a food processor. If you have a little more or a little less grated beet, it's okay.

Combine all ingredients in a bowl. Mix well with a rubber spatula. Chill for at least an hour before serving.

Serving Suggestion: *I like to serve this salad with dark pumpernickel bread.*

Note: *If you want to use non-fat or low-fat yogurt, follow directions in previous recipe for making thick yogurt cheese.*

Greek Eggplant Salad

Actually a fruit, not a vegetable, eggplant is rich in bioflavonoids. In Japan, pregnant women don't eat eggplant because it can cause miscarriage.

Did you know onions are known to help correct high blood pressure and are beneficial for colds and fevers, hay fever, asthma and lung conditions? That's because onions are a member of the garlic family.

Serves 4   *Bake at 400°*

1 eggplant, cubed (½-inch cubes)
1 zucchini, halved and sliced
1 onion, diced
1 green pepper, diced
¼ cup olive oil
2 teaspoons salt

1 teaspoon each of rosemary,
thyme and basil
¼ pound feta
splash balsamic vinegar or
lemon, *optional*

Preheat oven to 400°.

Prepare vegetables. Toss with olive oil and roast in oven on cookie sheet in a thin layer for 1 hour, or until eggplant is tender and lightly colored. Turn once or twice during baking. Take vegetables out of oven and spoon into a large mixing bowl. Add seasonings.

Once vegetables are cool, add feta. Add a splash of balsamic vinegar or lemon juice if you like.

Garbanzo Salad Italiano

Very Italian, colorful and de-lish. Your taste buds will do the watusi! Feel free to use Asiago or Fontina if you like more flavorful cheeses. Great to share with friends at a potluck or picnic.

Kale is a member of the cabbage family and can, like cabbage, be used to treat ulcers. Its calcium is easily assimilated, making kale wonder food when combating osteoporosis and bone loss disorders.

Serves 8

3 cups cooked garbanzo beans
1 cup mozzarella or provolone cheese, cubed
½ cup red onion, minced
½ cup celery, minced
¼ cup sliced pitted black olives
¼ cup sliced pitted green olives
2 diced carrots, steamed

½ (or small) bunch kale, cut into bite-sized pieces and steamed
½ cup olive oil
½ teaspoon garlic powder
½ teaspoon oregano
1 teaspoon salt
2 teaspoons poppy seeds

Combine all ingredients. Taste and adjust seasoning.

Marinated Vegetable Salad

A wonderful summer picnic salad. Dill has a slight caraway taste and tarragon tastes a little like licorice. They marry well with the other subtle flavors and promote good digestion.

Serves 4

3 cups 1-inch pieces wax beans,
steamed
1 zucchini, quartered lengthwise
and sliced
½ cup sliced mushrooms
1 cup marinated artichoke
hearts
1 red onion, diced
1 red pepper, diced

Dressing:
⅓ cup walnut or olive oil
3 tablespoons cider vinegar
2 tablespoons lemon juice
1 teaspoon dill weed
1 teaspoon sea salt
¼ teaspoon allspice
½ teaspoon garlic powder
¼ teaspoon oregano
¼ teaspoon tarragon

Combine the first 6 ingredients in a salad bowl. In a separate small bowl, mix together the remaining ingredients thoroughly to make a dressing. Pour over vegetables and toss gently. Refrigerate an hour to give the flavors a chance to blend.

Note: *Did you know that most vinegars today are no longer naturally fermented? If your vinegar says it's distilled (check labels on all products containing vinegar, too), then it's made biochemically in just 24 hours. Naturally fermented vinegars such as apple cider and balsamic have unique flavors and contain amino acids and other nutrients. Balsamic vinegar, which is dark in color and has a sweet, complex flavor from aging in wood barrels, is yummy, gourmet, and a little pricey! Apple cider vinegar has been touted for years for its health-giving properties. So save distilled vinegars for softening fabric or use as a disinfectant, cleaning agent (especially for glass) and the best wallpaper remover you've ever tried. But keep it out of your tummy!*

Sicilian Salad

This dish is great with anchovies, but try Bragg's Liquid Aminos for a vegetarian version. Some spas serve it together with a kettle of hot water so people can make themselves a pick-me-up midmorning and midafternoon. Just add a tablespoonful of liquid aminos to a cup of hot water.

Cauliflower contains a compound called "indoles" which stimulates our body's own natural defense to fight cancer.

Serves 8

1 head cauliflower, florets
4 cups chopped kale
4 cups escarole or other hardy
   greens
1 jar artichoke hearts
1 cup celery, sliced
1 cup cucumber, diced
2 tablespoons capers

Dressing:
1 cup olive oil
¼ cup lemon juice
¼ cup wine vinegar
6 cloves garlic
2 tablespoons anchovies,
   mashed, or Bragg's liquid
   aminos
salt and pepper to taste

Blend dressing.

Steam cauliflower and hardy greens in a small amount of water until tender, about 5 minutes. (Obviously, if you want to substitute a tender green like spinach, don't steam for more than a minute, or use raw spinach.) Drain both cauliflower and greens and place in a large salad bowl.

When vegetables are cool, toss together with remaining ingredients and dressing. Taste and adjust seasoning.

Pasta or Tortellini Primavera Salad

You have to use the best marinated sun-dried tomatoes to make this salad sing. We've yet to find any we like better than our own recipe (see Miscellaneous at end of book). Don't stint on the olive oil because it imparts a superior flavor and poly- and mono-unsaturated composition. Good for you!

Serves 8

1½ pounds rotini or tortellini
½ cup olive oil (more is
  optional)
¼ cup cider vinegar
1 large carrot, diced and
  steamed
1 bunch kale, minced, or 1
  bunch swiss chard, diced
2 cups broccoli, florets

2 young zucchini, halved and
  sliced
1 cup Romano, freshly grated
1 cup marinated sun-dried
  tomatoes, diced
1 teaspoon garlic powder
1 teaspoon oregano
1 teaspoon basil
salt and pepper to taste

Bring water in a large pot to boil. Add pasta and cook until al dente. You're on your own here as every pasta is different. Start checking it in 5 minutes so you don't overcook and test it often. You don't want mush; you want pasta that is slightly firm to the tooth, or al dente.

Drain pasta and place in a large mixing bowl. Add olive oil and cider vinegar. Toss and let sit.

In the same pot, steam carrot and kale in a cup or two of water for 5 minutes. (Bring water to a boil, add vegetables and cover pot.) Add broccoli and steam another 5 minutes, or until a fork can pierce the vegetable, but it is still bright green. Drain water by pouring vegetables into a colander.

Add vegetables together with remaining ingredients to pasta in bowl. Mix with a rubber spatula and season to taste.

Note: *The zucchini does not get steamed. Broccoli may not be your favorite vegetable, but dressed in this salad, it's yummy and it's said to stop the growth of tumors.*

Asian Noodle Salad
with Chiles

Mirin is a rice wine vinegar used extensively in Oriental and macrobiotic dishes. Ingredients are brown rice, koji (a culture also used in miso) and water. Make sure to read labels as some brands are adulterated with corn syrup.

Watercress is considered a cruciferous vegetable, a member of the cabbage and broccoli family. It's wonderful for anemia, calcium deficiencies and blood cleansing. I probably should have you garnish every salad and main dish with watercress. My mother used to and then made us eat the garnish!

Serves 6

1 pound rice noodles
¼ cup toasted sesame oil
¼ cup tamari soy sauce
1 tablespoon mirin
2 teaspoons salt
1 cup chopped fresh cilantro
1 bunch scallions, sliced
2 jalapeno chiles, minced

1 bunch arugula or watercress, stemmed and torn into bite-sized pieces
1 medium jicama, peeled and grated
1 medium carrot, grated
1½ cups roasted peanuts, coarsely chopped, to garnish

Cook noodles in large pot of rapidly boiling water just until tender. Rinse noodles with cold water until cool. Drain well. Transfer to a large bowl.

Combine sesame oil, tamari, mirin and salt. Add to noodles. Add remaining ingredients except peanuts. Mix well. Garnish with peanuts and serve.

Lite Chow Mein Salad

This light, easily prepared salad can quickly be turned into a main course. Just add tofu, shrimp or tamari roasted nuts or seeds. Dulse, a mild-flavored seaweed, is soft, chewy and delicious. It has good alkalizing properties and is important in weight control.

Serves 8–10

1 pound Chinese rice sticks or threads
⅓ cup toasted sesame oil
½ cup tamari soy sauce
3–4 cloves garlic, minced
12 dried shiitake mushrooms, soaked in hot water and thinly sliced
3 cups mung bean sprouts

3 cups diced bok choy
2 carrots, cut into thin sticks
1 zucchini, quartered and sliced
2 teaspoons dried ginger
1 teaspoon black pepper
2 tablespoons dulse flakes
dash cayenne, salt and more sesame oil to taste

In a large pot of boiling water, cook rice sticks for 4 minutes. Drain and mix with sesame oil and tamari in a large salad bowl. Add remaining ingredients and mix well with hands, making sure rice sticks are well coated and vegetables interspersed.

Season to taste with pepper (a dash of cayenne is fun!), salt and, if desired, a splash more sesame oil.

Serving Suggestion: *Chow Mein Lite travels well and tastes great the next day.*

Note: *Maine Coast makes a dulse flake which is easy to use and is available in natural food stores.*

Potato Feta Salad

Feast for the eyes and the palate. Keeps well for a couple of days. Oregano is known as wild marjoram and blends perfectly with tomatoes and most vegetables. Dried oregano, like all dried herbs, is stronger than fresh. Parsley is said to help in cases of indigestion and measles!

Serves 6

Dressing:
⅓ cup olive oil
2 tablespoons dill weed
2 tablespoons parsley
1 small red onion, thinly sliced
2 tablespoons lemon juice
2 teaspoons oregano
1 teaspoon garlic powder
1½ pounds potatoes

1 cup feta, crumbled
4 green onions, sliced
1 red pepper, diced
1 cup diced tomato
1 pickling cucumber
  (or zucchini)
2 cups romaine strips
½ cup black kalamata olives
salt and pepper to taste

Mix ingredients for dressing together.

Steam potatoes until tender. Drain and cool slightly. Cut into bite-sized pieces. Transfer to large bowl. Pour dressing over potatoes and toss gently.

When cool, add rest of ingredients. Toss gently. Add salt and pepper to taste.

Note: *Try using yellow potatoes like Yukon Golds or Yellow Finns.*

Potato, Tofu and Dulse Salad

Great way to learn to love seaweed, which is high in minerals. Dulse, in fact, contains all 43 trace minerals! Particularly good for hair and skin.

Tofu is an easily digested protein, good for healing and sensitive stomachs. Because it has no flavor of its own, it takes on whatever personality you give it, as in this recipe.

Serves 4

1 pound firm tofu
1½ cups cider or wine vinegar
2 tablespoons tamari soy
   sauce
2 tablespoons olive oil
4 large potatoes, diced
½ cup dulse flakes

1 teaspoon dill weed
1 cucumber, diced
2 cups peppers, diced
2 cups cherry tomatoes
salt and pepper to taste
more oil, yogurt, mayonnaise or
   Nayonnaise, *optional*

Dice tofu into 1-inch cubes and place in large salad bowl. Combine vinegar, tamari and olive oil and pour over tofu. Let marinate for at least 30 minutes.

Steam potatoes until fork tender, about 5 minutes. Pour into colander and cool. Toss potatoes with tofu. Add rest of ingredients and toss.

Taste and adjust seasoning. You may want to add a little more oil or some yogurt, mayonnaise or Nayonnaise.

Russian Potato Salad

This salad is colorful, delicious and a favorite with everyone. It's not gooked up with gooey mayonnaise and can travel safely to picnics, too. Best at room temperature.

Serves 8

2 small beets, scrubbed, cut into ½-inch cubes
8 new potatoes, red or white, scrubbed and cut into bite-sized pieces
4 carrots, quartered and diced
1 small red onion, minced
1 medium cucumber, diced
2 cups peas
2 teaspoons dry mustard powder
1½ teaspoons dill weed
1 teaspoon garlic powder
½ cup olive oil
salt and pepper to taste

Steam beets until fork tender (don't worry about peeling!). Drain and place in mixing bowl. Steam potatoes until tender. Add to bowl. Same with carrots.

When beets, potatoes and carrots are cool, add remaining ingredients. Adjust seasoning to taste and serve.

Note: When you buy prepared mustard, make sure you're getting just that; many commercial mustards now are made with turmeric and vinegar because it's cheaper. Don't buy mustards with oil, gums, flour, preservatives, artificial flavors or colors!

Broccoli, Lentil and Potato Salad

Claudia Vestal, the good customer whose fast fingers typed this book, says you can never have too many potato salad recipes because there are so many potato varieties to try like Yukon Golds and Yellow Finns. Remember in the Bible Esau sold his birthright for a bowl of lentils? This salad has lentils, too. They are a nutritional powerhouse!

Steamed carrots are useful in treating constipation. Because they are high in silicon, they are said to strengthen connective tissues.

Serves 8

2–3 cups water
1 cup lentils
1 pound potatoes, cut into
  ½-inch cubes
1 cup sliced carrots
2 cups broccoli, florets

Dressing:
1 small red onion, chopped
½ cup olive oil
1 teaspoon thyme
1 teaspoon salt
½ teaspoon pepper

Bring water to a boil. Rinse lentils, add to water and cook until tooth tender, about 20 minutes. Make dressing in a large mixing bowl. Put lentils in bowl and toss with rubber spatula to coat.

Bring 1 inch water to a boil in a large skillet. Put in potatoes and carrots and steam about 10 minutes. Add broccoli, cover and steam another 2–3 minutes until all vegetables are tender. Pour into colander and cool to room temperature.

Combine vegetables with lentils. Toss to coat.

Salad Oliver

A Russian version of coleslaw. It's nice to know that cabbage, according to the January 1927 *American Medicine Journal,* is "therapeutically effective in conditions of scurvy, diseases of the eyes, gout, rheumatism, pyorrhea, asthma, tuberculosis, cancer and gangrene. It is excellent as a vitalizing agent and blood purifier."

Serves 6

2 carrots, julienned
1 large potato, diced
2 hard-boiled eggs, chopped
1 small green cabbage, finely
   shredded

1 cup peas, uncooked
1 apple, peeled, cored and diced
¼ cup soy mayonnaise
1 teaspoon salt
½ teaspoon pepper

Prepare potatoes and carrots and steam together in a small amount of water (about 1 cup) for about 10–15 minutes. Potatoes should be soft, but not mushy. Drain and allow to cool.

Hardboil eggs by placing in a pot with water to cover. Bring to a boil, lower heat and simmer for about 5 minutes. Drain water and fill pot with cold water to cool eggs. Once you can handle them, roll between hands to loosen shells and peel.

In the meantime, cut cabbage in half and slice finely with a good sharp knife. Place cabbage in bowl with peas, apple and soy mayo. Add remaining ingredients and mix well with a rubber spatula. Adjust salt and pepper to taste.

Note: *We use a soy mayonnaise called Nayonnaise in the kitchen of our store which is lower in fat than regular mayo. It's another way to introduce soy products into your diet. Your family won't know or complain.*

Sesame Root Vegetable Salad

When we couldn't get parsnips, we tried rutabagas. They have the melt-in-your-mouth richness everyone loves. They're golden yellow inside. Rutabagas, members of the turnip family, are said to contain anti-cancer qualities and help clear congestion. However, one book I read said they should not be eaten by people with kidney problems.

Recent studies are showing that Jerusalem artichokes, also known as sun-chokes, have strong antioxidant properties. DeBoles pasta company uses some Jerusalem artichoke flour in their semolina pastas. Jerusalem artichokes were a staple in Native American diets.

Serves 4–6

4 tablespoons toasted sesame oil
½ teaspoon turmeric
1 cup sliced carrots
2 cups diced Jerusalem
** artichokes, peeled**

2 cups diced rutabagas
2 cups diced sweet potatoes
1½ cups water
4 tablespoons sesame seeds
salt and pepper to taste

In a skillet, gently warm sesame oil and turmeric. Stir until turmeric is fragrant, not browned, about half a minute.

Add vegetables and water. Simmer, covered, until tender, about 10 minutes. Drain if necessary. Toss with sesame seeds and seasonings to taste.

Serving Suggestion: *It makes a pretty main course over quinoa, rice or millet.*

Eggless Egg Salad

Eight ounces of tofu contain only 164 calories and supply the same amount of calcium as eight ounces of milk, but with far more absorbability. It also supplies the same amount of iron as two ounces of beef liver or four eggs. Here's the version of eggless egg salad we make in our deli. It's similar to recipes we've found in several cookbooks.

Serves 4

1 pound firm or extra-firm tofu	**½ teaspoon turmeric**
¼ cup Nayonnaise (soy mayo)	**1 stalk celery, chopped**
½ tablespoon lemon juice	**½ small onion, minced**
1 teaspoon dill weed	**1 tablespoon chopped parsley**
1 teaspoon prepared mustard	**lettuce, tomato or slice of onion**
½ teaspoon prepared horse-	**to garnish**
radish	

Ideally, one should remove tofu from water and press under a heavy plate or pot for an hour to remove as much water as possible. If you don't have time to press tofu, make this recipe anyway—it'll just be softer!

Crumble tofu into a bowl with your fingers. Add remaining ingredients and toss together lightly. Chill and serve on a bed of greens, stuffed into a pocket bread or on the sprouted whole-grain hamburger buns (Food for Life brand) we love in our kitchen. Garnish with lettuce, tomato or slice of onion.

Variations: Add chopped pickle relish if you like. Use tamari, black pepper and sesame salt if those flavors appeal to you. Add dulse flakes. Add minced green bell pepper. Add chopped scallions. Put in whatever you like. Be happy that you've made something high in protein, easy to digest and appetizing. And it doesn't cost an arm and a leg!

Cajun Chicken Salad

Whether you use white or dark meat is up to you. Dark meat, of course, has more fat, but some of us prefer it! Chicken is said to act as an energy tonic and improve the condition of bone marrow. Make sure your chicken is healthy chicken. No hormone-raised birds, please!

Celery is used to treat high blood pressure and is an especially safe remedy during pregnancy.

Serves 8

4 pounds boneless, skinless chicken, cut into bite-sized pieces
Dressing:
⅓ cup lemon juice
⅓ cup olive oil
¼ teaspoon cayenne pepper
1 teaspoon cumin
1 teaspoon thyme
1 teaspoon marjoram

4 stalks celery, diced
2 carrots, halved and thinly sliced
2 cups corn
1 small jicama, peeled and diced
1 bunch parsley, minced
2 cloves garlic, minced
salt and pepper to taste

In a skillet with 1-inch water, poach chicken in a steamer basket or wire colander that fits into the skillet for about 7–8 minutes, or until juice runs clear when chicken is poked with knife. Don't overcook or chicken will be tough.

Remove chicken from skillet and put in salad bowl. Make dressing, pour over chicken, toss and let chicken cool. Add remaining ingredients and season to taste.

Curried Chicken Salad

Use chicken in conditions where appetite is poor and there is diabetes, edema or general debility. According to Chinese medicine, celery and lettuce are said to be the only vegetables that combine well with fruit because they balance (dry) the "damp" conditions caused by fruits.

Serves 8

5 pounds boneless, skinless white meat chicken, cut into bite-sized pieces
½ cup olive oil, *optional*
2 cups seedless red grapes
2 cups seedless green grapes
4 stalks celery, diced

1 small jicama, peeled, diced
1 cup mango or papaya juice
2 teaspoons curry powder
½ teaspoon turmeric
2 tablespoons olive oil
salt and pepper to taste

Simmer 1-inch water in a skillet. Place chicken in a steamer basket or wire colander which fits into the skillet and cook for 7–8 minutes. (Alternately, you can toss the chicken with the olive oil and bake in a 350° oven for 20 minutes.)

Place cooked chicken in a large salad bowl and cool. Combine with remaining ingredients. Adjust seasoning to taste and refrigerate for an hour before serving.

Note: *You can substitute a curry paste for powder, which will give you a richer flavor because it has oil as a base.*

Almond Rice Pesto

In Ayurveda, a system of medicine, which originated in India centuries ago, almonds are said to strengthen the intellect and be important for reproductive and heart health because they are high in vitamin E.

Serves 6

2 cups brown basmati rice
3½ cups water
1 cup almonds
1 bunch parsley
2 cloves garlic

3 tablespoons lemon juice
3 tablespoons olive oil
½ European cucumber,
 chopped
salt and pepper to taste

In a pot with a tight-fitting cover, place rice and water. Bring water to a boil, cover pot, lower heat and simmer rice for 45 minutes. Turn off heat and let pot sit, covered, for another 10 minutes. Then turn rice out into mixing bowl to cool.

Blend remaining ingredients, except cucumber, using steel blade of a food processor. When rice is cool, mix well with pesto. Add cucumber and salt and pepper to taste.

Note: If you worry about smelling from garlic, parsley is a good antidote because its chlorophyll acts as an internal deodorizer! Or try chewing a sprig of parsley after a garlicky meal. Just be sure to brush the green flecks off your teeth.

Barley, Wild Rice and Vegetables

Creamy barley is offset by the dark grains of wild rice in this salad. I used to use parsnips only in soups, but have come to love them in dishes like this one. Parsnips are said to help clear liver and gall bladder obstructions. They can also be diced and simmered in water. Drink the broth to fight colds, coughs and shortness of breath.

Serves 6

1 cup barley
1 cup wild rice
4 tablespoons olive oil
1 red onion, chopped
4 cloves garlic, minced

2 parsnips, diced
4 cups mesclun or bitter greens
   like escarole or chicory, torn
   in bite-sized pieces
salt and pepper to taste

In a large pot, place barley and wild rice together with 4 cups water. (Use a much larger pot than you think you need because barley tends to bubble over, and this will save clean-up time.) Bring water to a boil, turn flame down to lowest it will go, cover pot and simmer grains for an hour.

In a skillet, gently warm olive oil. Saute onion, garlic and parsnips until onions are translucent, about 5–10 minutes. Scrape mixture into bowl.

If they have not absorbed all the water, drain cooked grains in a colander. Add to bowl. When grains are cool, add mesclun or bitter greens. Toss, taste, adjust seasoning and serve.

Note: *If you haven't yet discovered mesclun, a washed assortment of baby greens, you've got a treat in store. Not only does mesclun require no washing or tearing into bite-sized pieces, so it's quick when you're rushed, but it's colorful and a little spicy because part of the mixture is usually greens like arugula, tatsoi, radicchio and even edible flowers.*

Berry and Tuna Salad with Ginger

Wasabi is powdered Japanese horseradish, which is usually mixed with some water and served with food like sushi. It is very hot and will clear congestion. Find it in natural food or Asian food stores.

If you eat radishes regularly, they are said to prevent viral infections like colds and flus.

Serves 4

1½ cups wheat berries
Dressing:
2 tablespoons soy sauce
2 tablespoons olive oil
4 teaspoons wasabi powder
2 tablespoons tahini
2 tablespoons rice vinegar
1 teaspoon mustard
4 cloves garlic, minced

1 pound tuna
4 cups mesclun or sprouts
2 cups stemmed spinach
1 bunch radishes, sliced
2 cups minced green onions
2 tablespoons minced ginger to garnish

To cook wheat berries, or any grain berry, place in large pot and cover with 4–5 inches of water. Bring to boil, lower heat, cover pot and cook an hour or a little more. Berries will be soft, but still a little chewy.

While berries cook, combine dressing ingredients. Brush both sides of the tuna liberally with dressing and allow to marinate until berries are done. Set aside remaining dressing.

Broil or grill tuna until crusty on outside and rare within, about 4 minutes per side. Let fish rest a few minutes and then cut against grain into ⅓-inch-thick slices.

Toss salad greens, radishes and green onions together with berries. Place tuna on top and garnish with remaining dressing and ginger.

Bulgur and Wild Rice with Apricots and Pistachios

The colors make this salad look like confetti. Dried red and green bell peppers not only add color, but crunch. If you can't find dried peppers (we wouldn't be without them in our store), you can, of course, substitute fresh vegetables of any kind. It will change the salad, but maybe you'll come up with something even better!

Dried apricots are high in vitamin A, iron and copper. They are often used to treat anemia.

Serves 8

1 cup bulgur
1 cup boiling water
½ cup wild rice
½ cup minced dried apricots
½ cup shelled pistachios
½ cup dried red and green bell
  peppers

1 teaspoon cumin
½ teaspoon coriander
2 tablespoons lemon juice
¼ cup olive oil
salt and pepper to taste

Put bulgur into bowl and pour water over it. Let stand for 15–20 minutes, or until all water is absorbed. Then fluff with fork from time to time to allow heat to escape.

While bulgur is soaking, place wild rice in a pot together with 1½ cups water. Bring to a boil. Cover pot, lower heat and simmer for 45 minutes, or until tender. If necessary, drain rice well. Cool to room temperature.

In a large mixing bowl, combine all ingredients. Taste and adjust seasoning.

Bulgur with Black Beans, Feta and Dates

Bulgur wheat has been parboiled, dried and then cracked. It retains all the choline, niacin and minerals. It's used in salads, cereals, stews, pilafs and, in the Middle East, in some desserts. Combined here with black beans, nuts and feta, you've got a protein jolt with lots of complex carbs.

Serves 8

1½ cups bulgur
1½ cups boiling water

Dressing:
4 cloves garlic, minced
¼ cup lemon juice
¼ cup olive oil
½ teaspoon salt

2 cups cooked black beans
½ cup pine nuts
1 cup diced tomato
¼ cup chopped dates
1 cup crumbled feta
½ teaspoon black pepper
parsley or cilantro to
    garnish

Pour boiling water over bulgur and let stand until liquid is absorbed, about 30 minutes. Then fluff with fork from time to time to allow heat to escape.

Meanwhile, whisk together garlic, lemon juice, oil and salt. When bulgur is cool, add dressing and rest of ingredients. Toss gently until feta is evenly distributed.

Cover and refrigerate an hour before serving. Taste, adjust seasoning and garnish with parsley or cilantro.

Note: *Mixing with a rubber spatula doesn't crush beans or grains.*

Cajun Quinoa Salad

Colorful and great in summertime when you need something lighter. Quinoa is a super grain, which can be used as a diet staple because it is a complete protein including amino acids and a good source of complex carbs, too.

Serves 4

1 cup raw quinoa
Dressing:
2 tablespoons lemon juice
2 tablespoons olive oil
pinch cayenne pepper
½ teaspoon cumin
½ teaspoon black pepper
½ teaspoon salt (or to taste)

1 cup frozen corn kernels
1 red pepper, diced
½ cup pitted, diced black olives
½ cup diced red onion
1 cup minced flat Italian parsley

Bring 2 cups water to a boil. Add quinoa, stir and cover pot. Lower heat and simmer for 10 minutes. Turn off heat and let pot stand covered for another 10 minutes.

In the meantime, prepare the dressing and place in salad bowl. Dump hot quinoa into dressing and toss with rubber spatula. Let stand to cool. Fluff quinoa with spatula every 5–10 minutes.

When quinoa is warm (not hot enough to "cook" vegetables), add remaining salad ingredients. Toss gently and season to taste (some of us like more cayenne!).

Notes: *Lots of books tell you that you have to sort quinoa and check for small stones or wash it to remove the bitter flavor from the waxy coating on the grain. We do neither at our store and have never had a problem with stones or bitterness.*

Couscous Chick-Pea Salad with Feta and Olives

I know everyone doesn't share my love of feta and olives. Perhaps I was a goat herder in a former life. I love the way the tastes go with vegetables and grain, and I love the color contrast. Feast for palette and eyes. This makes a great summer picnic dish. Colorful to bring to a pot luck. Chick-peas, also known as cecci or garbanzo beans, have lots of protein.

Serves 4

1 cup boiling water
1 cup French couscous
½ teaspoon salt
2 cups cooked chick-peas
2 red peppers, diced
small bunch scallions, sliced
½ cup sliced carrots, steamed
½ cup pitted kalamata olives

¼ cup minced parsley
3 tablespoons apple cider
    vinegar
1 teaspoon dijon mustard
⅔ cup olive oil
¼ teaspoon garlic powder
6 ounces feta cheese, crumbled
1 teaspoon pepper

Pour boiling water over couscous and salt. Let stand about 20 minutes. Break up with fingers or toss with rubber spatula every 5 minutes to allow heat to escape. If using fingers, be careful because the grain holds heat.

Combine remaining ingredients and toss with couscous when cool.

Taste and adjust seasoning.

Lentils and Mushrooms

An unusual and delicious salad, with a nutritional wallop from shiitakes, which boost the immune system, and from protein-rich, fiber-rich lentils. Shiitakes are said to give eternal youth and longevity!

Serves 8

5 cups water
2 cups lentils
½ cup olive oil
6 ounces Fakin' Bacon or other
  tempeh or soy bacon, chopped
1 red onion, minced
1 large bunch kale, minced
1½ teaspoons thyme
1 teaspoon tarragon

½ pound fresh (or 1 cup dried)
  shiitake mushrooms
hot water to cover
1 pound other mushrooms of
  your choice
2 cups green beans, trimmed
½ cup water, if needed
salt and pepper to taste

Bring water to a boil in a pot. Add lentils, turn down heat to lowest setting, cover pot and simmer 25 minutes, or until lentils are tender to the tooth but still have a nice shape.

Meanwhile, in a large skillet, gently warm olive oil. Saute bacon together with onion, kale and herbs for about 5 minutes. Turn off heat and cover skillet until lentils are ready.

If using dried shiitakes, soak in hot water for 10 minutes. Squeeze and save liquid to use later in this dish or in soups or stews. Or drink it while you cook since it is said to stimulate the immune system! Thickly slice all mushrooms.

Add lentils to skillet together with mushrooms and beans. Cook for another 5 minutes, stirring so ingredients are well mixed and lentils don't stick to bottom of skillet. You may need to add ½ cup water or liquid from mushrooms. Taste and adjust seasoning.

Note: Shiitake mushrooms are often called oyster mushrooms when fresh. An advantage to using dried shiitakes is that you can keep them on hand and you don't have to worry about them spoiling.

Curried Couscous

This is a nice change from the usual couscous salad. Best served within hours of being made, otherwise the coconut gets soggy.

Serves 4

1 cup boiling water
1 cup French couscous
¼ cup shredded coconut
¼ cup toasted cashews
1 teaspoon curry powder
½ cup mango juice
1 tablespoon fresh ginger, minced

1 teaspoon salt
¼ teaspoon pepper
2 teaspoons toasted sesame oil
1 small head cabbage, shredded
3 carrots, grated
1 bunch scallions, sliced
salt and pepper to taste

In a mixing bowl, pour boiling water over couscous. Let stand for about 15 minutes, or until grain has absorbed water. Fluff with fork and let cool.

Add remaining ingredients. Taste and adjust seasoning.

Note: Want to always have fresh ginger on hand? You can freeze the whole root, take it out to thaw for 5 minutes and grate off what you want (refreeze the rest). Or grate ginger when you bring it home and freeze it in a glass jar or plastic bag.

Bean and Grain Main Dishes

Beans and grains are the world's staple foods. Their cultivation goes back tens of thousands of years. Beans contain protein, fats, carbohydrates, fiber, vitamins and minerals.

In this country, we rely mainly on wheat and rice. Typically, we process those grains so the part which can spoil—the part which is nutrient rich—is removed so products can sit on shelves longer. The bran we remove from wheat and rice, for instance, not only adds bulk to the digestive system, it also helps stabilize blood sugar by regulating the absorption of nutrients and sugars in the digestive tract. The bran we remove from grains to make them shelf-stable has been shown to reduce blood cholesterol as effectively as any known cholesterol-lowering drug.

Try the recipes in the following chapter. Not only will you get a chance to explore grains other than wheat and rice, you'll get a chance to eat vegetarian dishes. You won't miss the meat. You'll find vegetarian dishes are easier to digest and give your body a chance to recover when you're stressed. Because the body has to work less to process them, you'll have more energy for other things.

What about protein? you ask. Combining beans and grains, grain and dairy, beans and dairy or grains and nuts, for instance, yields complete protein. Nor do we need to eat those combinations at the same meal. It seems that eating them even the same day suffices.

Where can you get grains like millet and quinoa? At this writing, not at your local supermarket! You'll have to visit a natural food store where you can expect a culinary and gustatory adventure!

Turkish Vegetable Casserole

This dish works equally well with chicken or shrimp, but if you use tofu, you get those phyto (plant) estrogens said to be important in preventing breast and prostate cancer. Eggplant is said to prevent convulsions. This is a good company dish. Hearty peasant fare.

Serves 8   *Bake at 375°*

½ cup olive oil
2 large onions, chopped
4 cloves garlic, minced
1 eggplant, diced
2 stalks celery, sliced
2 carrots, sliced
2 tomatoes, diced

1 teaspoon thyme
1 teaspoon oregano
2 teaspoons salt
1 teaspoon pepper
4 potatoes, diced
4 cups spinach
2 pounds tofu or tempeh

Toss together all but last three ingredients in a large casserole dish. Stir to coat with oil (I like to mix with my hands). Cover tightly and bake in a 375° oven for 30 minutes.

In the meantime, steam the diced potatoes in a small amount of water until fork-tender. Add potatoes, spinach and drained tofu to casserole. Mix well. Taste and adjust seasoning. Continue baking, uncovered, for another 15 minutes.

Lemon Grill Charmoula

Charmoula is colorful and aromatic. Ordinarily lamb is used, not tempeh. This dish is a favorite with staff and customers at our store.

Serves 4–6   *Bake at 350°*

4 smallish potatoes, cut into bite-size pieces
1 green pepper, cubed
1 red pepper, cubed
1 eggplant, with skin, cubed
1 large onion, quartered, slices separated
½ cup olive oil
2 tablespoons olive oil

2 tablespoons lemon juice
4–5 cloves garlic
½ teaspoon paprika
pinch cayenne
1 teaspoon cumin
2 tablespoons dried parsley
1 package lemon grill tempeh
salt and pepper to taste

Prepare vegetables. Pieces should fit easily in one's mouth but be large enough to be attractive and speared easily with a fork! Toss veggies in ½ cup olive oil and spread in shallow pans. Roast at 350° until potatoes are tender and begin to brown. This can take upwards of an hour.

In the meantime, make the sauce by mixing the remaining olive oil with lemon juice, garlic (use a garlic press or make sauce in a blender or food processor), spices and herbs.

Cube lemon grill tempeh and add to vegetables when they are done. Tempeh doesn't need to be cooked, just heated through in 10 minutes. Remove pans from oven. Place charmoula in bowl and toss with sauce. Taste and adjust seasoning, using more cayenne if you like things hot, and salt and black pepper as needed. Serve in an attractive dish.

Note: *Lemon grill tempeh is made by several companies. We use one made by Lightlife. Tempeh is a staple in Indonesia made when presoaked and cooked soybeans are fermented and pressed into cakes. High in protein, tempeh may have gray or dark spots, which do not indicate spoilage but are part of the food. The enzymes produced during fermentation not only make tempeh easy to digest, but are said to actually improve digestive health.*

Tempeh Creole

The consistency of tempeh, the feel of it on the tongue, is different from foods most of us are used to. It doesn't feel like chicken, tofu, shrimp or beef. Can we acquire a taste for it? I think so, just as many of us have acquired a taste for mangoes, avocadoes, quinoa and even tofu. There are many kinds of tempeh. Some are multigrain. Others are already seasoned like Fakin' Bacon. You get the benefit of soy from all. Try incorporating tempeh in your menu every once in a while!

Serves 6 over brown rice, potatoes, white beans or orzo

¼ cup olive oil
2 packages tempeh
2 onions, chopped
4 cloves garlic
2 ribs celery, sliced
2 green peppers, chopped
2 cups diced canned tomatoes
1 lemon, sliced

¼ teaspoon cayenne, *optional*
¼ teaspoon black pepper
1 teaspoon salt
1 teaspoon chili powder
1 teaspoon basil
½ teaspoon thyme
4 bay leaves

Gently warm olive oil in a large skillet. Cube tempeh and saute together with onions, garlic, celery and peppers for about 5 minutes. Stir from time to time.

Add tomatoes and remaining ingredients. Lower flame, cover pot and simmer for 15 minutes. Remove dish from stove.

Taste and adjust seasoning.

Snappy Tempeh

Neutral in taste, unflavored tempeh absorbs whatever flavors you pair it with. You can bake tempeh, broil, stir-fry or use it in casseroles, salads, sandwiches, sauces, soups or dips. Mix it with vegetables or grains. It's good sauteed in a little oil or tamari. If you like ginger, you'll like this recipe. Besides its zippy taste, ginger helps the body break down protein foods and lessens problems with flatulence.

Serves 3–4

1 package unflavored tempeh
1 tablespoon minced fresh ginger
4 cloves garlic, minced
2 tablespoons toasted sesame oil
2 tablespoons tamari

3 tablespoons mirin or wine
**   vinegar**
1 teaspoon hot sauce,
**   *optional***
sliced scallions to garnish

Slice tempeh. Blend remaining ingredients, except scallions. Gently toss tempeh in marinade with a rubber spatula and let sit minimum 2 hours or overnight.

Broil tempeh for about 10–15 minutes, until crisp and lightly browned. Serve with a grain and your choice of steamed veggies. Garnish with scallions.

Variation: Serve as an appetizer with toothpicks and your favorite dipping sauce. Lots are available at natural food stores everywhere.

Root Vegetable "Curry"

Root vegetables like sweet potatoes have been important in the Western Hemisphere since prehistoric times; they have made an important contribution to supporting life. Make this "curry" as mild as you like since it actually has no curry powder and is simple, low in fat and yummy. We love not only its taste, but the way it looks. It's very colorful!

Serves 4

4 tablespoons olive oil
2 tablespoons minced or grated fresh ginger
6 cloves garlic, minced
1 teaspoon coriander
1 teaspoon cumin
½ teaspoon cardamom
pinch cayenne, *optional*
1 teaspoon chili powder
1 large onion, chopped

2 green peppers, chopped
2 carrots, sliced
2 parsnips, diced
2 sweet potatoes/yams, diced
1–2 cups papaya or mango juice
1 apple or pear, diced
¼ cup raisins/diced apricots (choose your favorite)
salt and pepper to taste

Gently warm olive oil in a large skillet. Add all ingredients through onion. Stir to coat onion and garlic. Saute 2–3 minutes.

Add vegetables and again stir to coat. Add juice and fruit to skillet. Cover and simmer over low heat for about 15 minutes, or just until vegetables are tender. Season to taste with salt and pepper.

Serving Suggestion: *We know this dish uses lots of spices, but they blend together beautifully, making the stew flavorful and delicious. Eat curry alone or serve over rice, quinoa or millet. You can garnish with pistachios, cashews or soy nuts.*

Note: *Don't peel carrots, potatoes, parsnips or fruit. Just scrub. It makes life easier and adds a few more vitamins to the dish.*

Oven-Roasted Vegetables

Don't peel any of the veggies in this dish. Rustic charm is the effect you want to create. Very gourmet, you know! So save labor and save those vitamins which are in or just under the skin! Serve with fish, poultry, couscous or rice. Roasted vegetables also make a terrific salad with a splash of balsamic vinegar.

Serves 6   *Bake at 400°*

1 small eggplant, cut into bite-sized pieces

2 red potatoes, cut into bite-sized pieces

1 large red onion, cut into 1-inch pieces

1 zucchini, cut into bite-sized pieces

1 summer squash, cut into bite-sized pieces

2 cups mushrooms, quartered

8 cloves garlic, crushed

½ teaspoon thyme

½ teaspoon rosemary

½ teaspoon oregano

4 tablespoons olive oil

salt and pepper to taste

Preheat oven to 400°.

Toss vegetables with garlic, herbs and olive oil. Spread in shallow baking pans or cookie sheets with sides. Roast for approximately 45 minutes, or until vegetables are tender and beginning to brown. (Sometimes potatoes are stubborn and take longer to roast. You can shorten the time by steaming them first, but then you'll probably need more oil as cooked potatoes are notorious for absorbing oil.) Stir occasionally.

Remove vegetables to serving bowl. Add salt and pepper to taste.

Serving Suggestion: *This dish heats up beautifully the next day, so you can prepare it ahead when you're having company or it's holiday time.*

Tofu Rancheros

This is our version of a recipe in *Nasoya Tofu* cookbook by John Panos. Tofu has cooling properties and lends itself to dishes with warming spices. Salsa works great here.

Serves 4

1 tablespoon toasted sesame oil
1 red onion, halved and sliced
2 carrots, diced
1 rutabaga, diced
1 bunch kale, diced, *optional*
½ pound frozen corn (more if you like)

1 pound firm tofu
1 cup salsa (our favorite brand is San Angel Chipotle)
1 tablespoon tamari soy sauce
salt and pepper to taste

Gently warm oil and saute onions. Add carrots, rutabaga and kale. Stir to coat. Saute for a few minutes. Add corn, tofu, salsa and tamari. Simmer until carrots are tender, about 10 minutes, stirring occasionally.

Adjust seasoning to taste.

Curried Barley and Pistachio Pilaf

Ayurvedic medicine, practiced widely in India, considers the pistachio a tonic for the whole body. Coriander kills bacteria and fungi and is good on cuts and wounds. Coriander is the dried form of cilantro. However, they are not interchangeable in recipes.

Serves 6

6 cups water
1 teaspoon salt
2 cups barley
1 carrot, diced
2 cups broccoli, florets
½ cup water
2 tablespoons olive oil

1 small onion, diced
1 tablespoon garam masala
2 teaspoons coriander
1 teaspoon cumin
1 teaspoon turmeric
1 cup shelled pistachios
½ cup currants, *optional*

Bring water and salt to a boil in a big pot (barley tends to bubble over). Add barley, reduce heat as low as it will go, cover pot and simmer for 1 hour. You may need to move the pot partially off the burner if it bubbles over.

Steam carrot and broccoli in water for 5 minutes. Set aside.

In a second skillet, gently warm olive oil. Saute onion until translucent, or about 5 minutes. Stir in rest of ingredients and saute another few minutes.

When barley is cooked, remove from heat. Place in a large bowl and fluff with a spatula. Add remaining ingredients and toss until thoroughly mixed.

Black Bean Stew

Beans with a grain are a wonderful source of protein and have lots of complex carbohydrates, which are great for boosting one's energy. And they have cholesterol-lowering soluble fibers. Try a piece of seaweed called "kombu" in the pot when cooking beans. Kombu helps break down carbohydrates in beans that are difficult to digest and cause gas.

Serves 8

1 pound dried black beans	1 16-oz. can tomatoes, diced
2 tablespoons olive oil	8 cups water
2 slices Fakin' Bacon	4 cups brown basmati rice
2 large onions, sliced	salt and pepper to taste
6 cloves garlic, minced	avocado slices, sprig parsley or
1 bay leaf	cilantro or grated cheese to
1–2 teaspoons crushed red pepper	garnish

Sort beans to check for stones and rinse. Pressure-cook for 20 minutes. (If you don't have a pressure cooker, cook beans as in chart in What You Need to Know in front of book.) If you don't want to cook beans, buy canned. You'll need 6 cups cooked beans.

Gently warm olive oil in a skillet. Saute Fakin' Bacon together with onions and garlic. Add bay leaf, hot pepper and tomatoes. Simmer sauce for 10 minutes and set aside.

Bring 8 cups water to a boil. Stir in rice. Cover and turn flame down to lowest. Simmer rice for 45 minutes. (Remember not to stir rice after it comes to a boil or it will become sticky.) Turn off flame and let rice sit, covered, for 10 minutes.

When beans are cooked, drain if necessary and stir into sauce in skillet. Taste and adjust seasoning. Place 1 cup cooked rice on each plate. Mound beans in center. If desired, garnish with avocado slices, a sprig of parsley or cilantro, or slather with grated cheese.

Bulgur Pilaf with Tahini Sauce

Bulgur is heavier than couscous and has more flavor. Both have been steamed and dried before being cracked, which makes them easy to use. Bulgur comes in varying degrees of coarseness. We like it coarse in our kitchen.

Garlic contains a compound that destroys aflatoxin, a carcinogen produced by mold that can grow on grains and peanuts.

Serves 4

2 cups cooked chick-peas	1 yellow summer squash,
1 cup bulgur	quartered and sliced
1 cup boiling water	4 cloves garlic
3 tablespoons olive oil	¼ teaspoon salt
1 onion, minced	2 teaspoons lemon juice
2 carrots, diced	½ cup tahini
1 zucchini, quartered and sliced	⅓ cup water

Pour boiling water over bulgur in a bowl and let sit for 15 minutes, until all water has been absorbed.

Gently warm olive oil in a skillet and saute onions and carrots for about 5 minutes. Add zucchini and stir for another minute or two, just until squash begins to soften. Remove skillet from flame. Set aside.

Break up bulgur with fork and gently toss to release heat.

To make sauce in a food processor using the steel blade, blend rest of ingredients.

Toss half of vegetable mixture with bulgur. Place in serving dish, spoon sauce over that, place remaining bulgur in center and remaining vegetables around the sides.

Chick-Peas, Swiss Chard and Spinach

Chard is said to correct calcium deficiency, improve digestion and act as a diuretic. As with spinach, you need only steam for a minute or two. I prefer red chard because its stems are more tender and it imparts a pretty color to any dish.

Serves 6–8

3 cups cooked chick-peas	**1 pound Swiss chard, rinsed**
6 tablespoons olive oil	**1 pound spinach, cleaned**
2 red onions, sliced	**2 tablespoons water**
6 cloves garlic, minced	**4 tablespoons lemon juice**
2 large tomatoes, chopped	**salt and pepper to taste**

Don't remember how to cook chick-peas? Consult the chart in What You Need to Know in front of book. Don't have time to cook them and don't have a jar tucked away in your freezer? Use canned beans. A little more or a little less is fine.

Gently warm olive oil. Add onion and garlic and saute until onion is softened, about 5 minutes. Add chick-peas and tomatoes. Cook 5 minutes. Add Swiss chard, spinach and 2 tablespoons water. Cover and simmer until chard is wilted, about 2 minutes.

Remove skillet from heat. Stir in seasonings and adjust taste.

Serving Suggestion: *This is as good hot as cold and makes a great picnic dish.*

Note: *If you don't have access to chard, use all spinach. If no spinach, feel free to use only chard!*

Curried Beans and Greens

Another simple dish with chick-peas. Chick-peas, also called garbanzo beans, probably originated in western Asia and traveled through India and the Middle East to the Mediterranean. Every culture loves them!

Garbanzo beans, shaped a little like the heart, are said to benefit that organ. They have more iron than any other legume.

Serves 8

1 pound dry chick-peas
1 bunch seasonal greens like
   kale or collards
1–2 cups water

16 cloves garlic, pressed
4 cups curry sauce (a favorite is
   Desert Curry sauce by
   Greater Galilee)

Check beans for stones and wash in a colander. Refer to the chart in What You Need to Know at the front of the book to cook beans. When done, drain.

Coarsely chop greens and steam with a cup or two of water until tender, about 10 minutes. Drain.

Toss all ingredients together and serve to rave reviews. It's that simple! Really!

Seven Vegetable Couscous

Saffron is the world's most expensive herb. Only two stamens per plant so it's harvested with tweezers. Don't be tempted to use more saffron because it will impart a bitter flavor to the dish.

Serves 8

1 cup chick-peas
2 cups boiling water
2 cups couscous
¼ cup olive oil
3 onions, chopped
½ teaspoon cinnamon
1 tablespoon fresh ginger,
    minced
4 saffron threads

6 parsnips, diced
6 carrots, diced
2 sweet potatoes, diced
½ head cabbage, sliced
1 bunch kale, cut into ribbons
salt and pepper to taste
1 bunch parsley, minced, to
    garnish

Cook chick-peas according to directions in What You Need to Know in front of the book. If you have a jar of cooked chick-peas in the freezer, use those. If you have no time and have canned chick-peas on hand, use those.

Pour 2 cups boiling water over couscous in a large serving bowl. Let stand for 10 minutes and then fluff with fork to release heat.

Gently heat olive oil in a large skillet. Saute onion, cinnamon, ginger and saffron until onion is soft and spices are aromatic. Add parsnips, carrots, sweet potatoes, cabbage and kale. Stir to coat with oil. Saute until a fork can pierce the carrots, about 5–10 minutes.

Toss together with couscous and chick-peas in the bowl. Taste and adjust salt and pepper. Garnish with parsley and serve.

Couscous with Pumpkin Sauce

Sweet potatoes or yams are high in beta carotene. The deeper the color, the more beta carotene. Basil is from the mint family and is good for stomach, lungs, spleen and intestines.

Serves 6

1 cup couscous
1 cup boiling water
½ teaspoon salt
½ teaspoon pepper
½ cup olive oil
1 package Fakin' Bacon, diced
1 red onion, minced
4 cloves garlic, minced

pinch red pepper
2 pounds sweet potatoes or pumpkin, diced
2 tablespoons basil
¾ teaspoon nutmeg
¼ teaspoon thyme
¼ cup pumpkin seeds
1 cup water
pumpkin seeds to garnish

Pour boiling water over couscous, salt and pepper and let it sit until water is absorbed, about 15 minutes. Crumble grain with fingers or fluff with fork.

In a skillet, gently warm olive oil. Saute Fakin' Bacon, onion, garlic, pepper and sweet potato. Stir almost constantly for 5 minutes, until sweet potato starts to soften. Add herbs, spices and a cup water. Lower heat, cover and simmer 15 minutes, or until sweet potato is very soft and you have a nice sauce. Toss couscous with sauce. Garnish with pumpkin seeds.

Kasha Chili

Kasha, or buckwheat, is rich in B vitamins and a member of the family that includes rhubarb, sorrel and dock. Combined with beans, it becomes a complete protein with lots of fiber. Try it—you'll like it.

Serves 4–6

2 onions, diced
2 peppers, diced
4 tablespoons olive oil
1 28-oz. can chunky tomato
   sauce
3 cups vegetable broth or water
1 15-oz. can pinto or kidney
   beans

1 tablespoon chili powder
4 cloves garlic, minced
1 teaspoon paprika
½ teaspoon cumin
¼ teaspoon pepper, or to taste
salt to taste
¾ cup whole kasha (buckwheat
   groats)

In a large skillet, saute onions and peppers in olive oil. Add tomato sauce, broth, beans and spices. Bring to a boil and add kasha. Cover, reduce heat and simmer for 10–15 minutes, or until kasha is tender.

Taste and adjust seasoning. If you like really spicy chili, add cayenne. Serve hot.

Serving Suggestions: *You can top with shredded cheddar cheese (regular or soy) before serving or serve as a dip with tortilla chips.*

Variation: *If you prefer black beans, use those. If you want to make lentil chili, use ½ cup dry lentils instead of canned beans. Let sauce and lentils simmer for 20 minutes before adding kasha.*

Lentils and Chestnuts

Chestnuts are the lowest in fat of all nuts and, as a matter of fact, almost fat-free. They are good raw, boiled or roasted. Here we use dried chestnuts because they are economical and easy to keep in the cupboard. Lentils and chestnuts makes a good vegetarian entree or a stuffing served along with the bird at holiday time. Chestnuts impart a sweetness to the dish.

Serves 4

**3 cups vegetable stock or
  water**
½ pound dried chestnuts
4 tablespoons olive oil

2 red onions, diced
1 cup dried lentils
1 teaspoon oregano
salt and pepper to taste

Place chestnuts and vegetable stock or water in a saucepan and bring to a boil. Simmer chestnuts until tender, about 20 minutes. Drain liquid into measuring cup and add water to make 2½ cups liquid.

Coarsely chop chestnuts. Put aside.

In a skillet with a cover, gently warm olive oil. Saute onions for 5 minutes. Add lentils, oregano, chestnuts, and liquid. Bring to a boil. Simmer, covered, for 20 minutes, or until lentils are tender and liquid is absorbed.

Adjust seasoning to taste.

Note: *Because this dish is monochrome in color, you can add carrots or a green vegetable like kale.*

Mejedrah with Steamed Veggies

Rice is the staple diet of over 50 percent of the world's population. This Lebanese dish couldn't be simpler. Combined with steamed vegetables, it's pretty to look at and satisfying to eat. And cauliflower is rich in vitamin C, potassium and fiber.

Serves 8

4 tablespoons olive oil
4 large onions, sliced
½ cup pine nuts, almonds or
   pistachios
1 cup brown lentils
3 cups water
1 cup brown basmati rice

½ teaspoon salt
½ teaspoon pepper
2 cups boiling water
4 carrots, sliced
4 cups broccoli, florets
1 head cauliflower, florets
2 cups water

Gently warm olive oil in a skillet. Saute onions until lightly browned, about 5 minutes. Add nuts and saute until they are golden, about 2 minutes. Remove onions and nuts and set aside. Add lentils to pan with water. Bring to a boil and simmer for 20 minutes, until soft but still whole. Add rice together with salt and pepper and 2 cups boiling water. Reduce heat to simmer, cover pot and cook another 40 minutes, or until rice is tender and liquid has been absorbed.

In the meantime, prepare vegetables and place in three separate piles in large skillet. Keep separate so when dishing out you can separate on plate. Add 2 cups water, bring to a boil, cover and simmer just until vegetables are crisp-tender, about 5 minutes.

Serving Suggestion: *Place some of each vegetable on one side of plate. On the other, place lentil and rice mixture. Garnish with onions and nuts.*

Barley Millet Pilaf with Shiitakes

Shiitake mushrooms stimulate the immune system, barley is said to stimulate the liver and lymphatic system and millet is the only grain good for the spleen, pancreas and stomach because of its alkalinity. In addition to these health credentials, this dish is delicious. Use it as a side or main dish or as stuffing cooked outside the bird.

Serves 6–8

1½ ounces dried American shiitakes	6 cups water
2 tablespoons olive oil	2 cups hulled barley
1 sweet red or white onion, chopped	1 cup millet
	2 teaspoons salt

Slice dried shiitakes. Use everything, stems, too. They are brittle when dry and easy to cut.

Gently warm olive oil in a large skillet with a tight-fitting cover. Add mushrooms and onions and stir until slightly softened, about 3–4 minutes.

Bring 6 cups water to a boil.

Add barley and millet to skillet with mushrooms. Stir for 1 minute to coat grains with oil.

Add boiling water and salt to skillet. Stir well, reduce heat to low, cover and simmer until the grains are tender, about 25–30 minutes. Fluff with a fork and serve!

Note: If you want to make this a company dish, add a diced carrot and chopped kale to the skillet together with barley and millet.

Millet, Mushrooms and Chestnuts

According to poet and mythologer Robert Graves, mushrooms were the original food of the gods. Alice nibbled on a mushroom during her adventure in Wonderland. Here are those chestnuts again! And millet is an excellent grain for those with sugar imbalance problems.

Serves 6

3 cups water
1 cup dried chestnuts
3 tablespoons olive oil
2 large onions, chopped
2 cups millet
4 cups boiling water
½ cup dried shiitakes, broken
   into pieces

4 celery stalks, sliced
1 bunch kale, cut into
   ribbons
2 teaspoons thyme
2 teaspoons rosemary
½ teaspoon nutmeg
1 teaspoon salt
1 teaspoon pepper

Bring 3 cups water to a boil and boil chestnuts until fairly soft, about 20 minutes. Drain, coarsely chop and set aside.

Gently warm olive oil in a large skillet. Add onion and saute for 5 minutes. Add millet, 4 cups boiling water and remaining ingredients, including chestnuts. Cover skillet and simmer on low for 40 minutes. Taste, adjust seasoning and serve. It's easy!

Millet, Sweet Potato and Broccoli

Millet, a primary food of the long-living Hunzas who inhabit a remote mountain region in Asia, was also an important food in biblical times. It has lots of protein and is the easiest grain to digest. Here, it makes a scrumptious salad or entree. Bring to potlucks, picnics or serve at home.

Serves 4–6

2 cups water
1 cup millet
2 cups cubed sweet potato, steamed
2 cups broccoli, steamed
½ red onion, chopped
2 stalks celery, sliced
1 cup cooked chick-peas

Dressing:
3 tablespoons toasted sesame oil
3 tablespoons tamari soy sauce
1½ tablespoons mirin or rice wine vinegar
salt and pepper to taste

Bring 2 cups water to a boil and stir in grain. Lower heat, cover pot and simmer for 45 minutes.

Cube sweet potato and steam using a rack in a saucepan or a steamer with a little water so potatoes won't become waterlogged. When tender, about 5 minutes, pour sweet potatoes into a colander in the sink. Use same pot and a little water to steam broccoli the same way.

Toss together all ingredients. Taste and adjust seasoning.

Suggestion: *If it's summertime, you may choose to use canned chick-peas. Otherwise, cook according to directions for cooking beans in What You Need to Know in front of book. Remember to save the water from steaming for soups or use as liquid for cooking grains.*

Vegetable Paella with Quinoa, Saffron and Curry

This dish is best the day it's made. Try rice in place of quinoa, although quinoa, called the "mother grain" by the Incas, has the highest protein content of all grains. And it has more calcium than milk.

Serves 4   *Bake at 400°*

4 zucchini, halved and sliced
1 large Japanese eggplant, cubed
¼ cup olive oil
10 cloves garlic, minced
1 teaspoon grated orange peel
1 teaspoon curry powder
2 red bell peppers, chopped
**   coarsely**
1 red onion, diced
1 teaspoon rosemary

2 cups quinoa
3 cups water or vegetable broth
2 saffron threads
½ teaspoon red pepper
1 jar marinated artichoke
**   hearts**
1 cup black pitted olives, halved
½ cup peas, uncooked
1 bunch scallions, sliced
¼ cup dried parsley to garnish

Combine veggies with 1 tablespoon oil, half the garlic, orange peel and curry powder and toss to coat. Oven-roast at 400° an hour.

Heat remaining oil in large kettle. Add peppers, onion, rosemary and remaining garlic. Saute 5 minutes. Add quinoa and stir 2 minutes. Add boiling water or vegetable broth, saffron and red pepper. Reduce heat and simmer for 5 minutes.

Add the artichokes and olives. Simmer until quinoa is done, about another 5 minutes. Add peas and green onion. Let dish stand, covered, another 10 minutes. Add oven-roasted veggies and toss to mix. Garnish with parsley. Taste and adjust seasoning.

Quinoa Pilaf

Quinoa (pronounced keen-wah) provides *all* essential amino acids and is high in protein, iron and the B vitamins. It's not a true grain but actually is a fruit. It cooks quickly, is versatile and takes on whatever flavor you give it. One of our favorite recipes is Quinoa with Pine Nuts and Apricots from our first cookbook.

Serves 4–6

4 cups water
2 cups quinoa
6-ounce package Fakin' Bacon
1 medium onion, chopped
4 cloves garlic, minced
2 stalks celery, minced
2 cups chopped kale

1 cup organic corn
2 tablespoons olive or sesame oil
2 cups cubed sweet potatoes
Spike or salt to taste
cayenne or black pepper to taste
2 tablespoons dried parsley
   flakes to garnish

Bring water to a boil in pot. Stir in quinoa, lower heat, cover pot and simmer for 10 minutes. Leave cover on pot and let it sit for another 10 minutes.

In a frying pan, saute Fakin' Bacon, onion, garlic, celery, kale and corn in oil for about 5 minutes.

Steam sweet potato cubes in a little water until soft, about 5 minutes. (Our favorite variety of sweet potatoes is the organic Red Garnet Yam.)

In a large mixing bowl, toss quinoa with sauteed veggies and sweet potato. Season to taste with Spike or salt. Feel free to add a little cayenne or black pepper if you like. Garnish with parsley.

Note: Spike, a seasoning sold in natural food stores, is derived mainly from dried vegetables. My nephew, Hank, loved it as a little boy and wouldn't eat anything without it. He called it "spite."

Brazilian Quinoa with Artichoke Hearts

Quinoa is great for vegetarians who crave nutrient-concentrated foods. It has been grown for thousands of years in South America, but is now being grown in the high mesas in Colorado. It needs a high, cold altitude. This recipe makes a great company dish and travels well to picnics!

Serves 6–8

2 tablespoons olive oil
2 cups quinoa
2 onions, chopped
6 cloves garlic, minced
3 cups vegetable stock or
  water
1 tablespoon dill weed
pinch saffron

12 marinated artichoke hearts
1 cup pitted black olives (oil
  cured or kalamata)
1 large sweet red pepper, diced
salt and pepper to taste
fresh parsley to garnish
½ cup chopped walnuts to
  garnish

Gently warm olive oil in a skillet with a tight-fitting cover. Saute quinoa, onions and garlic for 2 minutes. (If you prefer your quinoa fluffier and chewier, cook it separately following directions in What You Need to Know in front of book and then add remaining ingredients.)

Bring vegetable stock or water to a boil. Add to quinoa mixture in skillet together with dill and saffron. Cover skillet, lower heat and simmer for 10 minutes. Turn off heat and uncover.

Arrange artichoke hearts and olives on top. Cover skillet again and allow to sit for another 10 minutes. To serve, taste and adjust seasonings. Sprinkle with walnuts to garnish.

Spanish Rice with Artichoke Hearts

Use either marinated artichokes or those in water. When using marinated artichoke hearts, which are more luscious than their skinnier cousins, save the marinade to use with summer veggies. Be sure to look for marinated artichoke hearts without preservatives and in olive oil.

Serves 4–6

¼ cup olive oil
2 cups brown basmati rice
2 small onions, chopped
6 garlic cloves, minced
1 teaspoon salt
1 teaspoon pepper
5 cups vegetable stock or
   water

1 tablespoon dried dill weed
½ teaspoon saffron
1½ cups artichoke hearts,
   drained
½ cup chopped roasted peanuts
   to garnish
1 cup pitted black olives,
   drained and cut, to garnish

In a large skillet, add oil and saute rice, onions and garlic. Once the rice begins to color, add salt and pepper. Bring vegetable stock or water to a boil. Add to rice. Add dill and saffron.

Cover skillet with a tight-fitting lid and simmer on low for about 40 minutes, or until rice has absorbed liquid and is tender to the tooth.

Remove cover and arrange artichoke hearts on top. Cover skillet again and let pilaf stand for 10 minutes. Combine chopped peanuts and olives and sprinkle around the edge of the skillet as garnish to serve.

Alternately, once you have added vegetable stock or water to the rice mixture together with dill and saffron, you can transfer mixture to a flat casserole, cover and bake in a 375° oven for 50 minutes. Remove from oven, uncover and arrange artichoke hearts on top. Cover and bake another 10 minutes. Garnish with combined chopped peanuts and olives.

Jasmine Rice with Vegetables and Walnuts

Walnuts are rich in fiber and monounsaturated fat. Eating a few a day is said to serve as an antidote to heart disease. Toasted sesame oil adds a flavor and taste you'll love!

Serves 4

2 cups water
1 cup Jasmine, basmati or
   Texmati rice
½ cup walnut halves or pieces
1 pound or more vegetable
   pieces (use snap peas, asparagus, broccoli, whatever you
   like, in bite-sized pieces)

¾ teaspoon salt
½ teaspoon black pepper
4 tablespoons toasted sesame
   oil
2–4 tablespoons tamari soy
   sauce
½ small red onion, diced
salt and pepper to taste

Place water and rice in a pot. Bring water to a boil. Stir, cover and simmer until tender. White varieties of these rices take about 20 minutes; the whole grain, about 40–45. Turn off heat, and let pot sit covered another 10 minutes so rice can steam itself dry.

Turn rice out into a large bowl and fluff with a rubber spatula every few minutes until rice stops steaming.

If using sugarsnap peas or snow peas, stem and string and add to rice when hot. They don't need any more cooking than that. If using a vegetable which needs cooking like broccoli, steam for 2–3 minutes in a little water.

Combine rest of ingredients with rice. Toss well with a rubber spatula. Taste, adjust seasoning and serve. You may like more toasted sesame oil.

It's best to let this dish stand at room temperature for up to 4 hours before serving.

Azerbaijan Pilaf

Basmati rice smells like popcorn or flowers when it cooks. Like all brown rices, it's rich in B vitamins and a wonderful source of dietary fiber, which we all need to keep our insides toned and humming! And like all our dishes, the rice is combined with protein (nuts here), some fat and lots of flavor.

Serves 4–6

2 tablespoons olive oil
2 large carrots, sliced
1 red onion, sliced
⅓ cup slivered almonds
1 teaspoon cumin seeds

pinch saffron
1½ cups brown basmati rice
3 cups boiling water or vegetable
   stock
salt and pepper to taste

Gently warm olive oil in a 2-quart saucepan over medium heat. Add carrots and onions and stir for about 5 minutes, until onions and carrots are somewhat soft. Stir in almonds, cumin seeds, saffron and rice. Stir until rice is well-coated and takes on some color, about 2 minutes.

Add boiling water or stock. Reduce heat to lowest setting, cover pot tightly and simmer until liquid is absorbed, about 40 minutes. Turn off heat and let pot stand, covered, another 10 minutes.

Fluff rice with fork. Season to taste with salt and pepper. Transfer to serving platter.

Variations: *Substitute walnuts or pistachios for almonds. If you like, stir in ½ cup raisins.*

Basmati with Sweet Potatoes and Greens

Comforting, homey ingredients. But the addition of nutmeg gives it a different twist. Nutmeg, the inside of an evergreen nut, is said to relieve indigestion.

Serves 4

4 tablespoons olive oil
2 large onions, diced
2 cups sweet potatoes, cut into
  ½-inch cubes
2 cups basmati rice
½ teaspoon nutmeg

1 teaspoon salt
1 teaspoon pepper
4 cups boiling water or vegetable
  stock
3 cups Swiss chard or spinach,
  cut into ribbons

Gently heat olive oil in a large skillet. Saute onions. Add sweet potatoes, rice, nutmeg, salt and pepper. Stir to coat with oil. Add boiling water or stock and lower heat. Cover pot and simmer 25 minutes, until rice is tender.

Fold in greens. They will wilt. Serve. That's all there is to this dish. Good food in a hurry.

Negev Tofu

In the Middle East, garlic was thought to contribute to muscular strength and so it was added in large quantities to the diet of slaves who built the Pyramids.

Serves 4–6   *Bake at 400°*

¼ cup olive oil
½ cup lemon juice
4 cloves garlic, minced
1 teaspoon oregano
½ teaspoon salt
4 scallions, chopped
2 pounds extra firm tofu

Sauce:
½ cup sesame tahini
½ cup water
2 tablespoons olive oil
2 tablespoons lemon juice
2 cloves garlic
½ teaspoon salt
parsley and sesame seeds to
    garnish

Combine oil, lemon juice, garlic, oregano, salt and scallions in a nonmetal pan. Add tofu, cover and marinate for several hours, turning a couple of times.

In the meantime, using the steel blade of a food processor or a blender, blend the sauce.

Preheat oven to 400°. Cover tofu mixture with sauce and bake for 15 minutes, or until tahini is a pale gold.

Serve over rice or millet. Garnish with parsley and sesame seeds.

Note: *You can use this marinade for poultry or fish, too. The sauce is great over grains.*

Rye Berry Pilaf

Rye has been cultivated for more than 2,000 years. The protein in rye is said to be better nutritionally for women, in particular, than wheat. It promotes endurance and strength. (Many women who are prone to yeast infections are sensitive to wheat. Give rye a try!) This combination is yummy and colorful to boot.

Serves 6

2 cups rye berries
6 cups water
½ teaspoon salt
3 tablespoons olive oil
2 onions, minced

1 small purple cabbage, sliced
2 small potatoes, diced
1 rutabaga, diced
1 head kale, minced
salt and pepper to taste

Place berries, water and salt in pressure cooker. Bring to full pressure. Reduce heat and cook 45 minutes. Remove from heat, uncover and stir. If you don't have a pressure cooker, cook as for hulled barley in What You Need to Know in front of book.

Gently warm oil in a large skillet (or use a soup kettle with sides high enough so you can stir without vegetables leaping onto the stove). Saute onions until soft, about 5 minutes. Add cabbage, potatoes, rutabaga and kale and saute 5 minutes. Cover and simmer until tender, about 5 minutes. Add water if necessary to prevent sticking.

Place rye berries in mixing bowl and toss in vegetables. Season to taste with salt and pepper.

Variations: Any grain berry can be used in place of rye. Have you tried kamut or spelt?

Walnut, Spelt and Barley Pilaf

What is spelt? An ancient grain, a precursor to wheat, which has a higher protein content than wheat and a gluten analog different enough from it that many wheat-sensitive people seem to be able to handle spelt just fine. This simple dish can be served as a main dish or side dish. Try it piping hot or at room temperature.

Serves 4–6

¼ cup spelt berries
½ cup barley
1½ cups water
2 medium carrots, diced
3 tablespoons olive oil
1 small red onion, diced
½ cup roasted walnuts

½ teaspoon salt
2 cloves garlic, pressed, or
  ½ teaspoon garlic powder
1 teaspoon basil
cayenne to taste
parsley to garnish

In a large pot, bring grains and water to a boil. (Yes, a large pot. Barley tends to bubble over, and using a really big pot may save you having to clean the top of the stove!) Add carrots. Cover, reduce heat and simmer pilaf on low for about an hour. Do not stir while grains cook. When grains are tender, remove pot from heat and leave covered until ready to combine everything.

Gently warm olive oil in a little pan. Saute onion about 5 minutes, until translucent. Add walnuts, stirring a few minutes, until aromatic.

Drain grains and carrots in mesh colander, if necessary. Dump into mixing bowl. Add remaining ingredients and toss everything together gently. Adjust seasoning to taste. Garnish and serve.

Variations: This pilaf is chewy and slightly sweet because of the onions, carrots and grains. You can use other vegetables, like shredded kale, if you prefer. And you can choose other grains, like rye berries.

Wild Rice and Sweet Potato Pilaf

This dish is incredibly simple to make, tastes great and is colorful. It makes a wonderful side dish or it can be the main dish. Just garnish with a cup of nuts or sunflower seeds to add protein.

Wild rice, not a true rice, has more protein than other rices. It's rich in minerals and is hardy food for cold climates.

Serves 6–8

½ cup olive oil	3 sweet potatoes or yams, diced
2 red onions, chopped	2 cups green beans
2 cups water	1 teaspoon oregano
1 cup wild rice	salt and pepper to taste

In a skillet, gently warm olive oil. Saute onions until translucent, about 5 minutes. Place onions in mixing bowl and set aside.

Bring 2 cups water to a boil. Add wild rice, lower heat, cover pot and simmer for 50 minutes, or until water is absorbed and rice has opened and is light and fluffy. (Sometimes letting the pot sit, covered, after 50 minutes allows the rice to steam dry and open. Sometimes, water has to be drained off.)

Steam the sweet potatoes until tender, about 10 minutes. Add them to mixing bowl with onions. Add rice. Steam green beans in the same steamer using the same liquid for about 2–3 minutes. Add to bowl.

Using a rubber spatula, gently toss vegetables and rice together. Add oregano and salt and pepper to taste.

Note: Save liquid from steaming vegetables and drink it when cool. Or save for cooking grains or add to soups. Do this every time you steam vegetables!

Cheesy and Pasta Main Dishes

Not all pasta dishes are cheesy. Japanese pasta dishes are wonderful without dairy. You'll find a mixture of ethnic pasta dishes in this chapter; many are without cheese. However, those that contain cheese have lots of it.

Why? I like cheese. When I eat it, a little just doesn't do it for me. Nor do I believe, if you can eat cheese, that it's bad for you when it's part of an interesting and varied diet.

Is cheese fattening? For the most part, yes. There *are* less fattening cheeses out there, but the more I read, the less concerned I am about fat and the more concerned I am about simple carbs and refined sugars which are converted to saturated fat in the body. These are the problem. *It's sugar that scares me, not cheese, olive oil or nuts.*

If you're tired, cut back on dairy foods because they're harder for the body to process and may increase your sense of fatigue.

What to do if you want to make a cheesy pasta dish and can't eat dairy? Use soy and rice cheese alternatives. In fact, more and more alternatives and new products are being introduced every day. Try them to find what you like and can use. Substitute.

For dishes like lasagnas you can substitute tofu for some or all of the cheese. If you cut out cheese completely, you'll need to play with other ingredients like garlic and herbs in order to compensate for tofu's blandness. Enjoy the challenge!

Cheesy Small Potatoes and Haricots Verts

Originally from Central America, green beans were probably brought to Europe for cultivation by French explorers in the 17th century. Potatoes are high in potassium and may help prevent high blood pressure and strokes.

Serves 8   *Bake at 350°*

1½ pounds small red-skinned potatoes
¾ pound haricots verts or other green beans, trimmed
1 onion, chopped
4 cloves garlic, minced
1 tablespoon basil
¼ cup olive oil
1 pound shredded mozzarella or monterey jack cheese
basil to garnish

Steam potatoes until tender. Cool and cut into quarters. If beans are very long, cut in half. Steam until crisp-tender, about 5 minutes. Drain.

Combine potatoes, beans, onions, garlic and basil in a casserole and top with shredded cheese.

Bake in a 350° oven until cheese is melted and bubbling, about 15 minutes. Sprinkle with basil and serve.

Note: Can you substitute soy or rice cheese for regular cheese? Of course, you can!

Egyptian Kosherei

Our variation of an authentic dish. We're true to the original in spirit only! This version is just a lot of fun to make and eat.

Sweet rice is softer, stickier and sweeter than other varieties. When you toast it, it puffs up like popcorn. Black Thai rice is a sweet rice that cooks up to be purple crimson glop. Very dramatic. Like all whole grain rices, it's nutritious and high in B vitamins.

Serves 8

1 cup lentils	½ pound elbow pasta
3 cups water	1 tablespoon olive oil
¼ cup olive oil	4 cups diced tomatoes
1 onion, chopped	1 bunch scallions, sliced
salt and pepper to taste	4 cloves garlic, minced
1 cup water	½ teaspoon salt
½ cup black Thai rice or	⅛ teaspoon cayenne
any other sticky, glutinous rice	1 teaspoon cumin

Cook lentils in 3 cups water until soft, about 25 minutes. Drain if necessary. In the meantime, gently warm olive oil in a small skillet and saute onion until soft, about 5 minutes. Scoop onions into lentils. Add salt and pepper to taste.

At the same time, combine 1 cup water with rice in a small pot. Bring to a boil, lower heat, cover pot and simmer 45 minutes.

Concurrently, boil water in a large pot, cook pasta until al dente, about 5–7 minutes. Drain and toss with olive oil.

While all the above cooks, combine the rest of the ingredients to make the sauce.

For a dramatic presentation, serve in a clear glass dish with high sides to show off different colored layers. Spoon lentils in first. Cover with layer of sticky rice, then layer of pasta. Spoon sauce over the top, saving about a third to serve at the table. People always want more!

Cheesy Black Bean Burritos

No time to make the chili that goes into these burritos? There are some great canned chilis at natural food stores with no junk added. Using canned beans is another shortcut. However, if you have time, here's how to do it from scratch, since making chili, like making bread, is therapeutic. Black beans have an earthy aroma and are about my favorite beans.

Serves 8   *Bake at 350°*

6 cups cooked black beans
2 tablespoons olive oil
16 cloves garlic, minced
2 tablespoons chili powder
2 teaspoons ground cumin
1 pound carrots, diced
2 green peppers, diced
2 jalapeno peppers, seeded and
   minced

2 cups diced tomatoes
1 teaspoon salt
16 whole wheat tortillas
1 pound pepperjack cheese,
   sliced in 16 pieces
2 cups favorite salsa to
   garnish

Gently warm olive oil in a kettle and saute garlic for 2 minutes. Add chili powder and cumin and stir 1 minute. Add vegetables and stir. Cover and simmer vegetables until carrots are tender, about 10 minutes.

Add beans to kettle, but don't mix. Let them sit on top of vegetables so vegetables get really soft and beans don't burn. Simmer chili, covered, 15 minutes.

Remove pot from heat and stir chili until everything is well mixed. Taste and adjust seasoning.

Using the steel blade of a food processor, blend chili in batches, turning each batch into a second bowl.

Using a half-cup measure, plop a heaping half-cup of blended chili onto the center of each tortilla. Place a piece of cheese on top of the chili and fold over both sides of tortilla to the middle. Place in lasagna pan with folded side facing up. When all the burritos are filled and in the pan, cover with foil and heat in a 350° oven for 30 minutes.

Serving Suggestion: *Place two burritos on each plate and garnish with your favorite salsa. A steamed green vegetable alongside looks nice and tastes great.*

Variations: *You can make these burritos without any cheese, with soy or rice cheese or even with cooked shrimp or chicken in lieu of or in addition to cheese. Try using spelt tortillas. Feel free to use corn.*

Lasagna with Basil and Walnuts

This is reminiscent of Cheesy Vegetable Lasagna in my first book. However, this lasagna does use considerably less cheese than my original. (Mary Kadlik, a friend and cook at the store, finds this hard to believe!) Don't make this when you need to fit into a dress two sizes too small by the weekend. No matter, your mouth and soul will be happy.

Don't forget that walnuts help lower cholesterol. So perhaps the cholesterol in cheese is cancelled? Fat chance!

Serves 8   *Bake at 350°*

1 pound lasagna noodles
1 tablespoon olive oil
Pesto:
¼ cup basil leaves
¼ cup Italian parsley
¼ cup walnuts
8 cloves garlic
2 tablespoons pecorino Romano
½ cup olive oil

¼ cup pecorino Romano, grated
1 pound mozzarella, grated
½ pound provolone, grated
1 pound ricotta cheese
4 cups cauliflower and broccoli, florets, steamed crisp-tender

Cook lasagna noodles in boiling water for 5 minutes. Rinse in colander under cold water and drain. Put back into pot and add 1 tablespoon olive oil. Stir to coat to prevent sticking.

Using the steel blade of a food processor, make pesto by blending basil, parsley, walnuts, garlic, 2 tablespoons Romano and olive oil.

Layer half the noodles in a lasagna pan.

Mix half the pesto and half the other cheeses with all the ricotta. Spoon mixture over noodles in pan. Top with vegetables, remaining noodles and rest of pesto mixture, in that order. Distribute remaining cheese evenly over top and cover with foil. Bake at 350° for 45 minutes. Let stand 10 minutes before cutting. Voila!

Variation: You can substitute any vegetable you prefer for cauliflower and broccoli. If you use soft and tender vegetables like chard or zucchini, don't steam first. Simply cut and use. They'll cook enough in the oven.

Mexican Lasagna

There's something about the combination of potatoes, pasta and cheese which is irresistible. In this case, they make a hearty lasagna with less than the amount of cheese I usually use. My family always teases me that my pasta dishes are really cheese soups. If you like things hotter, just add more peppers!

Serves 8   *Bake at 350°*

**1 pound boiling potatoes,
    steamed until tender**
½ teaspoon cinnamon
½ teaspoon ground cloves
½ teaspoon chili powder
1 teaspoon garlic powder
½ teaspoon cumin
1 pound ricotta or soft tofu
**1 cup pecorino Romano,
    grated**
1 pound cheddar, grated
2 cups diced tomato
4 cloves garlic, minced

1 red bell pepper, minced
1 green bell pepper, minced
**1 tablespoon cilantro or parsley,
    chopped**
1 small chili pepper, minced
**1 large bunch greens, chopped,
    *optional***
1 stalk celery, minced, *optional*
1 carrot, minced, *optional*
1 pound lasagna noodles
**1 pound pepperjack and/or
    mozzarella, grated**
1 teaspoon oregano

Allow potatoes to come to room temperature. Mash together with cinnamon, cloves, chili powder, garlic powder, cumin and ricotta or tofu. Add Romano and grated cheddar.

Make sauce by combining tomatoes, garlic, peppers, parsley or cilantro and chili pepper. Throw in any optional ingredients. Simmer for 5–10 minutes in a saucepan. Set aside.

Meanwhile, bring water in a large pot to a boil and add lasagna noodles. Cook until al dente, about 5–7 minutes. Drain noodles into colander and lay half in large lasagna pan. Separate remaining noodles so they don't stick together until you're ready to use them.

Spoon potato cheese mixture onto noodles in pan. Cover with remaining noodles and sauce. Top with cheese and sprinkle with oregano. Cover with foil and bake at 350° for 45 minutes. Uncover and bake another 15 minutes so cheese browns around edges. Let lasagna sit for a few minutes before serving.

Fettucine with Greens and Garlic

This dish can be tossed together in no time. It's a great way to introduce greens to your family and friends. My favorite greens are kale and collards because they're hardy enough to be cooked in the same pot with the pasta, which saves time and washing another pot. If you've a lawn of dandelion greens that are unsprayed, feel virtuous if you use them!

It's nice to know that garlic, in addition to all its other attributes, is said to lift mood and have a mild, calming effect.

Serves 4

2 large bunches greens (use your favorites), rinsed and torn into bite-sized pieces
1 pound fettucine
½ cup olive oil
12 cloves garlic, minced
1 cup cooked cannellini beans or red kidney beans
1 cup pecorino Romano, grated
1 teaspoon black pepper
lemon wedges

Bring a large pot of water to boil. Add greens and stir until they just begin to soften, about a minute. Add pasta and cook until it is al dente, about 5–7 minutes.

In the meantime, gently warm olive oil in a skillet. Add garlic and saute. Add beans and simmer just until they're warmed through.

Drain pasta and greens into a colander. Place in large bowl and add oil and garlic mixture. Toss. Add Romano and black pepper and toss again.

Serve with extra bowl of Romano and pass lemon wedges at the table.

Variation: Soy or rice parmesan works well as a substitute for Romano here or in any recipe.

Fusilli Rutica with Romano

Pasta and beans are a combination that always seems to work, and this recipe is no exception. Make a great meal with a green salad tossed with an olive oil vinaigrette or fruity balsamic vinegar and berries for dessert.

Chick-peas are good for those with weak digestion. For those allergic to wheat, there are pastas made from rice, corn, quinoa or spelt. They work wonderfully in this dish and others!

Serves 4

½ cup olive oil
3 onions, chopped
4 cloves garlic, minced
½ teaspoon red pepper flakes
3 ounces Fakin' Bacon
1 red and 1 yellow pepper, diced
2 cups tomato, diced
½ cup pitted green olives
½ cup pitted black olives

2 tablespoons capers
½ teaspoon oregano
½ teaspoon basil
2 cups cooked chick-peas
1 pound fusilli
1 cup pecorino Romano, grated
salt and pepper to taste
parsley to garnish

To make sauce for pasta, gently warm olive oil in a large skillet. Saute onion, garlic, pepper flakes, Fakin' Bacon, peppers, tomatoes, olives, capers and herbs for 5 minutes. Add chick-peas and simmer another 15 minutes. Pour sauce into large bowl ready for pasta.

In the meantime, in a large pot, bring several quarts of water to a boil. Cook pasta until al dente, about 5–7 minutes. Drain and add to sauce. Toss with Romano. Taste and adjust seasonings and parsley to garnish. Serve with more Romano at table.

Orzo Pilaf with Mushrooms

Orzo is rice-shaped pasta. You can choose between orzo made of semolina flour or something more exotic like we stock at Debra's Natural Gourmet made of chick-pea flour. Chick-peas, or garbanzo beans, are high in protein and have a substantial, meaty taste.

You are only as healthy as your immune system is strong and can ward off disease. Shiitake mushrooms boost immune function as does garlic.

Serves 4

4 tablespoons olive oil	**1 cup orzo**
8 cloves garlic, minced	**pinch rosemary**
2 cups sliced shiitake, portabella	**4 tablespoons pine nuts**
or crimini mushrooms	**salt and pepper to taste**
2 cups water or vegetable broth	**parsley to garnish,** *optional*

Gently warm olive oil in a deep skillet. Add garlic and mushrooms and saute for about 5 minutes.

Add water or vegetable broth and bring to a boil. Stir in orzo. Reduce heat, cover and simmer for about 15 minutes. You may want to stir occasionally. Orzo will absorb the water and be tender.

Remove from heat and add rosemary and pine nuts. Season to taste and serve. Need a little green? Garnish with chopped parsley or a sprinkling of dried parsley flakes.

Orzo with Broccoli, Feta and Olives

Broccoli, like other vegetables of the cabbage family, is said to help prevent breast cancer because it speeds up removal of estrogen from the body. And it adds a nice splash of color to this dish. Feel free to substitute squash or cauliflower, although broccoli has goodly amounts of chromium that helps regulate insulin and blood sugar.

Serves 4

1½ cups orzo
2 cups broccoli, florets
¼ cup olive oil
3 tablespoons pine nuts
1 cup crumbled feta (about 3.5 ounces)

¾ cup black olives (kalamata are nice)
½ cup Romano, grated
1 tablespoon basil
1 tablespoon garlic
pinch cayenne
salt and pepper to taste

Bring water in a large pot to a boil. Add orzo and cook until tender but firm to the tooth, about 5–8 minutes. Drain and place orzo in a large bowl for mixing.

Steam broccoli in another pot or vegetable steamer until crisp-tender, about 5 minutes. Drain and add to bowl with remaining ingredients. Toss everything together to coat. Season to taste and serve with more Romano to pass.

Soba with Seaweed

Hijiki is a seaweed with a nutty taste and a crisp texture. It's protein- and calcium-rich with lots of B vitamins, all of which are easily absorbed by the body. I like the way its dark color contrasts with carrots and earth-tone pasta!

What are soba noodles? Long, thin Japanese noodles made of buckwheat or a mixture of buckwheat and wheat flours. Western pasta is made by forcing hard winter wheat dough through a pasta machine and then drying it quickly with heat. Soba, which cooks faster than Western-style pasta, is made with spring wheat. The dough is rolled out and noodles are cut and dried slowly.

Serves 4   *Bake at 350°*

2 ounces hijiki seaweed
2 tablespoons toasted sesame oil
1 onion, minced
2 carrots, minced
1 pound tofu, cubed

1 tablespoon sesame seeds
1 tablespoon poppy seeds
⅓ cup tamari
8 ounces soba noodles
tamari and pepper to taste

Soak hijiki in enough boiling water to cover for 30 minutes. Squeeze "dry." (Use water in soups, to cook rice or drink.)

Meanwhile, gently warm sesame oil in a skillet and saute onions and carrots for about 5 minutes. Set aside.

Cube tofu and toss in a bowl with seeds and tamari. Place mixture on baking sheet with sides and toast in 350° oven for about 20 minutes.

Bring water in a large pot to boil and cook pasta until al dente, usually about 3–5 minutes. Drain in colander and run under cold water to cool. Place pasta in a large bowl.

Add everything to pasta and toss to mix well (I usually end up using my hands). Adjust seasoning to taste by adding a little more tamari or some pepper.

Udon Noodles with Peanut Sauce

This dish is also delicious served cold the next day. Udon noodles lend themselves to cold dishes and differ from soba in that they are thicker and flatter. Made from wheat, udon sometimes has rice flour added, which makes a lighter pasta.

Serves 4

⅓ cup smooth natural peanut butter
⅓ cup sesame tahini
⅓ cup canola oil
¼ cup tamari

2 tablespoons mirin (rice wine vinegar)
pinch cayenne
1 pound udon
1 pound tofu, cut into cubes
tamari to taste

Using the steel blade of a food processor or blender, mix together peanut butter, tahini, oil, tamari, mirin and cayenne. If sauce curdles, add a little cold water while blending.

Bring a large pot of water to boil. Add udon and cook for 3–5 minutes. Drain in colander and cool under running water. Thoroughly drain again. Toss with sauce. Add tofu. Taste, adjust seasoning by adding a little more tamari and serve at room temperature.

Note: Another method of cooking udon and soba noodles is to bring 3–4 quarts water to boil, add the pasta, stir and, when water returns to a full boil, add a cup of cold water. Repeat this step two or three more times. Drain and rinse as above. This method is said to yield a superior noodle.

Linguini with Sicilian Pesto

I love the taste of this dish and also the fact that it can be kept covered in the oven for a good hour or two before serving. Or made ahead and refrigerated a day or so before you need to heat and serve. All you have to do after taking the dish out of the oven is to garnish. No last minute mess with company watching! And it uses almonds, the king of nuts.

Serves 4   *Bake at 350°*

1 cup almonds
8 cloves garlic
1 cup packed, coarsely chopped
  basil leaves
1 cup diced tomatoes
1 teaspoon black pepper
pinch cayenne

½ cup olive oil
1 pound linguini
Garnish:
1 cup black olives
1 cup diced tomatoes
basil leaves

Using the steel blade of a food processor, puree almonds, garlic, basil, tomatoes together with peppers and olive oil. Although you can use this sauce right away, I like the way it tastes best when given the chance for flavors to marry in the refrigerator, covered, for at least an hour.

Cook linguini in a large pot of boiling water until tender but still al dente, 5–7 minutes. Drain, return pasta to pot and add sauce. Toss to coat (hands work best, believe me!). Transfer to an oven-safe serving dish. Cover and bake for 30 minutes at 350°, or up to 2 hours at 300°. To serve, garnish with black olives, diced tomatoes and basil. Pass grated pecorino Romano at the table.

Mexican Chipotle Pasta

Great for everyone who doesn't eat wheat, but loves pasta. Delicious for the rest of us, too. Corn, like many other things natural, is said to promote anticancer and antiviral activity. If you're not fond of kale, try it anyway. You might find you like it in this dish. Or you can always substitute spinach or other greens.

Serves 6

¼ cup olive oil
3 onions, chopped
8 cloves garlic, minced
2 Chipotle peppers, crumbled
1 bunch kale, chopped into bite-sized pieces
2 carrots, diced
1 cup water

2 cups peanuts, coarsely chopped
2 stalks celery, diced
3 tablespoons minced fresh coriander or parsley
1 pound corn pasta or corn and quinoa pasta
salt and pepper to taste
extra peanuts to garnish

Gently warm oil in a skillet and saute onions and garlic. Stem, seed and crumble Chipotle peppers and add to skillet. Steam kale and carrots in 1 cup water until carrots are tender, about 5 minutes. Drain and add to skillet together with peanuts, celery and coriander. Cook another 1–2 minutes.

Meanwhile, cook pasta in large pot of boiling water until al dente, about 5–8 minutes, depending upon variety of pasta used, temperature, moisture in air and so on. Drain and place in a large bowl for mixing or add to skillet if it's large enough to accommodate everything. Toss. Taste and adjust seasoning. If you really love peanuts, use extra to garnish.

Note: What are Chipotle peppers? Smoked jalapenos. Very nice!

Maruzzine and Lima Bean Sauce

I like Romano cheese better than Parmesan because it's more pungent. To me, Parmesan always tastes a little rotten! If you can't eat dairy, there are soy or rice Parmesans which are really good. It's interesting to note that while limas have more starch, they also have less fat than other beans.

Serves 4–6

4 tablespoons olive oil
1 package Fakin' Bacon, cut into pieces
2 small onions, chopped
4 cloves garlic, minced
1 large bunch kale or collards, cut into ribbons

2 cups cooked lima beans
1 pound maruzzine or any other shell-like pasta
pinch oregano
½ cup grated pecorino Romano
pepper to taste

Gently warm olive oil in a skillet. Saute Fakin' Bacon together with onions, garlic and green vegetable for about 5 minutes, or until onions are translucent. Set aside.

Sort limas to check for stones and wash. Cook lima beans as in What You Need to Know in front of book. (It's fine if limas are *real* soft as they will be part of sauce.)

To make sauce, drain limas and add to skillet with greens. Stir.

Bring water in a large pot to boil, add pasta and cook until al dente, about 7 minutes. Drain and put pasta into a deep bowl for mixing. Stir in lima bean sauce. Toss with Romano, taste and adjust seasonings. Serve hot and pass more Romano at the table.

Zucchini Ole! with Cilantro and Rosemary

Great in the summertime when everyone's garden produces too many zucchini. Serve with crusty bread or baked potatoes to soak up the juices.

Rosemary is said to prevent food poisoning, fight infection and ward off headaches.

Serves 6   *Bake at 400°*

4 tablespoons olive oil
2 onions, chopped
6 small-medium zucchini, sliced
**   1-inch thick**
1 tablespoon cilantro, minced
2 jalapeno peppers, seeded
1 tablespoon rosemary

6 cloves garlic
½ cup tomato paste
2 cups plum tomatoes
1 pound cheddar or pepper jack
**   cheese, grated or diced**
rosemary or cilantro sprigs to
**   garnish**

Preheat oven to 400°.

In a large ovenproof skillet, gently warm olive oil and saute onions and zucchini. Remove skillet from heat and spread onions and zucchini evenly over bottom of pan.

Using the steel blade of a food processor or blender, make pesto by blending cilantro, peppers, rosemary, garlic, tomato paste and tomatoes. Transfer to a saucepan and simmer over medium heat for 5 minutes.

Spoon pesto over zucchini and top with cheese. Lay some rosemary or cilantro leaves on top for decoration. Cover skillet with aluminum foil or skillet cover and bake for 45 minutes.

Tortilla Pie

This dish is filling and hearty, great for a Super Bowl crowd or any cold winter day. Choose a zippy or mild salsa and use yellow, blue, white or any fat-free chips. Can't do cheese? Use soy cheese. Textured vegetable protein is made from soy beans, retains a nubby, chewy texture like hamburger and does not require cooking.

Serves 4   *Bake at 350°*

3 cups kidney, red or black beans **½ cup salsa**
¼ cup olive oil   **1 tablespoon ground cumin**
6 large garlic cloves, minced   **1 tablespoon chili powder**
2 cups textured vegetable   **8-oz. bag corn chips**
** protein (known as TVP)**   **8 oz. grated cheddar**
1 16-oz. can diced tomatoes   **8 oz. grated pepperjack cheese**

Sort beans to remove stones and rinse. Cook as in What You Need to Know in the front of the book. You can also pressure-cook or use organic canned beans.

In a large skillet, gently warm olive oil. Saute garlic. Add beans, TVP, tomatoes, salsa, cumin and chili powder. Heat through and simmer for 5 minutes.

In a lasagna pan, spoon in half the bean mixture. Crumble half the corn chips over beans. Sprinkle with half the cheese. Repeat the layering—beans, chips, cheese. Bake at 350° until cheese melts and pie is heated through, about 30 minutes.

Pad Thai

This version of Pad Thai—who doesn't love Pad Thai?—was bequeathed to us by Christina, who cooked with us briefly and who got it from the cooperative where she once worked. Be sure to use the toasted sesame oil which is made from toasted sesame seeds. It imparts a most individual and unique flavor to dishes.

Serves 6–8   *Bake at 350°*

1 pound firm or extra firm tofu   **3 tablespoons ketchup**
¼ cup tamari soy sauce   **⅓ teaspoon crushed red peppers**
1-pound package rice noodles   **3 eggs**
⅓ cup canola oil   **⅔ cup peanuts, chopped**
¼ cup toasted sesame oil   **pinch cayenne**
8 cloves garlic, minced   **minced scallions and/or extra**
3 tablespoons fish sauce   **peanuts to garnish**

Drain tofu by removing it from the package and pressing it by putting a heavy pot on top for 30 minutes. Cube and toss with tamari. Place on cookie sheet in 350° oven for 30–45 minutes, or until tofu is lightly browned and somewhat dry.

Meanwhile, bring a large pot of water to boil and cook rice noodles for about 5–7 minutes. Be careful not to overcook. Rice noodles go from underdone to overdone in a minute! Rinse noodles and put into large mixing bowl.

In a skillet, gently warm oils and saute garlic. Add fish sauce, ketchup and crushed red pepper. Crack eggs into a bowl and whisk briefly. Add eggs slowly to hot oil mixture in skillet, whisking the whole time. Sauce will be fragrant and aromatic. Pour sauce over noodles and mix with hands. (Though messy, mixing with hands is the only way to make sure all noodles are well-coated with sauce.) Add tofu cubes and peanuts and mix again.

Taste and adjust seasoning. Serve garnished with minced scallions or extra peanuts.

Tandoori Noodles

I love the fragrance of this dish as it cooks and the taste and the crunch of the pasta which gets crisp in the oven as it bakes!

Live cultures in yogurt are important in the digestive tract and have a natural antibiotic effect. They replenish friendly bacteria destroyed by prescribed antibiotics.

Serves 6   *Bake at 350°*

1 pound whole wheat or spelt
   fidelini
1 pound onions, sliced in ¼-inch
   rounds
2 pounds yellow potatoes, sliced
   in ¼-inch rounds
2 cups plain yogurt
1 teaspoon hot chilis

4 cloves garlic, minced
2 teaspoons fresh ginger, grated
1 teaspoon each cardamom,
   cinnamon, coriander, cumin,
   nutmeg and turmeric
pinch cayenne
1½ cups water or vegetable stock
2–4 tablespoons olive oil

Bring water in a large pot to a boil. Add pasta and cook until al dente, about 7 minutes. Drain in colander.

Toss all the rest of the ingredients together and spread evenly in a shallow baking dish.

Pour water or vegetable stock over top. Bake in 350° oven for 1½ hours, until lightly browned on top. Drizzle with 2–4 tablespoons olive oil. Bake 15 minutes more.

Radiatore with Broccoli, Yams and Peppers

Studies indicate that yams and sweet potatoes help prevent lung cancer, even in ex-smokers, because of their high beta-carotene content. Dark orange vegetables interrupt the process in the body that leads to lung cancer.

Serves 4

½ cup olive oil
4 cloves garlic, minced
¼ teaspoon cayenne
1 large red pepper, sliced lengthwise into strips

1 pound pasta
1 pound yams, diced
2 cups broccoli

Gently warm olive oil in a skillet. Saute garlic and cayenne until onion is soft, about 5 minutes. Add pepper strips and saute for 5 more minutes. Set aside.

Bring a large pot of water to a boil. Add pasta, stir and cook for 2 minutes. Add cubed potatoes to pot and cook 4 minutes. Then add broccoli and cook 2 minutes more. Yep, it's that easy!

Drain and place pasta, potatoes and broccoli in a large mixing bowl. Spoon sauce over mixture and toss well. Serve with grated cheese.

Note: *Do not serve to former President Bush or to my father, Sidney Stark, neither of whom like broccoli!*

Pasta with Olive Salsa and Shiitake Mushrooms

Do you know that shiitake mushrooms don't lose nutrient value when cooked? In addition to their ability to stimulate our immune system, shiitakes help lower the level of fat in the blood, which, in turn, lowers blood pressure and reduces fatigue.

Serves 4

1 pound pasta
Salsa:
½ cup olive oil
4 cloves garlic, minced
½ pound shiitake mushrooms, sliced
4 tomatoes, diced
2 squash, cut into 2-inch strips

1 cup black olives, coarsely chopped
1 tablespoon basil
1 teaspoon oregano
½ teaspoon thyme
1 teaspoon black pepper
grated pecorino Romano to garnish

Bring water to a boil in a large pot. (While water is coming to a boil, prepare vegetables for salsa.) Add pasta to boiling water and stir. Cook until pasta is al dente, about 7–10 minutes.

In the meantime, gently warm olive oil in a skillet. Add garlic and saute for 2 minutes. Add remaining ingredients except Romano and simmer 5 minutes.

Drain pasta in colander and pour back into pot. Toss with half the salsa.

Serve on plates and top with remaining salsa and a spoonful of Romano. Pass more Romano at the table.

Tunisian Polenta

Lentils are one of the oldest cultivated crops known to humanity. No wonder, because they are de-lish and strengthen adrenals, heart, circulation and kidneys! Make polenta, like in Polenta Pie, using the recipe from our first book, which is reprinted here.

Serves 8   *Bake at 350°*

⅓ cup lentils
2 cups water
4 cloves garlic, minced
½ teaspoon cumin
½ teaspoon coriander
½ teaspoon caraway seeds
½ teaspoon salt
¼ teaspoon red pepper flakes
salt and pepper to taste

1 potato, diced
1 carrot, diced
1 rutabaga, diced
½ head small cabbage, thinly
  sliced
1 tablespoon lemon juice
2 cups grated melting cheese,
  optional

In a large skillet, combine lentils and 2 cups water. Bring to a simmer and cook, partially covered, until lentils are tender, about 25 minutes. Add seasonings and vegetables. Reduce heat to low and simmer, uncovered, stirring occasionally until vegetables are tender and most of liquid has evaporated, usually about 10–15 minutes. Taste and adjust seasoning.

Spoon mixture over polenta, add cheese on top and heat in oven at 350° until cheese melts, about 10–15 minutes. Or simply spoon lentil/vegetable mixture on polenta and don't top with cheese. It's flavorful enough to stand on its own.

Polenta:

3 cups water
1 cup cornmeal
½ cup corn grits

2 tablespoons olive oil
1 teaspoon black pepper
¼ cup grated pecorino Romano

Bring water to a boil. Add cornmeal and corn grits, stirring with a wire whisk until no lumps remain. Add olive oil, pepper and Romano and simmer polenta 10 minutes. Stir often to prevent sticking. Remove from heat, and spoon into greased 12 x 17-inch baking pan and press down so covers whole pan like a pie crust. Set aside.

White Bean and Squash Stew

I always keep canned cooked navy and great northern beans in my cupboard in case I have to throw a dish together quickly. Both are beneficial to lungs and skin and can be used in this recipe.

Winter squash is high in vitamin A and potassium. It can be stored in a cool place for several months.

Serves 8

3 cups dried white beans	**2 cups diced tomatoes**
1 cup orzo	**1½ teaspoons sage**
¼ cup olive oil	**8 cups cubed squash, peeled**
6 ounces Fakin' Bacon, diced	**salt and pepper to taste**
2 large onions, diced	**2 cups grated asiago, cheddar,**
2 carrots, diced	**mozzarella or provolone,**
2 stalks celery, diced	***optional***
6 cloves garlic, minced	

Follow directions for cooking beans in What You Need to Know in front of book or use canned beans.

Bring water in a pot to a boil and add orzo. Cook for about 5–7 minutes, or until tooth-tender. Drain and set orzo aside.

Gently warm olive oil in a skillet. Saute Fakin' Bacon together with onion, carrots, celery and garlic for about 10 minutes.

Add remaining ingredients, as well as beans and orzo, to skillet, cover and simmer for 15 minutes, or until squash is tender. Taste and adjust seasoning. Transfer stew to large bowl. If desired, top with grated cheese.

Kasha Varniskes

Buckwheat is among the oldest of cultivated grains. It grows quickly, is hardy and serves as a staple in the Balkan countries. Used as a porridge, with pasta, as an accompaniment to meats or as a filling in dumplings, buckwheat is really not related to wheat. It's especially high in rutin, one of the bioflavonoids important for capillary strength.

Serves 6–8

1½ cups buckwheat groats
1 teaspoon salt
3 cups boiling water
4 small onions, diced

½ cup olive oil
8 oz. pasta bows
1 teaspoon salt
1 teaspoon pepper

Stir buckwheat kasha and salt into boiling water. Lower heat, cover pot and simmer for 15 minutes, or until kasha is fluffy and dry.

In a large skillet, saute onion in olive oil.

Cook pasta in a large pot of boiling water according to directions on package, or for about 5–7 minutes until al dente.

Drain pasta and add to onions. Add kasha, salt and pepper. Mix thoroughly.

Serving Suggestion: *Serve with a green salad for a simple, hearty meal.*

Poultry Main Dishes

Am I a vegetarian? No. I feel better when I eat meat from time to time as part of a balanced whole foods diet. I just make sure that the meat I buy has been raised without antibiotics or growth hormones and that the animals were raised humanely.

Human beings do have the digestive ability to utilize nutrients from meat. In the wild, even monkeys and gorillas hunt and eat meat when the opportunity arises.

Do I think one has to eat meat? No. As a group, vegetarians are healthier than those who eat meat. Most of us eat too much meat. However, there is no one right way to eat. There are people who need meat, and there are people who shouldn't eat any.

It seems funny to introduce the poultry chapter this way. It seems funny to say that you can substitute tofu or tempeh for chicken or turkey in most of the recipes that follow. But you can!

When you prepare poultry, put a pinch of turmeric, a yellow root from the ginger family, onto the uncooked bird. A pinch doesn't change the flavor of the dish and will protect you from harmful bacteria poultry might harbor due to improper handling. Turmeric is said to kill *E. coli* and other bacteria on contact.

I haven't bought commercially raised poultry in over 20 years. Naturally raised birds taste different. They smell different when they cook. They are not diseased and pumped full of antibiotics. Buy the best birds you can.

Snappy Chicken

Here's a recipe which uses ginger, garlic and hot oil—all things to get your metabolism moving. Ginger contains a substance called gingerol, which resembles the chemical makeup of aspirin and keeps blood from coagulating.

Makes 10 servings   *Roast at 375°*

**5 pounds chicken, whatever
    parts you like**
**4 tablespoons fresh ginger,
    minced**
10 cloves garlic, minced

⅔ cup tamari soy sauce
4 tablespoons toasted sesame oil
**¼ cup rice wine vinegar (or white
    wine or sherry vinegar)**
½ teaspoon cayenne

Preheat oven to 375°.

Rinse chicken and pat dry. Whisk together other ingredients. Pour over chicken. Marinate for 2 hours.

Place chicken on baking sheets in 375° oven and bake until brown and crispy, turning once.

Note: I like my chicken well done so I bake it 45 minutes to an hour, depending upon the parts I've chosen and whether or not I use chicken with skin. Chicken is done when juice runs clear when poked with a knife. White meat, skinless and boneless, is usually ready to eat in 30 minutes.

Note: Be sure to serve this finger-licking, lip-smacking chicken with napkins!

Note: This marinade is great for tofu, too. You can bake tofu as described here or saute in skillet about 5 minutes, turning once. (Marinate a few pounds at a time; it can be stored for about a week and a half in your fridge.)

Chicken Fricassee
with Chestnuts

Another one-dish meal that's simple to prepare. Chestnuts are considered warming, so this dish is great when there's a chill in the air.

Serves 4

½ cup dried chestnuts
4 tablespoons olive oil
8 cloves garlic, minced
4 chicken legs, thighs or breasts
1 small sweet potato, cubed
1 large potato, cubed
1 cup sliced shiitake or porta-
　bella mushrooms
1 bunch greens like kale,

arugula, or swiss chard,
　coarsely chopped
1 teaspoon thyme
½ teaspoon sage
½ teaspoon marjoram
1 teaspoon each salt and
　pepper
2 cups vegetable or chicken
　broth

Place dried chestnuts in a pot of water. Bring to a boil, and boil uncovered for about 20 minutes, or until soft when pierced with a knife.

Gently warm olive oil in a large skillet. Saute garlic and chicken, turning frequently, until chicken is browned, about 10 minutes. Add chestnuts, potatoes, mushrooms, greens, herbs, salt and pepper to skillet. Stir just until everything is lightly coated with oil.

Pour in vegetable or chicken broth. Cover skillet and simmer until chicken is cooked and potatoes are soft, about 15 minutes.

Place a piece of chicken on each plate and spoon vegetables alongside. Pour juice over all and serve to the hungry troops.

Note: *This dish, too, lends itself well to tofu or tempeh. The only change is don't brown with garlic; just add to skillet together with vegetables.*

Rosemary Chicken Thighs

Rosemary is particularly good with root vegetables like carrots and parsnips. Add it at the beginning of cooking as it needs a while for its flavor to permeate. Strong and aromatic, it should be used sparingly so it doesn't overpower your dish!

Onion is said to inhibit allergic reactions, so if you have allergies, eat those onions!

Serves 4   *Bake at 375°*

4 chicken thighs   **2 parsnips, diced**
1 tablespoon olive oil   **8 cloves garlic, minced**
2 onions, chopped   **1 teaspoon rosemary**
2 carrots, diced   **1 teaspoon thyme**
2 stalks celery, diced   **1 cup broth, if not oven-baked**

In a large mixing bowl, toss everything with olive oil and herbs. Place vegetables in the bottom of a baking pan and top with chicken. Roast at 375° for 1 hour, until vegetables and chicken are tender and vegetables lightly browned.

Note: If you don't want to cook this dish in the oven, gently warm olive oil in a large skillet. Add chicken thighs and brown on all sides, about 10 minutes. Remove chicken from skillet and set aside. Add remaining ingredients and saute until vegetables are brown, about 8 minutes. Return chicken to skillet. Pour broth over chicken, cover and simmer-stew until chicken is done and liquid evaporated, about 30 minutes.

Note: Vegetarian chicken is made from wheat-gluten and tempeh products (made from soy) and works great in this dish, too.

Chicken Tagine and Couscous

Tagine is a Moroccan stew usually cooked in a shallow clay pot. This makes a terrific party dish, and you can tell people you're also warding off colds and flus with garlic, ginger, cayenne and turmeric.

Serves 8

3 tablespoons olive oil
3–4 pounds boneless chicken, cut into bite-sized pieces
½ teaspoon salt and pepper
2 onions, diced
12 cloves garlic, minced
1 tablespoon paprika
2 teaspoons ginger
½ teaspoon turmeric
¼ teaspoon cayenne
3 lemons, cut lengthwise into 6 pieces each
2 cups chicken or vegetable broth

1 cup pitted kalamata olives
1 cup pitted green olives
salt and pepper to taste
2 tablespoons olive oil
1 large red onion, diced
1 red bell pepper, diced
4 carrots, halved and sliced
2 parsnips or rutabagas, diced
¼ teaspoon turmeric
3½ cups water
2 cups couscous
½ teaspoon salt
½ teaspoon pepper

Gently warm olive oil in a large skillet. Season chicken with salt and pepper and add to skillet together with onions, garlic and spices. Cook over high heat until chicken is lightly browned, about 10 minutes.

Add lemons and chicken or vegetable broth. Bring to a boil, lower heat, cover skillet and simmer until chicken is tender, about 30 minutes. Add olives. Taste and adjust seasoning.

Meanwhile, in another skillet, heat oil and saute onion, pepper, carrots and parsnips. Add turmeric and water. Bring to a boil. Mix in couscous, salt and pepper. Stir, cover skillet, remove from heat and let stand 10 minutes.

Fluff couscous with fork and use to bed chicken on plates when serving.

Note: This dish, too, can be roasted in the oven. Toss chicken, vegetables, lemons and olives with spices (all except turmeric), olive oil, salt and pepper and roast at 350° for an hour, or until vegetables are tender and chicken nicely browned. Make couscous separately by bringing water to boil, adding turmeric, salt and pepper and mixing in couscous. Cover pot, remove from flame and let stand 10 minutes before serving.

Chicken with Lentil Sauce

Marinating the chicken in citrus gives it a flavor perfectly complemented by the lentil sauce. Lentils, good source of protein, are eaten the world over. India produces more than 50 varieties of lentils. Garlic is a good addition to lentils, always!

Serves 8   *Bake at 400°*

Marinade:
½ **cup orange juice**
¼ **cup olive oil**
⅓ **cup lemon juice**
6 cloves garlic, minced
2 bay leaves

3 pounds boneless, skinless
  chicken

Lentil Sauce:
2 tablespoons olive oil
1 red onion, minced
6 cloves garlic, minced
1 cup lentils
2 cups vegetable or chicken broth
½ teaspoon thyme
½ teaspoon rosemary
pinch cayenne
salt and pepper to taste

Combine first 5 ingredients as marinade in a large bowl. Add chicken and turn to coat. Cover and refrigerate overnight.

To make sauce, gently warm olive oil in a skillet with a cover. Saute onions and garlic. Add lentils, water and herbs. Bring water to a boil and then simmer until slightly thickened, about 25 minutes, stirring from time to time. Season to taste. Let stand at room temperature.

Preheat oven to 400°. Place chicken on baking sheet and bake for 15–20 minutes, or until juices run clear when chicken is pierced by a knife.

To serve, warm lentil sauce. Toss chicken with half the sauce and spoon remaining sauce onto plates and top with chicken.

Note: *This recipe works well with seafood, too. Depending on the type of seafood you choose, shorten baking time to approximately 10 minutes. You can also saute shrimp or scallops.*

Roasted Garlic Chicken

Garlic, garlic, garlic. Where would we be without garlic!?! Protects us from infection, detoxifies and strengthens. Makes everything taste great.

Why do we use turmeric in so many poultry dishes? Turmeric is said to kill *E. coli* and other bacteria on contact.

Serves 6   *Bake at 350°*

3 pounds boneless, skinless white meat chicken, cut into bite-sized pieces
15 cloves garlic, minced
½ teaspoon turmeric

⅓ cup olive oil
⅓ cup lemon juice
1 teaspoon salt
1 teaspoon pepper

Toss chicken with other ingredients. Cover and marinate for at least an hour, but preferably overnight.

Preheat oven to 350°. Let chicken come to room temperature.

Place chicken in lasagna-style pan in oven for 20 minutes. Turn once or twice while baking. When you prick chicken, juice should run clear. That's how you know chicken is done.

Note: *This also makes a wonderful appetizer. Serve it with a plum dipping sauce to be a little exotic. Garlic chicken tastes great hot, warm or cold.*

Chicken with Brown Rice and Cumin

Dark meat makes this dish with brown rice a rich-tasting, satisfying meal with a green salad. If you want to use up leftover turkey, this recipe works great. However, if you substitute white meat turkey, add during last 10 minutes of simmering so it won't be tough.

Serves 6

3 tablespoons olive oil
12 cloves garlic, minced
2-inch piece ginger, minced
1 teaspoon salt
1 teaspoon black pepper
3 onions, diced
1 teaspoon ground cumin
½ cup dried tomatoes, diced

½ cup dried shiitake mushrooms, diced
1 cup raw brown rice
2 pounds boneless chicken thighs, cut into bite-sized pieces
2 cups water
parsley to garnish

Gently warm olive oil in a large skillet. Add garlic, ginger, salt, pepper, onions, cumin, tomatoes and mushrooms. Stir to coat and saute until onions are soft, about 5 minutes. Add rice and chicken. Stir to coat. Add water and bring mixture to a boil. Cover, reduce heat to low and simmer 45 minutes, or until rice has absorbed all liquid and is tender.

Taste and adjust seasoning. Sprinkle with parsley and serve.

Variation: You can simplify the flavors in this dish by omitting mushrooms, dried tomatoes and even ginger. Kids probably prefer it that way. You might even want to leave out the cumin.

Chicken Stew with Herbs

Here's an incredibly simple recipe using chicken or "mock" chicken. If you use the fake chicken (see note), you'll need to increase the amount of olive oil by a ¼ cup—more or less to suit yourself.

Serves 4–6

¼ cup olive oil
1 pound boneless chicken, cut
   into bite-sized pieces
8 cloves garlic, minced
1 onion, chopped
1 16-oz. can diced tomatoes
2 cups diced potatoes

2 tablespoons lemon juice
1 teaspoon dried tarragon
1 teaspoon dried basil
1 bay leaf
6 peppercorns
2 tablespoons dried parsley to
   garnish

Gently warm olive oil in a skillet. Saute chicken together with garlic and onions for about 5 minutes. Stir once or twice to prevent sticking. Add remaining ingredients and cover skillet. Simmer 20 minutes, until potatoes are tender.

Garnish with parsley and serve.

Variation: Leave out tomatoes and use another vegetable such as carrots, cauliflower or parsnips. Add ½–1 cup water or vegetable broth to compensate for lack of liquid from tomatoes.

Note: By "mock" chicken, we mean the stuff made from wheat, soy or something other than the bird. You can find it in freezers in natural food stores. It takes about 45 minutes to thaw. Fun to use in lots of things.

Indonesian Chicken with Peanut Sauce and Apples

The peanut is actually a legume that originated in South America. It has more folic acid than any other nut and is said to harmonize the stomach. Peanuts are great for increasing the milk supply of nursing moms.

Serves 4

Sauce:
½ cup smooth peanut butter
1 teaspoon ginger, minced
4 cloves garlic, pressed
2 tablespoons lemon juice
2 tablespoons soy sauce
⅓ cup water
2 tablespoons peanut oil
½ teaspoon black pepper

1½-pound chicken, cut into pieces
2 Granny Smith apples or Asian pear apples, minced or thinly sliced
1 tablespoon lemon juice
1 bunch arugula or watercress, stemmed
4 scallions, thinly sliced
2–3 cups cooked grain like rice, quinoa, millet or barley

Make sauce by blending in a blender or food processor until smooth. Spoon over chicken and turn to coat well. Set aside an hour to give flavors a chance to permeate.

Broil chicken with apples or saute in a large skillet, just until chicken is cooked through. Toss with lemon juice, arugula and scallions.

Place some cooked grain on each plate. Top with chicken and serve.

Turkey Potato Parsnip Pie

Homey, satisfying, you'll love it! Once again, if making for kidlets, you may have to simplify the recipe and leave out the shiitakes. They are an acquired taste! They are also a natural source of interferon, a protein which appears to boost immune responses against many illnesses. Tomatoes and tomato sauce contain the antioxidant called "lycopene," which is good for preventing prostate cancer.

Serves 4   *Bake at 325°*

1 pound potatoes
½ pound parsnips or rutabagas
¼ cup olive oil
½ teaspoon salt
½ teaspoon pepper
½ teaspoon nutmeg
1 pound ground turkey
8 cloves garlic, minced
1 onion, chopped

1 cup tomato sauce
½ teaspoon marjoram
8 shiitake mushrooms (substitute white if you prefer)
1 bunch greens, chopped, *optional*
½ teaspoon pepper
salt and pepper to taste

Scrub potatoes and parsnips (don't bother to peel) and steam until tender. Mash with olive oil and seasonings. Set aside.

In a large skillet, combine turkey with rest of ingredients. Cook over medium heat until turkey is brown and breaks apart with spoon, about 8 minutes.

Taste mixture and adjust seasoning.

Spoon turkey mixture into casserole baking dish. Top with mashed potato-parsnip mixture. Smooth top. Bake at 325° until potatoes are heated through and golden brown, about 25 minutes. Let stand 5 minutes before serving.

Noodles and Meatballs with Spinach and Pine Nuts

Pine nuts are used widely in the Middle East and Italy. They have a chewy, sweet flavor and more protein than any other nut!

Serves 6

4 tablespoons olive oil
1 onion, minced
8 cloves garlic, minced
1 pound spinach, chopped
½ cup pine nuts
1 cup fine whole grain bread
   crumbs
2 pounds ground turkey or
   chicken
1 egg

½ teaspoon nutmeg
½ teaspoon allspice
1 teaspoon salt
1 teaspoon pepper
4 tablespoons olive oil
⅓ cup water
4 cups favorite tomato sauce
1 pound ribbon noodles
pecorino Romano or soy or rice
   Parmesan, grated

Gently warm olive oil in a skillet. Saute onion and garlic. Add spinach and pine nuts and cook until spinach is dry, about 3–5 minutes. Using the steel blade of a food processor, blend spinach mixture. In a large bowl, combine mixture with bread crumbs, ground turkey, egg, nutmeg, allspice, salt and pepper. Form into 1-inch balls.

Add remaining oil to skillet and add meatballs. Brown on all sides. Add ⅓ cup water and simmer covered until meatballs are tender and cooked through, about 20 minutes. Add more water as necessary during cooking. Then add tomato sauce and let meatballs stand in covered pot for 5 minutes for flavors to meld.

Meanwhile, cook pasta in a large pot of boiling water until al dente, 6–8 minutes. Drain and return to pot. Toss with half the meatballs.

Serving Suggestion: *Divide pasta between plates and top with remaining meatballs and sauce. Pass pecorino Romano or soy or rice Parmesan at the table.*

Shiitake Chicken and Sweet Potatoes

The sweetness of yams provides a surprise in this hearty dish, which is also earthy tasting because of the mushrooms. Sweet potatoes and yams have more carbohydrate than any other vegetable and lots of fiber. Hot peppers like jalapenos are used to protect the lungs.

Serves 6   *Bake at 400°*

1 cup dried shiitake mushrooms, soaked in hot water and thickly sliced

2½ pounds boneless, skinless chicken, cut into bite-sized pieces

2 tablespoons olive oil

1 onion, diced

4 cloves garlic, minced

1 jalapeno chili, seeded and minced

3 sweet potatoes, scrubbed and cubed

1 teaspoon thyme

1 red and 1 green sweet bell pepper, diced

1 teaspoon salt

1 teaspoon pepper

Preheat oven to 400°.

In a large baking pan, combine all ingredients and bake covered for 30 minutes. Uncover and bake until chicken is browned and sweet potatoes are soft, another 30 minutes or so.

Adjust seasoning to taste.

Variations: *You can also brown chicken in skillet with garlic and onions. Then place all ingredients in casserole and bake covered until chicken and potatoes are tender.*

Variations: *Leave out mushrooms and add diced tomatoes instead. Or leave out peppers and throw in a handful of seaweed like hijiki, which has first been soaked in hot water to soften.*

Grilled Chicken with Black Beans

Hot peppers improve circulation, aid digestion and stop bleeding from ulcers.

Serves 4–6

2 pounds chicken fillets	**1 teaspoon black pepper**
2 tablespoons olive oil	**2–3 cups cooked black beans**
2 tablespoons lemon juice	**1 cup favorite salsa**
2 jalapeno peppers, minced,	**chopped cilantro or parsley to**
some seeds left in	**garnish**
10 cloves garlic, minced	

Put chicken fillets in a shallow nonaluminum pan. Whisk together olive oil, lemon juice, jalapeno peppers, garlic and black pepper. Pour over chicken in pan and toss to coat well. Cover and marinate in refrigerator at least 2 hours. Overnight is best.

Grill chicken over moderately hot fire or broil until nicely browned, or until juices run clear when pierced with knife, about 5 minutes per side.

Meanwhile, in a small pot, heat beans together with salsa.

Divide chicken on warm plates and spoon black beans beside it. Garnish and serve.

Variation: You can marinate chicken and then toss together with black beans and salsa mixture. Simmer together as a stew in a skillet until chicken is cooked and black beans heated about 5 minutes per side.

Serving Suggestion: Great served with warm tortillas.

Open-Faced Turkey Tostadas

Finger food for casual entertaining or for Sunday evenings. Fun for kids. Fun for adults. Yum! Who cares if this is messy to eat!?!

Use refried beans you made yourself or bought in a natural food store so you don't get added junk. Beans are a powerhouse of nutrition and you want to keep them that way! No lard or preservatives, please!

Serves 8   *Bake at 350°*

8 tortillas (any kind you like)　　**3–4 teaspoons chili powder**
4 cups refried beans　　**2 teaspoons cumin**
7 cups diced, cooked turkey　　**2 cups diced tomatoes**
**　(chicken is fine, too)**　　**1 bunch scallions, sliced**

Spread tortillas on cookie sheet with sides to save oven-cleanup. Spread about a half a cup of refried beans on each tortilla.

Combine turkey with rest of ingredients. Spoon 1-cup turkey mixture over each tortilla.

Bake at 350° until mixture is heated through, about 10 minutes.

Variations: *Top with your favorite shredded cheese. Most kids will eat anything topped with melted cheese! Make this dish vegetarian by using tofu, textured vegetable protein or "fake" chicken in place of turkey or chicken. Use soy or rice cheese instead of real cheese. It all works!*

Mediterranean Chicken with Chick-Peas and Kalamatas

A lot of ingredients, I know, but worth their inclusion. Turmeric colors chicken nicely, kills many harmful bacteria on contact and has a ginger/pepper flavor. It's used in many curry powders.

Serves 6

3 pounds boneless, skinless chicken, cut into bite-sized pieces
2 teaspoons salt
1 teaspoon pepper
1 teaspoon ginger
½ teaspoon cinnamon
2 saffron threads, crumbled
1 teaspoon turmeric
12 cloves garlic, minced

¼ cup plus 1 tablespoon lemon juice
¼ cup olive oil
2 cups tomatoes, diced
3 cups cooked chick-peas
3 cups cooked orzo
2 cups kalamata or brine-cured olives
parsley and lemon wedges to garnish

Mix chicken with herbs, spices, garlic, lemon juice and olive oil. Cook over high heat until browned, about 10 minutes. Add tomatoes and simmer, covered, until chicken is tender and done, about another 10 minutes.

Add chick-peas, orzo and olives and simmer until just heated through.

Serve garnished with parsley and lemon wedges.

Variation: Make this dish nightshade-free by leaving out the tomatoes. You can substitute zucchini, summer squash or even sweet potatoes.

Mustard Chicken with Cabbage and Apples

The colors of the cabbage make this dish a visual treat. But cabbage has therapeutic properties as well, the most well-known of which is its ability to heal due to its high sulfur content. Drinking a ½ cup of freshly made cabbage juice a few times a day for two weeks is said to heal stomach ulcers.

Mustard seeds, used in Indian, African and Asian dishes, are primarily cultivated in the Mediterranean. Mustard is said to be warming, pungent and stimulating, and it strengthens digestion. Serve this dish to cries of delight.

Serves 6   *Bake at 350°*

3 pounds skinless, boneless white meat chicken, cut into bite-sized pieces
2 tablespoons Dijon mustard
1 teaspoon sage
1 teaspoon thyme
1 teaspoon salt
1 teaspoon pepper

4 tablespoons olive oil
2 onions, chopped
¼ cup cider vinegar
2 tablespoons parsley
½ small head red and green cabbage, shredded
3 apples, cored and sliced
salt and pepper to taste

Rub chicken with mustard, sage, thyme, salt and pepper. Set aside to marinate for at least an hour or better overnight.

Spread chicken in a shallow baking pan and roast at 350° for about 20 minutes. Turn once or twice.

Gently warm olive oil in a large skillet. Saute onions until translucent. Add remaining ingredients. Cook, stirring occasionally, until cabbage and apples are tender, about 10 minutes.

Toss chicken, cabbage and apples together. Adjust seasoning to taste.

Moroccan Chicken and Couscous Pilaf

For some reason lima beans have gotten a bad rap in this country. However, they are said to be healthful for liver and lungs and to clear the skin. Another plus for limas is that they neutralize acid conditions largely attributed to overreliance on refined foods.

Serves 6

2 tablespoons olive oil
1¼ pounds chicken, cut into
   bite-sized pieces
2 onions, chopped
pinch saffron
2 carrots, sliced
2 parsnips or turnips, diced
½ cup boiling water
2 cups boiling water
½ teaspoon salt
1 cup couscous

2 tablespoons olive oil
1 cup cooked chick-peas
½ cup cooked lima beans
½ cup raisins
2 zucchini, thickly sliced
1 cup string beans or kale, cut
   into bite-sized pieces
½ cup black olives
¼ teaspoon cayenne
salt and pepper to taste
fresh parsley to garnish

Gently warm 2 tablespoons olive oil in a large skillet. Saute chicken until lightly browned, about 5 minutes, and remove from pan. Using the same pan, saute onions, saffron, carrots and parsnips, until just tender. Return chicken to skillet, along with ½-cup boiling water. Reduce heat, cover and simmer for about 30 minutes, until chicken is cooked and tender.

Meanwhile, combine 2 cups boiling water, salt and couscous and simmer on low until all water has been absorbed, about 5 minutes. Add 2 tablespoons olive oil. Turn off heat, stir and cover. Let steam for 10 minutes.

Meanwhile, add chick-peas, lima beans, raisins, zucchini, green beans and olives to the skillet with chicken and vegetables. Simmer another 5 minutes. Add salt and pepper to taste. Serve chicken mixture over couscous. Garnish with parsley.

Variation: For some reason, many people don't like raisins. You can substitute minced dried apricots, peaches or nectarines, too. All are good sources of iron.

South American Chicken Stew

The sweet potato, as used in this dish, is common in South America. When first introduced to Europe in the 1500s, sweet potatoes or yams were treated as ornamental plants. Thank heaven that custom has changed! When I am stressed, I find a baked sweet potato for breakfast or as a snack gives me energy and is easy for my body to digest.

Serves 6

¼ cup olive oil
3 pounds chicken, cut into bite-
　sized pieces
6 cloves garlic, minced
½ teaspoon paprika
2 bay leaves
3 carrots, chunked
1 parsnip, chunked

6 whole little potatoes
2 sweet potatoes, cut into chunks
⅓ cup barley
2 cups water
1 cup corn
2 cups green beans, cut
1 teaspoon salt
1 teaspoon pepper

In a large soup kettle, gently warm olive oil. Saute chicken and garlic. Add paprika, bay leaves, carrots, parsnips, both kinds of potatoes, barley and 2 cups water. Turn heat down and simmer about 30 minutes.

Then add corn and green beans and cook 5 minutes more. Add salt and pepper to taste and serve in large soup bowls.

Stifado of Mexican Chicken, Okra and Orzo

Okra is hated by many because it is slimy, but I don't think you'll find it so here. Okra is said to be beneficial for those who suffer from inflammatory intestinal disorders where soothing and mucilaginous are the operative words!

This dish also works well with shrimp, scallops or tofu. Some flavored tofus are especially terrific here. My favorite is lemon-garlic.

Serves 6

3 tablespoons olive oil
12 cloves garlic, minced
1 small red onion, diced
⅓ cup red wine vinegar
2 tablespoons tomato paste
1 tablespoon chili powder
2 bay leaves
1 large red pepper, diced
1 large green pepper, diced
6 stalks celery, diced

2 pounds boneless, skinless chicken, cut into bite-sized chunks
3 cups diced tomatoes
2 cups okra, sliced
8 ounces orzo, cooked
1 teaspoon salt
1 teaspoon pepper
cayenne pepper, cilantro or balsamic vinegar to taste

In a skillet, gently warm olive oil and saute garlic and onion for a few minutes. Add all ingredients but tomato, okra and orzo and saute for 15 minutes, stirring so chicken is coated and won't stick. Add tomatoes and okra and simmer for another 5 minutes.

Meanwhile, bring water to a boil in another pot and cook orzo until tooth-tender, about 7 minutes. Drain and add to skillet with chicken. Add salt and pepper.

Taste and adjust seasoning. You may want to add cayenne pepper, cilantro or balsamic vinegar. Allow stifado to sit in skillet for 10 minutes to give the flavors a chance to marry.

Seafood Main Dishes

Seafood is an easily digested and rich source of essential fatty acids. Eating seafood once or twice weekly may lower your risk of heart disease.

Buy fish from a reputable market. Don't buy fish that smells fishy, because it's not fresh. Be aware that some markets dip fish in a water/bleach solution to hide the fact that their fish isn't fresh. Ask questions because there's no law that requires markets to post a sign warning you. Be sure to keep fish cold and use within a day or two.

Which fish is best to eat? Saltwater fish are said to be better than fish from streams because our streams are polluted. Small fish are said to be safer than large fish, because large fish have had more years of exposure to pollutants. Farm-raised fish are likely not to be contaminated but usually contain less essential fatty acids than their wild counterparts.

If you are worried about parasites in fish, freeze it. Freezing fish for 24 hours will kill parasites. (So will cooking fish to an internal temperature of 140°F.) One of my favorite fish is a frozen Icelandic haddock which we use a lot in our kitchen in the store.

Of course, you can substitute tofu or tempeh for fish in the recipes in this chapter.

Baked Halibut with Creole Mustard Sauce

If you prefer a more assertive-tasting fish, this sauce also works nicely with mackerel or bluefish. (To make this dish vegetarian, substitute tempeh, tofu or beans!) Serve with steamed chard or spinach and baked potato.

Serves 8

½ cup olive oil
⅓ cup coarse-grained mustard
1 tablespoon Dijon mustard
1 large tomato, diced
1 large onion, diced
1 green pepper, diced
1 stalk celery, diced

1 teaspoon pepper
½ teaspoon basil
dash cayenne pepper
2 tablespoons lemon juice
8 halibut filets, about 6 ounces
  each

In a large skillet, gently warm olive oil and mix in all the sauce ingredients. Simmer until thick, stirring frequently, about 5 minutes. Add fish to skillet in a single layer. Cover pot and simmer until done, about 10 minutes. Do not turn fish.

To serve, place fish in center of each plate and spoon vegetable sauce over it.

Serving Suggestion: *Place greens to one side and potato to the other. Voila!*

Note: *Buying frozen fish isn't a bad idea because at least you know it's been frozen fresh. Many markets have the horrible habit of dipping fresh fish in a chlorine solution to retard spoilage.*

Broiled Haddock with Lemon and Tarragon

A quick, easy fish dish. Serve with a baked potato or white beans and steamed greens. Tarragon has an aniselike flavor and is delicious. A Dutch study of men who ate 7 to 11 ounces of fish weekly found they had a 50 percent lower death rate from heart disease than men who didn't consume fish. So eat fish!

Serves 6

3 tablespoons lemon juice
3 tablespoons olive oil
1 teaspoon tarragon

6 fish filets, about 6–8 ounces per
    person
salt and pepper to taste

Preheat broiler.

Whisk together lemon juice, olive oil and tarragon. Brush fish with mixture. Place skin side down on broiling pan. Broil, without turning, until opaque in center, about 6 minutes.

Transfer fish to plates and drizzle with salt and pepper. Serve with accompaniments.

Haddock with Pine Nuts and Capers

Fish is easier for our body to digest than chicken, beef or lamb because it has less connective tissue and there's less work for our digestive system.

This fish dish goes great with a green salad and a loaf of crusty brown bread. Capers are the pickled flower buds of a bush that grows in the Mediterranean. Parsley, too, is Mediterranean in origin and it's rich in vitamins A, B, C and E as well as some minerals.

Serves 4

¼ cup olive oil
4 pieces of fish, 6–8 ounces each
½ teaspoon salt
½ teaspoon pepper
1 red onion, diced

¼ cup pine nuts
¼ cup drained capers
¼ cup lemon juice
¼ cup minced parsley
1 cup pitted French green olives

Gently warm olive oil in a skillet. Sprinkle salt and pepper on fish and cook about 2 minutes per side. Transfer fish to plate and set aside.

Add onion to same skillet and saute for a few minutes. Add remaining ingredients to skillet and cook for another minute or two, stirring frequently.

Return fish to skillet and gently spoon sauteed ingredients over pieces. Cook until fish is cooked through, about 2 minutes.

To serve, transfer fish to plates and drizzle sauce and juices over top.

Variation: *You can try this dish with almost any whitefish filets. You can even substitute fresh New England bluefish.*

Fish with Lebanese Salsa

The salsa makes this dish, so don't skip it. Feel free to substitute whatever fruit you have on hand as long as the quantities are approximately the same. One-time staffer Connie Donofrio used melon and kiwi one day in our kitchen, and it was great!

Serves 8   *Bake at 400°*

8 potatoes, cut into bite-sized pieces
2 eggplants, cut into bite-sized pieces
2 yellow squash, chunked
2 red onions, chunked and separated
1 cup olive oil
2 pounds fish filets
salt and pepper to taste after roasting

Salsa:
2 lemons, peeled, seeded and pith removed, diced
1 medium red onion, diced
1 bunch parsley, minced
1 bunch cilantro, minced
½ cup lemon juice
¼ cup olive oil
2 tablespoons capers
1 pear, diced
1 peach, diced
1 apple, diced
salt and pepper to taste

Preheat oven to 400°.

Toss vegetables with olive oil and oven-roast for 45 minutes in shallow baking dishes. In a separate dish, place fish in a single layer and bake for 15 minutes, or until it flakes. Turn once during baking. Stir vegetables and let them continue to roast while the fish bakes.

Combine ingredients for salsa.

To serve, toss fish with half the salsa. (Yes, fish will probably break up into pieces—it's okay.) Add salt and pepper to taste. Spoon onto plates and mound vegetables alongside. Use remaining salsa as garnish.

Flounder with Greens and Almonds

Brown rice provides more fiber, vitamin E, protein, phosphorus, riboflavin and calcium than white rice. Flounder is a low-fat salt water fish. Don't you and those you care about deserve the best?

Serves 6   *Bake at 400°*

4 tablespoons olive oil
1 medium onion, chopped
½ teaspoon dill
1½ pounds fresh spinach or chard, chopped
1 cup cooked brown rice
1 tablespoon lemon juice

6 flounder filets, about 6–8 ounces each
2 tablespoons olive oil
½ cup almonds, roasted, chopped coarsely, to garnish
ground black pepper to garnish

Gently warm olive oil in a skillet. Saute onion until tender, about 5 minutes. Add dill and spinach and saute until spinach wilts, another 3–5 minutes. Add rice and lemon juice. Heat through, about 5 minutes.

Place ⅓–½ cup filling on each fish filet. Roll and secure ends with toothpicks. Arrange rolled fish filets in a shallow baking pan and brush with olive oil. Bake in a 400° oven for 20 minutes.

Serve garnished with almonds and pepper grindings.

Baked Salmon with Lemon and Capers

Salmon is one of the "fatty" fish whose oil seems to be essential in keeping blood pressure on an even keel. Salmon is also said to boost levels of good cholesterol because its fat is high in omega-3 essential fatty acids which also keep hearts healthy.

This dish goes beautifully with crisp tender asparagus and brown basmati rice or a baked potato. Don't skip the capers.

Serves 6   *Bake at 350°*

6 salmon steaks   **½ teaspoon each salt and pepper**
4 tablespoons olive oil   **¼ cup capers**
4 tablespoons lemon juice   **¼ cup parsley, chopped**

Preheat oven to 350°.

In a baking pan large enough to hold the steaks in a single layer, arrange salmon. Mix together olive oil and lemon juice with fork or whisk. Brush salmon with mixture and sprinkle with salt and pepper. Cover pan with foil and bake about 30 minutes, or until fish flakes easily when tested with a fork.

Transfer fish to dinner plates and drizzle any remaining oil over steaks. Sprinkle with capers and parsley. Lay asparagus (4–6 spears is a nice serving) beside salmon on plate and place potato or rice to side.

Baked Shrimp with Garlic and Cheese

Shrimp, like all seafood, is a source of selenium. If you've got the moody blues in winter, you may be deficient in selenium. Shrimp are also rich in iodine, so don't overeat shrimp if you are prone to skin troubles.

This is a real, to-hell-with-the-waistline dish. The first time I ate shrimp swimming in melted cheese with lots of garlic was Mexico City and I was 11 years old. I've never forgotten the pleasure!

Serves 4   *Bake at 400°*

1 pound shrimp, shelled and deveined
8 cloves garlic, minced
1 cup marinated artichoke hearts, drained
½ pound mushrooms, sliced
½ teaspoon thyme

1 tablespoon parsley, chopped
1 tomato, diced
½ teaspoon black pepper
1 pound pepperjack, asiago, cheddar or your favorite cheese, shredded

Preheat oven to 400°.

Combine all ingredients in a small baking dish and bake in oven until cheese starts to bubble and shrimp turn pink, about 10 minutes.

To serve, spoon baked shrimp and cheese over pasta or rice. Pass grated pecorino Romano at the table.

Grilled Bluefish with Squash and Spices

Bluefish are a fatty fish. Researchers have found that those who eat fatty fish on a regular basis (twice weekly) have less arteriosclerosis and fewer deaths from heart disease than those who don't.

Use green and yellow squash here for their pretty colors. Zucchini and yellow summer squash are said to have cooling, refreshing properties. They help us tolerate summer heat and act as diuretics.

Serves 8

Marinade:
3 tablespoons balsamic vinegar
3 tablespoons lemon juice
1 tablespoon paprika
1 teaspoon curry powder
½ teaspoon chili powder
½ cup olive oil

8 good-sized bluefish filets (8 ounces per person)
1 pound zucchini, sliced into ½-inch rounds
1 pound yellow or summer squash, cut into ½-inch rounds
4 red onions, quartered and separated
1 teaspoon pepper
½ teaspoon salt

Prepare barbecue to medium high heat.

Meanwhile, whisk together vinegar, lemon juice, paprika, curry powder, chili powder and olive oil.

Brush bluefish and vegetables with marinade. Grill fish and vegetables until just cooked through, about 3 minutes per side for fish and vegetables. Sprinkle with salt and pepper and serve over rice or with corn or potatoes.

Variation: *Place tofu in marinade for a few hours and grill it with vegetables instead of fish.*

Grilled Tuna with Anchovies

Great with ripe tomatoes and steamed corn. Garnish with pine nuts. Yummy!

Serves 8

½ cup olive oil
8 cloves garlic, minced
1 tin anchovies
¼ cup lemon juice
2 teaspoons oregano

8 tuna steaks, about 6–8 ounces
  each
1 small bunch green onions,
  sliced
½ teaspoon black pepper

In a skillet over medium heat, gently warm olive oil. Add garlic and saute a minute. Add anchovies and stir until they dissolve, about 2 minutes. Whisk in lemon and oregano.

Prepare barbecue or preheat broiler. Brush fish with dressing and grill or broil fish until cooked through, about 5 minutes per side. To serve, spoon on remaining dressing. Garnish with green onions and sprinkle with pepper.

Variation: You can substitute 4 tablespoons tamari, Bragg's liquid aminos or Dr. Bronner's mineral bouillon for anchovies.

Note: Because fish is perishable, store in fridge at 32°F (not higher than 40°F) to be safe.

Island Shrimp with Jalapenos and Thyme

Onion, garlic, green onions, all part of the aphrodisiac lily family, are combined here with a jolt of jalapeno. Not only are peppers a richer source of vitamins A and C than oranges, lemons or grapefruit, but they are believed to protect the lungs.

Thyme may provide protection against free radicals, those gone-crazy molecules that attack healthy cells in the body.

Serves 4

1 large onion, minced
8 cloves garlic, minced
3 tablespoons chopped parsley
3 tablespoons chopped green onions
1 small jalapeno, seeded and minced

½ teaspoon thyme
1 teaspoon lemon juice
4 tablespoons olive oil
5 large shrimp per person
salt and pepper to taste

In a large skillet, gently warm olive oil. Saute all ingredients except shrimp until onions and garlic are soft, about 5 minutes. Add shrimp and stir until they just turn pink. Spoon shrimp and sauce onto plates.

Serving Suggestion: *This dish goes well with brown basmati rice and steamed diced pumpkin or sweet potato. You'll need 2 cups of each to feed four people.*

Pecan-Crusted
Oven-Baked Fish

In ancient Rome, dishes with nuts were presented to newlyweds to promote fertility. Sweet and savory, pecans have more vitamin A than any other nut—about 130 mg per 4 ounces. They were a staple food among Native Americans.

Serve this succulent fish with tiny green beans or new sugar snap peas steamed for a minute. Accompany with couscous or polenta.

Serves 6   *Bake at 400°*

½ cup olive oil   ½ teaspoon black pepper
4 tablespoons lemon juice   1 teaspoon salt
½ teaspoon garlic powder   6 haddock filets, 6–9 ounces each
½ teaspoon marjoram   2 cups pecans, toasted
½ teaspoon oregano

Preheat oven to 400°.

Combine all ingredients except nuts and pour over fish filets.

Blend 1 cup pecans so that it has almost the consistency of flour. Chop the other cup coarsely. Dip each fish filet into ground pecans. Lay in a single layer in a shallow baking pan and top with chopped pecans. Bake at 400° for 20 minutes.

Picnic Shrimp with Mushrooms

Skewers of succulent shrimp and mushrooms, served shish kebab style, make a special entree. Seafood is a good source of minerals as is poultry when raised outdoors and chemical-free.

Serves 8

½ cup olive oil
32 large uncooked shrimp,
  peeled and deveined
16 small shiitake mushrooms
  (or buttons if you prefer)

1 pound turkey sausage, cut into
  ½-inch rounds
1 tablespoon thyme
8 cloves garlic, minced
¼ teaspoon cayenne pepper

Soak 8 bamboo skewers for 30 minutes in water.

Combine all ingredients in a large bowl. Let stand 1 hour at room temperature. On each skewer thread 2 mushrooms, 4 shrimp and 4 pieces of sausage. Start and end each skewer with a mushroom and alternate shrimp and sausage in between. Save marinade in bowl.

Heat grill to medium high. Arrange skewers on grill and brush with reserved marinade. Grill until shrimp are cooked through, turning and basting with marinade, about 8 minutes.

Transfer to plates.

Serving Suggestion: *Serve with rice and a cucumber dill salad.*

Red Snapper with Tomatoes and Sweet Potatoes

Sweet potatoes and fish are a delicious, if surprising, combination! The bright green of parsley as garnish makes this dish beautiful. I like to serve it with steamed greens alongside.

Serves 4

2 tablespoons olive oil
2 medium onions, chopped
6 cloves garlic, minced
2 jalapeno peppers, seeded and minced
2 sweet potatoes, diced
2 cups diced tomatoes
2 tablespoons tomato paste

1 cup water
1 teaspoon thyme
½ cup lemon juice
4 red snapper filets, 6–8 ounces each
3 tablespoons chopped fresh parsley to garnish
black pepper to taste

In a large skillet, gently warm olive oil. Saute onions, garlic, peppers and sweet potatoes until onions and garlic are soft, about 5 minutes. Add tomatoes, tomato paste, water, thyme and lemon juice. Simmer another 5 minutes. Potatoes should be soft or just about ready.

Lay fish filets on top of vegetable mixture. Cover pot and simmer 5 minutes. Spoon stew onto plates and garnish with parsley. Season to taste with pepper.

Salmon Curry

Curry powders are mixtures of coriander, turmeric, cumin, chili and other aromatic spices. They can be mild, medium or hot. Curry paste usually contains fresh chiles, onion and ginger root as well as the dry spices listed above. They'll get your metabolism going and boost your immune system!

Serves 6

3 cups water
1½ cups brown basmati rice
3 tablespoons olive oil
1 onion, minced
1 green pepper, minced
1 stalk celery, sliced
1 tomato, diced

6 cloves garlic, minced
3 teaspoons curry powder
3 tablespoons olive oil
1 pound salmon filets
4 teaspoons lemon juice
black pepper
lemon wedges to garnish

Bring water to a boil. Stir in rice, cover pot, lower heat and simmer 45 minutes. Turn off heat and let rice sit in pot, covered, while preparing dish.

In a skillet with a cover, gently warm olive oil. Add onion, pepper, celery, tomato, garlic and curry powder. Stir to coat everything and saute for 5 minutes. Arrange salmon filets over vegetables. Drizzle lemon juice over all and sprinkle with black pepper. Cover skillet and simmer for 10 minutes.

To serve, place some rice on plate. Place salmon to side and spoon vegetables and sauce over both. Garnish with lemon wedges.

Scallops and Papaya Salsa

Papayas contain bromelain, an enzyme that aids digestion. A proteolytic enzyme, bromelain works to break down proteins exclusively. Bromelain is also used to treat inflammation from sports injuries and degenerative diseases.

The colors and flavors of fruit salsa in this recipe provide a jazzy, colorful counterpoint to the creamy, pale scallops. You can also serve hot.

Serves 4

¼ cup olive oil
8 cloves garlic, minced
1 pound scallops

Salsa:
1 red onion, minced
1 jalapeno or serrano chile, minced
2 cups papaya, diced
2 tablespoons lemon juice
1 teaspoon basil
1 teaspoon cilantro, minced
salt and pepper to taste

In a skillet, gently warm olive oil. Add minced garlic and scallops and saute for no more than 5 minutes.

Combine remaining ingredients for salsa in a nonreactive bowl (use stainless steel, glass or ceramic).

When scallops are cool, add to salsa and refrigerate at least an hour or overnight. Serve cold.

If you prefer this dish hot, add salsa ingredients to scallops in skillet and simmer until onion is soft, about 5 minutes. Remove from heat and spoon onto plates.

Serving Suggestion: *Good for a picnic or party or for a light summer dinner with crusty, whole grain bread.*

Scallops with Thai Curry Sauce

The protective ingredients in curry are said to help prevent harmful bacteria from growing. That's one reason curry is used in countries where refrigeration is virtually unknown.

Serves 2

1 tablespoon toasted sesame oil
1 tablespoon curry powder
4 cloves garlic, minced
½ cup canned coconut milk
½ pound scallops
1 zucchini, halved lengthwise
   and sliced

1 carrot, halved and sliced
1 jalapeno chile, seeded and
   chopped
1 teaspoon salt
½ teaspoon black pepper

Gently warm toasted sesame oil in a skillet. Add curry powder, garlic and coconut milk. Simmer a few minutes. Add rest of ingredients and simmer another 5 minutes, or just until scallops are heated through and vegetables are still crisp-tender.

Remove skillet from heat. Divvy scallops and sauce between plates.

Serving Suggestion: *Side with potato or couscous. Make sure to mash potato into sauce so none is wasted.*

Smoked Fish Paella

Saffron is the strands of the dried stamens of the Asian crocus. It can take 75,000 hand-harvested stamens to make just 1 pound of saffron, which has a delicate aroma. Because it is so flavorful and so expensive, a little goes a long way!

Serves 8

¼ cup olive oil
1 onion, chopped
2 carrots, diced
8 cloves garlic, minced
1 cup brown rice
1 cup water
1 cup tomato juice
1 cup tomatoes, diced
1 teaspoon black pepper

2 strands saffron
4 ounces smoked salmon
4 ounces smoked mackerel
4 ounces smoked bluefish
½ jar artichoke hearts
1 cup kalamata or french herbed
   olives, pitted
1 cup peas

Gently warm olive oil in a large skillet. Add onion, carrots and garlic and saute until onions begin to soften, about 5 minutes. Add rice and stir to coat.

Add water and tomato juice to skillet and bring mixture to a boil. Add diced tomatoes, black pepper and saffron. Stir and lower heat, cover skillet and simmer mixture 45 minutes, or until rice is tender and liquid is absorbed.

Break up smoked fish and add it and remaining ingredients to skillet. Toss together gently, cover and let stand for 10 minutes. Adjust seasoning to taste and serve.

Variation: You can substitute whatever smoked seafood you like for those listed above. You can also make this a vegetarian dish without seafood. In that case, you might want to use a seasoned tofu or tempeh product.

Seafood with Vegetable Sauce

A light and easy seafood rendition. Feel free to substitute salmon for shrimp or scallops. Serve with white beans or a baked potato and crusty brown bread to sop up the juices.

Fennel is a sweet herb used as an appetite suppressant. It's used, too, for acid stomach and abdominal pain.

Serves 4

4 tablespoons olive oil
½ pound carrots, diced
½ pound fennel bulb, chopped
1 large onion, chopped
6 cloves garlic, minced
2 cups diced tomatoes
2 threads saffron
1 cup fish stock or clam juice
½ teaspoon thyme

½ teaspoon basil
1 teaspoon parsley
1 bay leaf
12 ounces firm white fish, cut into 1-inch pieces
12 medium uncooked shrimp, peeled and deveined
12 scallops
salt and pepper to taste

Gently warm olive oil in a large skillet over medium heat. Add carrots, fennel, onion and garlic. Saute until tender, about 5 minutes.

Add tomatoes and saffron and saute for another 5 minutes. Add stock and herbs. Simmer uncovered until mixture thickens slightly, about 10 minutes.

Add fish to skillet and cook until heated through, about 4 minutes per side. When you have turned fish and are cooking the second side, add remaining seafood for the last 4 minutes. Shrimp will just turn pink. Season to taste with salt and pepper.

Seafood Stew with Clams

An easy and impressive stew. Yep, this, too, goes great with crusty brown bread to sop up the juices.

Thyme has a high tannin content, which may impart a bitter taste to dishes if you use too much. It's good for chronic respiratory problems, colds, flu and sore throats.

Serves 4

3 cups bottled clam juice
2 large onions, chopped
6 cloves garlic, minced
2 teaspoons thyme
12 clams, scrubbed
1 pound firm fish filets, cut into
** pieces**
12 shrimp

12 scallops
2 tablespoons olive oil
1 medium head cabbage, thickly
** sliced**
2 carrots, diced
2 parsnips, diced
ground pepper and chopped
** parsley to garnish**

Using a soup kettle or heavy pot, bring clam juice to a boil. Add onion, garlic and thyme and simmer for 15 minutes. Add clams. Cover pot and cook until clams open, about 5 minutes. Using a slotted spoon, transfer clams to a large bowl. Discard any that don't open.

Add fish and other seafood to same pot and simmer until seafood is just cooked, no more than 3 minutes. Using slotted spoon, transfer seafood to bowl with clams.

Add olive oil to pot together with vegetables. Simmer until carrots are tender, about 10 minutes. Return seafood to pot for a minute and stir to heat through. Divide mixture between large shallow soup bowls or pasta plates. Garnish with grindings of pepper and parsley.

Shrimp and Potatoes in Green Sauce

Another dish that works equally well with tofu or chicken. If you don't have access to tomatillos, use green tomatoes or plain, regular red tomatoes. Won't be quite the same, but what the heck!

Serves 2

1 tablespoon olive oil
1 small onion, diced
4 cloves garlic, minced
1 pound tomatillos, husked
1 jalapeno, minced
1 teaspoon cumin
½ teaspoon oregano

½ teaspoon salt
5–6 jumbo shrimp per person
2 smallish red potatoes per
    person, quartered, steamed
    until tender
2 small zucchini, sliced

Gently warm olive oil in a skillet. Saute onion and garlic until translucent, about 5 minutes. Stir occasionally.

Simmer tomatillos in a pot with about an inch water until just soft. Puree together with jalapeno, cumin, oregano and salt. Add to skillet. Cover and simmer for 10 minutes. Sauce will thicken slightly.

Add rest of ingredients. Simmer, uncovered, until shrimp turn pink, about 5 minutes.

Note: *If you're using tomatoes, obviously you don't have to husk or peel them. If time is really short, use canned tomatoes.*

Sole with Tomatoes, Olives and Capers

I used to think capers, the flower buds of a Mediterranean shrub, pickled in salt water and vinegar were an affectation until I broke down and used them in a recipe. Now I love them and toss them in lots of dishes. You will, too.

Serves 6

½ cup olive oil
12 cloves garlic, minced
1 small onion, chopped
3 cups diced tomatoes
12 pitted Italian or French green olives, chopped
12 pitted kalamata olives, chopped
2 tablespoons capers

2 tablespoons balsamic vinegar
2 teaspoons rosemary
2 teaspoons basil
2 small zucchini, diced
6 sole filets, 6–8 ounces each
8 ounces orzo
1 tablespoon olive oil
1 teaspoon black pepper

In a large skillet, gently warm olive oil. Add garlic and onion and saute 5 minutes. Add ingredients up to fish. Cook gently another 5 minutes.

Add fish, cover skillet and simmer an additional 5 minutes. Fish should be done.

Meanwhile, bring water to boil in a large pot. Add orzo and cook until al dente, 5–7 minutes. Drain and toss with olive oil and black pepper.

To serve, spoon orzo onto plates. Spoon fish beside it and add sauce over both.

Tamarind Shrimp

Simple and different. Serve with Asian noodles tossed with sesame oil. Tamarind is a fruit called "garcinia cambogia" which is eaten in the Far East. Its extract, hydroxy citric acid, is being used in this country to help fight the battle of the bulge. Hydroxy citric acid seems to both burn fat and block it from being stored.

Serves 6

1½ cups water
4 tablespoons tamarind concentrate
1½ cups mirin
⅔ cup tamari soy sauce
2 tablespoons ginger, minced

12 cloves garlic, minced
1 teaspoon crushed red pepper
30 shrimp
15 mushrooms
3 green peppers, halved and
quartered

Prepare grill to medium high.

In a large saucepan, combine water and tamarind. Whisk until tamarind dissolves. Add mirin, tamari, ginger, garlic and red pepper. Boil until reduced to 2 cups, about 10 minutes. Pour half the sauce into a small serving bowl. Set aside.

With the pan off the burner, toss in shrimp, mushrooms and green peppers in remaining sauce. Stir to coat, then place shrimp and vegetables on grill basket. (Alternately, you can skewer everything, but a basket is quicker and easier.)

Grill shrimp and vegetables until just cooked through, about 3 minutes per side. Baste once or twice with sauce.

Serve with extra sauce to spoon over dish or use for dipping.

Note: *Mirin, in case you don't know or you've forgotten, is rice wine vinegar! Find it in Asian and natural food stores.*

Breads and Breakfast Goodies

Breakfast should be relaxed and leisurely. Yet, for most of us, it isn't. We don't have time to sit down and eat breakfast. Either we go without breakfast or have a donut or bagel washed down with a cup of coffee. So we have to plan ahead so a healthy breakfast is ready and easy to grab.

A good breakfast sets the tone for the day and can keep you humming. Days when I know I don't have time to make oatmeal, for instance, I'll make a blender drink or take waffles out of the freezer. I try to plan ahead by cooking a big pot of grains or oatmeal on the weekend. It's easy to warm a little each morning with some water in a pot and add mix-ins.

When my son, Adam, is over, or when I have other company, I make pancakes or waffles. They're easy to make from scratch. (Any extras I make and freeze are those I heat on rushed mornings.)

Don't spill out sour milk of any kind (cow, soy, rice or oat). Save it in jars in the fridge and use for pancakes, waffles, muffins. Pioneer women used to let a bowl of milk sour in the cupboard to make baked goods rise. Sour milk doesn't make you sick, and you won't taste it in the final product.

A word about breads: Baking yeast keeps forever if it's stored in the freezer. If the bread, muffins or sticky buns you bake don't get eaten immediately, freeze for later use. Storing baked goods in the refrigerator dries them out. Freezing is the way to go. Slice bread before you freeze it, and then you can take out a slice at a time to pop in your toaster.

Grease pans with a mixture of half liquid lecithin and half canola oil, described at the end of the introduction to the dessert chapter. In the end you'll be glad you took the time for this precaution.

Good Morning Waffles

Wheat germ is the heart of the wheat kernel and it's rich in nutrients like vitamin E and octacosanal, an oily substance which boosts stamina and endurance. Make sure you store yours in the freezer to keep it fresh.

Makes about 16 waffles

1 ¼ cups whole wheat pastry
    flour
1 cup wheat germ
½ cup ground sunflower seeds or
    almonds
1 teaspoon salt
1 tablespoon baking powder
2 cups sour milk (soy, rice or oat
    milk)

3 tablespoons Sucanat, honey or
    maple syrup
½ cup canola oil
4 eggs
2 teaspoon vanilla extract
    (substitute 1 teaspoon
    almond extract if using
    ground almonds)

Preheat waffle iron. Follow instructions for your machine. (I use a lecithin-canola oil spray on my grids.)

Combine everything together in a large bowl and mix quickly using a wire whisk. Use a ⅓-cup measure to pour waffle batter onto grids. Serve waffles with fresh fruit, jam, honey or maple syrup.

Variation: If you want to make your waffles gingery, cut the milk to 1½ cups, use ⅔ cups Barbados or sorghum molasses, reduce the other sweetener to 2 tablespoons and add 2 teaspoons ginger and 1 teaspoon cinnamon. Leave everything else the same.

Variation: Want to make your waffles Scandinavian? Substitute rye flour for whole wheat and use orange extract instead of vanilla and/or orange marmalade instead of the sweetener. You can also add 1 teaspoon fennel or caraway seeds. Or a pinch of cardamom.

French Toast Baked in an Oven

I don't avoid eggs. Studies done on twins, one of whom stayed in Scotland, Ireland or France while the other moved to the United States, showed that the twins who stayed in Europe and ate lots of eggs had no problems with cholesterol. The twins who came to this country did, despite the fact that eggs were virtually eliminated from their diets.

Egg yolks contain lecithin, a substance also found in soybeans, which is used to combat "bad" cholesterol. I could never figure out why, then, eggs and particularly egg yolks are considered "bad" for you.

Serves 4   *Bake at 400°*

2 tablespoons maple syrup
½ stick butter, melted
8 slices whole grain bread
½ cup milk (soy, rice or oat milk)
4 eggs

½ teaspoon cinnamon
¼ teaspoon nutmeg
⅛ teaspoon salt
4 tablespoons maple syrup
cinnamon to garnish

Preheat oven to 400°.

Whisk 2 tablespoons maple syrup into melted butter. Pour into baking pan. Place bread slices on top.

Whisk together rest of ingredients. Pour over bread and bake in hot oven for 20 minutes, or until set.

Invert toast when serving. Sprinkle with more cinnamon, if you like. Serve with maple syrup.

***Variation:** Cinnamon raisin bread makes especially nice French toast. Using stale bread makes this recipe perfect.*

Whole-Grain Pancakes

The combination of flours in these pancakes gives a well-rounded and varied nutritional boost for the morning! Spelt is a precursor to wheat with a higher protein content and a gluten analog different enough from that in wheat so that many wheat-sensitive people seem to be able to handle spelt just fine. Use it exactly as you would wheat.

Serves about 4

1 cup buckwheat or oat flour
1 cup whole wheat pastry or
  spelt flour
1 teaspoon baking powder
¼ cup wheat, oat or rice
  bran

¼ cup honey, barley malt or
  maple syrup
⅓ cup canola oil
2 eggs
2 cups sour milk (soy, rice or oat
  milk)

Combine dry ingredients in a mixing bowl. Combine liquid ingredients in a large bowl. Add dry to wet and stir lightly to form a thick, lumpy batter.

Brush a pancake griddle with butter or oil. Heat to medium high and pour pancakes in ⅓ cupfuls. Cook about 3 minutes per side, or until bubbles appear and begin to pop on surface. Flip.

Serve pancakes with honey, maple syrup, jam or fresh fruit.

Variation: Add 1½ cups of a favorite fruit like blueberries (add pinch nutmeg and 1 teaspoon vanilla), diced apples (add 1 teaspoon cinnamon and 1 teaspoon allspice) or peaches (add 1 teaspoon almond extract and pinch nutmeg).

Variation: Add 1½ cups shredded vegetables like carrots and zucchini, 1 teaspoon cinnamon, pinch nutmeg and ½ cup currants or raisins.

Variation: Blend in 2 mashed bananas, 1 cup chopped dates, 1 teaspoon vanilla extract, 1 teaspoon cinnamon and 1 cup rolled oats.

Hot Whole-Grain Cereal

Nothing like a bowl of hot cereal, especially on a cold morning! And this bowl, which you can vary any way you like, takes only minutes to make because you'll be using rolled, flaked grains or grains that cook quickly like quinoa. If you prefer the whole grain berry, you'll need to put them up overnight in a crockpot (remember those!) or allow a good hour or two for them to cook in the morning.

Makes enough for an army, but then you have cooked cereal on hand to just warm the next morning. (You can also spoon cooked cereal in portions into glass jars and tuck away in freezer.)

6 cups water
½ cup rolled oats
½ cup barley flakes

½ cup rye flakes
¼ cup quinoa
¼ cup buckwheat groats

Bring 6 cups water to a boil in a large pot (large enough to prevent the cereal from bubbling over onto your stove top). Stir in grains, lower heat, cover pot and move it partially off the burner. Simmer for 10 minutes. Turn off heat and let pot sit, covered, for 5–10 minutes depending on how you like it. Or you can eat it right away, if you prefer.

Variations: *Yes, you can choose to add other grains or change the proportions. For added nutrition, stir in wheat germ or wheat or oat bran. How about flax seeds? In a glass jar, put ½ cup flax seeds to 2 cups water. Mix a spoonful or two into your hot cereal. Store jar in fridge.*

Serving Suggestions: *Vary additions. You might like raisins and milk (or soy, rice or oat milk). You might like butter or flax seed oil and salt. How about a spoonful of tahini? Or almond or pistachio butter? Try tamari soy sauce and sesame seeds. Add honey, maple syrup, molasses or fruit to make your cereal sweet. If you like coconut and dried apricots, mix those in. It's your bowl of cereal, so have it the way you like it.*

Breakfast Berries with Yogurt and Oats

The bacteria in yogurt breaks down milk sugar to lactic acid, which makes yogurt easier to digest than cow's milk. Yogurt made from goat's milk is even more digestible because it most resembles human milk. It also contains more calcium. Make sure you're getting live cultures in your yogurt because they aid digestion and stimulate the immune system. The label needs to say that it has active yogurt cultures or living cultures. If it doesn't, look for another brand. Be sure to get a nutritional bang for your buck!

Serves 6   *Bake at 300°*

1 quart yogurt
2 cups blueberries or rasp-
   berries
½ cup rolled oats

½ cup wheat germ
½ cup Sucanat
1 teaspoon cinnamon

Preheat oven to 300°.

In a casserole baking dish, spoon out yogurt. Cover with berries.

Mix together rest of ingredients. Sprinkle over berries. Bake in oven for 10 minutes, or until topping is lightly toasted.

Debra's Peanut Chocolate Granola

This is the first of the new granolas I've developed since the first cookbook. The maple syrup I use is from Butternut Mountain Farm in Vermont. I use only their grade B, a thick, rich, luscious grade of syrup. None of that grade A syrup, which is simply sweet and runs on your plate!

Makes 12 servings   *Bake at 275°*

2 cups rolled oats
1 cup rolled rye
1 cup rolled barley
⅔ cup shelled peanuts
½ cup maple syrup

⅓ cup canola oil
2 teaspoons vanilla
⅔ cup bittersweet chocolate chips

Preheat oven to 275°.

In a large bowl, mix grains and peanuts together with maple syrup, canola oil and vanilla. Make sure grains are well-coated.

Spread granola in shallow pans and bake in oven until golden brown and dry, about 1½ hours. Stir every 15–20 minutes. Baking time varies due to weather, the size of your pans, your oven and the grains themselves.

Remove from oven and stir. Let cool completely before adding chocolate chips.

Store in air-tight containers.

Note: *This granola makes a good trail mix or topping for ice cream.*

Debra's Chocolate
Berry Granola

I searched high and low to find dried cranberries that were not sweetened with sucrose or fructose. I discovered New England Cranberry Company has terrific organic fruit-sweetened cranberries. The chocolate chips we use are organic, too, made by Tropical Source. What makes this granola nutritious—in addition to being delicious—is that the protein in oats is easily assimilated and helps lower cholesterol.

Makes 12 servings   *Bake at 275°*

2 cups rolled oats
1 cup rolled rye
1 cup rolled barley
½ cup maple syrup
⅓ cup canola oil

2 teaspoons vanilla
⅓ cup dried cranberries
½ cup freeze-dried cherries
⅔ cup bittersweet chocolate
**   chips**

Preheat oven to 275°.

In a large bowl, mix grains together with maple syrup, canola oil and vanilla. Make sure grains are well-coated.

Spread granola in shallow pans and bake in oven until golden brown and dry, about 1½–2 hours. Stir every 15–20 minutes. Baking time varies due to weather, the size of your pans, your oven and the grains themselves.

Remove from oven and stir. Let cool completely and add fruit and chocolate chips.

Store in air-tight containers.

Debra's Maple-Raspberry-Blueberry Granola

This is my concession to low-fat granola. Beautiful to look at, it turns your milk (soy, rice or oat milk) purple. The puffed corn is what kids are nuts about. Coated with maple syrup and roasted, it's crunchy and sweet.

Makes 12 servings   *Bake at 275°*

3½ cups wheat flakes   **¼ cup canola oil**
1 cup puffed corn   **½ cup freeze-dried raspberries**
1 cup maple syrup   **½ cup freeze-dried blueberries**
1 teaspoon vanilla

Preheat oven to 275°.

In a large bowl, mix wheat flakes and corn with maple syrup, vanilla and canola oil. Make sure grains are well-coated.

Spread granola in shallow pans and bake in oven until golden brown and dry, about 1 hour. Stir every 15–20 minutes. Baking times vary due to weather, size of pans, your oven and the grains themselves.

Remove from oven and stir. Let cool completely and add freeze-dried fruit.

Store in air-tight containers.

Variation: I also like this granola with rye instead of wheat. Rye has a higher amount of lysine, which means it is a more complete protein than wheat.

Strawberry Smoothie

Perfect for hot days when you want something to soothe and refresh the spirit and it's too hot to eat. Light on the tummy.

What kind of green stuff? Any powder that contains ingredients like barley, wheat grass, spirulina, or chlorella. Although it adds a nutritional wallop, you may omit it if it's too way out for you. But first take a look at some powders in natural food stores and consider the benefits.

Serves 2

1 cup mango juice
1 cup black cherry juice
1 cup strawberries (frozen)
1 banana, sliced (frozen)

2 tablespoons green stuff
1 tablespoon brewer's yeast,
  optional

Place juice in blender. Add rest of ingredients. Blend until smoothie is thick and shake-like.

Variation: If you don't have strawberries, use grapes, peaches, apricots, nectarines—whatever. Organic, of course! Stores like ours carry a variety of frozen organic fruits, if you don't want to bother freezing your own.

Serving Suggestion: Pour into tall glasses, or make it special by using a long-stemmed wine glass. Add a straw and pretend you're on vacation!

Note: I freeze my fruit because I love the thick, just-like-an-ice-cream-sundae richness frozen fruit gives smoothies. Bananas lend a creamy goodness, and strawberries make the smoothie look loverly.

To freeze berries, stem, rinse and put on cookie sheet in freezer. To freeze bananas, peel, slice and place on cookie sheet. When frozen, store in plastic bags.

Breakfast Protein Blast

An energy blast! Bee pollen is famous for increasing strength and endurance. It has all the amino acids a body needs, helps the immune system and is cleansing to the blood. Start with no more than ½ teaspoon daily. Increase up to 1 tablespoon daily.

Flax seeds are the richest source of omega-3 essential fatty acids and are also high in omega-6 essential fatty acids. Not only is flax oil good for the heart, arteries and immunity, but it makes skin beautiful. If you have dry skin or cracks around your mouth or nails, try flax seed oil.

Makes 1 super nutritious protein shake

2 cups vanilla yogurt or vanilla
 soy, rice or oat milk
1 cup favorite juice
1 frozen banana
1 teaspoon flax seed oil

1 teaspoon bee pollen granules
1 tablespoon protein powder
1 tablespoon green food powder
 like barley or wheat grass
1 tablespoon brewer's yeast

Put all ingredients in a blender. Blend. Serve very cold.

Variation: *Feel free to add more frozen bananas if you like your drink thicker and sweeter. Or add more juice if you like your drink thinner.*

Carob Eggnog Shake

When using eggs in blender drinks, coddle first. Bring water to a boil, lower egg into water and count to 30. Lift egg out, cool under running water and crack into blender. This quick cooking is enough to kill harmful bacteria.

Makes 2–4 servings

2 ripe bananas
2 cups milk
1 coddled egg
4 tablespoons carob powder

2 teaspoons honey
½ teaspoon vanilla extract
dash cinnamon
6–8 ice cubes

Blend until frothy. Serve immediately in tall glasses.

Creamy Mango Shake

A quick, easy breakfast or pick-me-up. My favorite brewer's yeast is one available in natural food stores made by Lewis Laboratories. It has a nice mild flavor, considerably different from the usual brewer's and nutritional yeasts. It's the only one I'm aware of grown on sugar beets, which may account for the difference.

Makes 2 servings

1 cup mango juice
1 frozen banana, sliced
¼ teaspoon ground cardamom

½ cup frozen soy milk (in cubes)
1 heaping tablespoon protein
    powder or brewer's yeast

Combine all ingredients in blender and process until smooth. Serve immediately.

Green Giant Smoothie

Good for stabilizing blood sugar and helps fill those nutritional holes!
Spirulina, a microalgae, contains more nutrients than any other single
grain, herb or plant. Its nutrients help cleanse, heal and curb the appetite
because they stabilize blood sugar. Chlorella has a hard cell wall which
makes it harder for the body to utilize, but it's high in RNA and DNA and
is said to protect against the effects of ultraviolet radiation.

Makes 1 super-green drink

1 teaspoon spirulina and
  chlorella powder or 2 teaspoons liquid chlorophyll
2 cups yogurt or soy, rice or oat
  milk

2 cups tomato juice
1 tablespoon brewer's yeast
1 teaspoon bee pollen granules
pinch cayenne, *optional*

Put all ingredients in a blender. Blend and serve cold.

Quick Coffeecake

It feels virtuous to find a use for milk that has soured, instead of pouring it down the drain. In fact, pioneer granny used to sour her milk deliberately for baking by keeping it in a bowl in the cupboard.

Serves 8–12   *Bake at 325°*

1 cup date pieces in oat flour
1 cup sour milk, soy or rice milk
2 cups Sucanat or other sweet-
ener
2 ¼ cups whole wheat pastry
flour

½ cup canola oil or butter
1 teaspoon baking soda
1 teaspoon cinnamon
½ teaspoon salt
1 egg, lightly beaten
¼ cup chopped nuts

Preheat oven to 325° and grease a 9 x 9-inch baking pan. (We use a mixture of liquid lecithin and canola oil.)

Combine dates and sour milk and set aside.

Place Sucanat and 2 cups flour in a bowl. Add oil or butter and cut in using two knives to make a crumbly mixture. Set aside ¾ cup to use for topping.

In another bowl stir together remaining flour, baking soda, cinnamon and salt. Add to mixture in other bowl.

Add egg to milk and dates. Stir wet ingredients into dry ingredients briefly, just so everything is moistened. Pour batter into pan. Mix nuts with reserved topping and sprinkle over cake before popping into oven. Bake 45 minutes, or until a sharp knife inserted in the center comes out clean.

Variation: Feel free to use spelt or rye flour in place of whole wheat flour.

Lemon Bread

Honey has antiseptic, antibacterial and laxative properties. Use raw, un-filtered honey because it contains some vitamins, minerals, bee pollen and live enzymes. Many commercial honeys are not only heated and fil-tered, but they are mixed with sugar water or corn syrup, which is not easy to detect.

Makes 4 small or 2 large loaves   *Bake at 350°*

3 cups whole wheat pastry flour
½ cup wheat germ
2 teaspoons baking powder
1 teaspoon salt
1 cup oil
1½ cups honey

4 eggs
zest of two lemons or 2 teaspoons
   dried lemon peel
1 cup buttermilk or sour milk
½ cup lemon juice
¾ cup chopped walnuts

Preheat oven to 350° and grease 4 small or 2 large teacake pans.

Mix all dry ingredients together. Combine oil and honey in food processor until light. Add eggs, lemon zest, buttermilk and lemon juice. Add dry ingredients to food processor and mix in with several pulses. Add walnuts and pulse 3 or 4 times. Do not overmix.

Spoon batter into pans and bake for 45 minutes. Remove pans and cool on rack. Turn bread out of pans.

Serving Suggestion: *Slice and serve with fresh strawberries and rasp-berries.*

Note: *If your raw honey crystallizes and you need to liquefy it for bak-ing, put the jar in a bowl of warm water. You can also store honey in a warm place. Germs won't grow in honey, and it will keep forever in your cupboard.*

Whole Wheat Scones

If not eaten immediately, these are good toasted the next day! Whole wheat pastry flour is made from whole grain soft wheat, which is higher in carbohydrates and good for pastries, cakes, cookies and muffins. Currants are dried from small black grapes. They are seedless and almost always sold unsulphured. Many raisin-haters seem to like currants. Go figure!

Makes 16 scones   *Bake at 450°*

2 cups whole wheat pastry flour
2 cups tapioca, oat or light buck-
   wheat flour
1 teaspoon salt
5 teaspoons baking powder
½ cup currants
½ cup finely chopped nuts

½ cup butter
½ cup honey
2 cups sour milk or soy, rice or
   oat milk
¼ cup currants to garnish
¼ cup finely chopped nuts to
   garnish

Preheat oven to 450° and grease two baking sheets.

Combine flours, salt, baking powder, currants and nuts in a mixing bowl. Cut in butter and honey using a fork and a butter knife, or your fingers. Make sure butter is well-distributed. Add milk and stir just until batter is moistened.

Press batter onto baking sheets in 4 circles. Score each crosswise into 4 sections. Sprinkle with remaining nuts and currants to garnish and press them down lightly into dough.

Bake for about 12 minutes, until scones are lightly browned. Cool slightly on rack and then break each into 4 pieces. Split and serve with butter and jam.

Cranberry Bran Muffins

Oat bran is a great source of soluble fiber, which helps lower cholesterol. If you have high cholesterol and want to avoid drugs to lower it, try ⅓ cup daily for six weeks.

Makes 12 muffins   *Bake at 375°*

1½ cups dried cranberries
1 cup oat bran
1 cup sour, soy or rice milk
⅓ cup honey
¼ cup canola oil
¼ cup molasses

2 eggs
1 cup whole wheat pastry flour
½ cup wheat germ
1 teaspoon baking powder
½ teaspoon baking soda
1 teaspoon cinnamon

Preheat oven to 375°. Line muffin cups with muffin papers or grease with mixture of half liquid lecithin and half canola oil.

In a large bowl, combine dried fruit with bran, sour milk, honey, oil, molasses and eggs. Let stand for 10 minutes.

Meanwhile, mix dry ingredients together. Add to wet ingredients and stir just until moistened. Don't overmix. The batter will be somewhat lumpy.

Spoon batter into muffin cups. Bake for about 20 minutes, or until lightly browned and a knife inserted in the center comes out clean.

Variation: You can substitute raisins, currants, dates or dried cherries for dried cranberries.

Note: Mix up a jar of half liquid lecithin and half canola oil and keep on hand for greasing pans. This mixture prevents whole grain flours from sticking.

Marie's Apple-Raisin Muffins (wheat/egg/dairy-free)

Flax seeds contain essential fatty acids similar to those in fish oil. Flax seed can be used as a tea or ground to sprinkle on cereal, yogurt or salads. One-time staffer Marie Taft made these muffins which are moist and a little sticky.

Makes 12 muffins   *Bake at 350°*

½ cup flax meal (directions
  below)
¾ cup water
¼ cup canola oil
½ cup honey
1 tablespoon molasses
½ cup soy or rice milk
1 apple, finely chopped
½ cup raisins

1 cup rolled oats
3 cups spelt flour
2 teaspoons baking powder
1 teaspoon baking soda
1 teaspoon cinnamon
¼ teaspoon cloves
¼ teaspoon nutmeg
raisins to garnish

Preheat oven to 350° and grease muffin wells with a mixture of half liquid lecithin and half canola oil.

To make flax meal: Grind ½ cup flax seeds in blender or food processor. Add 1½ cups water. Blend until a thick consistency is reached. (This makes enough for several batches of muffins. Store extra in glass jar in refrigerator.)

In a bowl mix ½ cup flax meal with water, oil, honey, molasses, soy milk, apple and raisins. Mix dry ingredients together in a large mixing bowl. Stir flax batter lightly into dry ingredients. Spoon into greased muffin wells. Place a few raisins on top of each muffin to garnish. Bake 30–35 minutes.

Jammin' Muffins

Using different jams as sweeteners in your muffins allows you to change their flavor. My favorite jams to use are raspberry, plum, pineapple or strawberry. Yum.

Makes 12 muffins   *Bake at 400°*

1½ cups whole wheat pastry or spelt flour
½ cup oat, rice or wheat bran
2½ teaspoons baking powder
½ teaspoon salt
1 teaspoon cinnamon

2 cups fruit-sweet jam
1 egg
1 cup milk or soy, rice or oat milk
5 tablespoons oil or melted butter

Preheat oven to 400°. Line muffin tins with paper liners.

Mix the dry ingredients together in a large bowl. Add the wet ingredients and stir just until moistened. The batter will still have lumps. Overmixing makes muffins tough!

Fill muffin cups two-thirds full. Bake for 25 minutes, or until muffins are lightly browned and the tops spring back when lightly pressed.

Serving Suggestion: *Want to make your muffins look fancier? Want people to know what kind you made? Place an identifying ½ teaspoonful jam on top of each muffin as you take muffins out of the oven.*

Pecan Muffins

A member of the hickory family, pecans contain "good," mono-unsaturated fat, which actually lowers "bad" cholesterol. I love pecans so much I always have a jar full in my freezer for baking! These muffins are a real treat in a holiday bread basket.

Makes 12 muffins   *Bake at 400°*

1¾ cups whole wheat pastry
flour
¼ cup wheat germ
1 teaspoon baking powder
1 teaspoon baking soda
1 cup maple syrup

1 cup sour milk or soy or rice
milk
½ cup canola oil
2 eggs
2 teaspoons maple extract
1 cup pecans, toasted

Preheat oven to 400°. Line muffin cups with muffin papers or grease with mixture of half liquid lecithin and half canola oil.

Using the steel blade of a food processor and 2 on/off turns, mix the dry ingredients. Add wet ingredients and incorporate with several quick on/off turns.

Add pecans and chop into batter, using several quick on/off turns. Pulse, don't blend.

Alternately, you can chop pecans and mix with dry ingredients. Whisk together wet ingredients and spoon into dry. Stir just until combined.

Divide batter among muffin cups and bake until knife inserted in the center comes out clean, about 20 minutes. Cool for 10 minutes before serving.

Note: *You should always feel free to substitute in recipes. If you don't have maple extract, use vanilla, although the flavor won't be as pronounced.*

Sweet Potato Muffins

You'll find many recipes using yams or sweet potatoes throughout the book. They're rich in beta carotene, have lots of fiber and are easy to digest. In addition to giving muffins a rich color, they are great for preventing strokes. A study showed eating ¾ cup sweet potato, 1½ cups carrots or 3 cups cooked spinach daily shaved 40 percent off stroke rates.

Makes 12 muffins   *Bake at 350°*

1 cup whole wheat pastry flour
1 cup oat or barley flour
2 teaspoons baking powder
½ teaspoon salt
1 teaspoon cinnamon
¼ teaspoon nutmeg
¼ teaspoon cloves
¼ teaspoon allspice
½ cup milk or soy or rice milk

1 egg
½ cup honey
¼ cup canola oil
2 teaspoons vanilla
2 cups sweet potato, baked or simmered until soft
½ cup raisins or walnuts
cinnamon, raisins or walnuts to garnish

Preheat oven to 350°. Line muffin tins with paper liners.

Combine the dry ingredients in a large bowl. Using the steel blade of a food processor, blend wet ingredients using on/off turns of the processor until no lumps of sweet potato remain. (You don't have to worry about peeling them.)

Spoon wet mixture into dry and stir together just to moisten. Add raisins or walnuts. Spoon into muffin cups. Top each muffin with a pinch of cinnamon and a raisin or walnut.

Bake 25 minutes, or until muffins spring back when touched.

Wheat Germ and Banana Muffins

Make sure you keep wheat germ in the refrigerator or freezer because it can turn rancid quickly. Freezer is best. The embryo of wheat, wheat germ is high in B vitamins, proteins, vitamin E and iron.

Makes 12 large muffins   *Bake at 400°*

**1½ cups whole wheat pastry
  flour**
¾ cup Sucanat or honey
1 tablespoon baking powder
¾ teaspoon salt
1 cup wheat germ
1 teaspoon cinnamon

3 large ripe bananas
**½ cup sour milk or soy or rice
  milk**
2 eggs
¼ cup canola oil
1 tablespoon vanilla extract

Preheat oven to 400°. Line muffin tins with muffin papers.

Mix dry ingredients together in a bowl. Using the steel blade and on/off turns of a food processor or a blender, puree bananas with wet ingredients.

Combine the two using a rubber spatula, but don't overmix! Spoon batter into muffin cups, dividing it equally.

Bake until tops are golden brown and tester inserted into the center comes out clean, about 25 minutes.

Note: *If you want to use less wheat, substitute a flour like spelt and corn germ for wheat germ. Corn germ is harder to find, but it's supposed to be higher in some nutrients than wheat germ. For instance, it has 10 times more zinc. I like the fact that it's not so perishable.*

Sesame Corn Sticks

Buy brown unhulled sesame seeds. Not only do they have a nutty flavor and are high in calcium and other minerals, but they can be sprouted. Canola oil is good for baking and has little saturated fat and lots of mono-unsaturates. Some believe mono-unsaturates are superior to polyunsaturates for lowering cholesterol. You'll love these corn sticks.

Makes corn sticks, muffins or 8-inch square pan   *Bake at 350°*

¼ cup whole wheat pastry flour
¼ teaspoon salt
¾ teaspoon baking soda
1 cup cornmeal
½ cup wheat or oat bran
¼ cup unhulled sesame
   seeds

1 cup milk, sour milk, soy, rice
   or oat milk
2 tablespoons maple syrup
¼ cup canola oil
1 egg
¼ cup unhulled sesame seeds to
   garnish

Preheat oven to 350°. Grease corn-stick, muffin or 8-inch square cake pan with a mixture of half liquid lecithin and half canola oil.

Mix dry ingredients in a large bowl. Whisk together wet ingredients in another bowl and add all at once to dry. Stir until dry ingredients are moistened. Fill pans two-thirds full. Garnish with extra sesame seeds.

Bake about 20 minutes. Knife inserted in center should come out clean, or corn sticks will spring back when lightly touched.

Maple, Cardamom and Oatmeal Loaves

Cardamom is a member of the ginger family, and it is grown in tropical climes. It's an expensive spice because pods ripen at different times. Therefore, there is no single harvest. Very labor intensive! Some use cardamom as a breath freshener. It's also said to energize.

Makes 2 loaves   *Bake at 350°*

1 cup rolled oats
2 cups milk, sour milk, soy, rice
  or oat milk, scalded
1 tablespoon baking yeast
¼ cup warm water
½ cup maple syrup

1 teaspoon salt
1 teaspoon cardamom powder
¼ cup canola oil or melted
  butter
6 cups whole wheat or spelt
  bread flour

Place oats in a mixing bowl and pour milk over oats. Stir and let stand until mixture cools to room temperature.

Dissolve yeast in warm water. (Whisk yeast into water. I like to use a 4-cup measure so it won't splash out and I can pour it easily.) Add to oats together with maple syrup, salt, cardamom and oil. Gradually beat in the flour.

Transfer dough to a clean bowl, which has been lightly coated with a mixture of half liquid lecithin and half canola oil. Cover and let rise in a warm place for an hour, or until doubled in bulk.

Punch down. Knead until smooth and elastic. The dough will no longer be sticky. Divide in two. Place in greased loaf bread pans and shape into nicely rounded loaves. Let rise another hour.

Preheat oven to 350°. Bake for about 45 minutes, or until loaves sound hollow when pans are thumped on bottom. Turn loaves out to cool on a rack.

Orange Sticky Buns

What is it about sticky buns that makes them so irresistible? They mess up our hands and mouth, but who cares? These are chock-a-block full of everything we need for breakfast, too.

Makes 16 buns   *Bake at 375°*

1 tablespoon baking yeast
¼ cup warm water
½ cup soft butter or canola oil
⅓ cup honey
1 teaspoon salt
1 cup milk or soy, rice or oat milk, scalded
4½ cups whole wheat (spelt or rye) pastry flour
2 eggs
2 teaspoons orange extract

1 teaspoon cinnamon
⅓ cup rolled oats

Orange filling:
1 stick butter or margarine, melted
1 cup honey
2 teaspoons cinnamon
4 teaspoons grated orange peel
1 cup chopped nuts, dates or apricots

In a measuring cup, sprinkle yeast over water and whisk to mix. Set aside.

In the work bowl of a food processor, using the steel blade and quick on/off turns, combine butter with honey and salt. Pour in scalded milk and process with several quick on/off turns. Cool to lukewarm.

Add in flour, eggs, orange extract, cinnamon and yeast mixture with quick on/off turns. In 10 seconds, the dough will begin to form a ball. Stop processor and add oats. Pulse 3 or 4 times.

Grease a large bowl with a mixture of half liquid lecithin and half canola oil and place dough in bowl. Turn to coat. Cover and allow dough to rise in a warm place (or just cover with plastic wrap) until double in bulk, about 1 hour. Punch down dough. Turn out onto lightly floured surface. Cover and let rest 10 minutes.

Combine ingredients for the orange filling in a small bowl. In each of two 8 x 2-inch round pans, place one-fourth of the orange filling. Tilt pans to coat.

Divide dough in half. Roll one half on floured work surface to form a rectangle about 16 x 12 inches. Spread half the remaining orange filling over rectangle. Roll as for jelly roll and cut into eight 2-inch slices. Repeat with other half of dough.

Place 8 slices, cut side down, in each pan. Cover and let rise in warm place until double in bulk, about 45 minutes.

Bake at 375° for 25 minutes. Immediately remove buns from pans. Serve with the bottoms turned up.

Honey Sesame Rolls

These rolls are fairly sweet. As in all recipes, feel free to use spelt flour instead of wheat. Or try rye flour, though it makes things heavier.

There's a new whole wheat white flour that is whole grain (includes the germ and bran) but has the lightness of white flour. If your family prefers lighter breads, look for whole wheat white in your natural food store.

Makes about 8 rolls   *Bake at 350°*

4 cups whole wheat bread flour   **¼ cup sesame tahini**
1 tablespoon baking yeast   **2 tablespoons olive oil**
1½ teaspoons salt   **1 egg with 1 tablespoon water**
½ cup honey   **for glaze**
1½ cups warm water   **sesame seeds to garnish**

Using the steel blade of a food processor, mix flour, yeast and salt with several quick on/off turns of processor. Add honey, water and tahini and pulse until dough cleans sides of work bowl. This takes less than a minute.

Grease bowl with oil. Place dough in bowl and turn to coat. Cover and let rise until doubled in bulk, about 2 hours.

Punch dough down, form into eight rolls and put in a greased muffin tin. Cover rolls and let rise another hour. Score tops of rolls with a scissors cross-wise. Brush with egg mixed with water and sprinkle with sesame seeds.

Meanwhile, preheat oven to 350° and bake rolls for 25 minutes. Let cool on rack and serve with butter or jam.

Variations: *Prefer rolls savory, not that sweet? Cut honey to tablespoon or less. Try mashed garlic or toasted sesame oil in place of tahini. Use olive oil instead of tahini and a pinch each of basil, oregano and thyme with 4 tablespoons Romano. Hey, the possibilities are endless!*

Garlic and Herb Focaccia

Why whole-grain flours instead of white? White flour has been stripped of fiber and over 80 percent of its essential nutrients. It's been stripped of anything live that can spoil and will prevent a product from sitting on supermarket shelves for an indefinite period. Don't be fooled by the term "enriched," which means an essentially dead flour has been pumped up with some synthetic nutrients so we don't drop dead from malnutrition! Also, don't be fooled when buying baked goods. Wheat flour means white flour. Look for the term "whole wheat" or "whole rye."

Makes 1 loaf   *Bake at 400°*

1 cup whole wheat bread flour
2 tablespoons baking yeast
½ cup warm water
¼ cup olive oil
12 cloves garlic, minced
2 cups whole wheat bread flour
1 cup warm vegetable stock or
  water

½ teaspoon salt
1 teaspoon pepper
1 teaspoon oregano
1 teaspoon basil
½ teaspoon thyme
olive oil for pans and for brushing

In the work bowl of a food processor, using a steel blade, whirl 1 cup whole wheat bread flour, baking yeast and warm water for a second or two. Cover bowl with towel and let sponge rise in a warm place until doubled in bulk, about an hour.

In a small pan, gently warm olive oil and saute garlic for a minute or 2, until it is aromatic and begins to brown. Set aside.

Into sponge, using on/off turns of the processor, add half the garlic and remaining flour with vegetable stock or water. Add salt, herbs and spices, incorporating with several quick on/off turns. Cover and let rise in warm area until doubled in bulk, about 45 minutes.

Preheat oven to 400°. Brush a 9 x 13-inch baking pan with shallow sides with olive oil. Spoon in batter, smoothing with a rubber spatula. Top with remaining garlic. Bake until bread is golden brown, about 35 minutes. Cool in pan on rack for 10 minutes.

Twisted Loaf with Olives and Cornmeal

Doesn't this make you think of a summer picnic in the Tuscan country-side? Just add ripe tomatoes, goat cheese and a bottle of wine.

Makes 1 large loaf   *Bake at 350°*

1 teaspoon baking yeast	20 pitted French green olives,
2 cups warm water	coarsely chopped
5 cups whole wheat bread flour	pinch rosemary
2 teaspoons salt	pinch marjoram
¼ cup corn meal or corn grits	½ cup cornmeal
2 tablespoons olive oil	1 egg yolk with 1 tablespoon
20 pitted kalamata olives,	water for glaze
coarsely chopped	sliced olives to garnish, *optional*

In the work bowl of a food processor (or bowl of a mixer equipped with a dough hook), sprinkle yeast over warm water and stir to dissolve. Let stand 10 minutes.

Using on/off turns of the processor, mix in 4½ cups of the flour together with salt and ¼ cup corn meal. Process until dough is soft and just beginning to clean the sides of the work bowl, about 10 seconds. Dough will be sticky. (If using a mixer, add flour ½ cup at a time. Knead with dough hook about 5 minutes.)

Grease a large bowl with olive oil and spoon dough into bowl. Turn to coat. Cover bowl and let dough rise in warm place until doubled in bulk, about 1½ hours.

Place dough back in work bowl. Using the white plastic blade of the processor or the dough hook of a mixer, add olives and herbs. Knead in. Processor takes seconds; mixer about 5 minutes.

Return dough to oiled bowl to rise, again covered in a warm place for another 1½ hours, or until doubled in bulk.

Punch dough down and turn onto lightly floured surface. Cut into thirds. Roll each third into an 18-inch rope. Place ropes beside each other on surface and pinch the three ends together, tucking under the loaf. To braid, take one rope and weave it over center rope and under side rope. Do same with other side. Continue weaving this way. Pinch ends together and tuck under.

Sprinkle baking sheet with cornmeal. Place loaf on baking sheet and cover with towel. Let rise again for about 30 minutes. Bread will double in volume. Brush with egg mixture and garnish with sliced olives.

Place in 350° oven and bake for 40 minutes, or until bread is nicely browned and sounds hollow when hit on side.

Page's Sesame Millet Bread

Page Loeser is our bread expert. Sundays, after she walks the dog and feeds her husband Rudy, she bakes bread for the week.

With the amount of baking yeast in this bread, it rises quickly. Count on a total of 3–3½ hours until you can pop some in your mouth!

Makes 2 delicious, nutritious, somewhat crumbly loaves!   Bake at 350°

3½ cups milk or soy milk
¼ cup canola oil
¼ cup honey or rice syrup
2 tablespoons baking yeast
3 cups unhulled sesame seeds

1½ cups millet
6 or more cups whole wheat bread flour
2 teaspoons salt

Mix milk, oil and sweetener in a small saucepan and heat to 115° (mixture will be hot on wrist). Stir in yeast and let stand for a few minutes.

Partially grind sesame seeds and millet by half-cupfuls in blender or coffee grinder. Mix 6 cups flour, sesame seeds, millet and salt in a large bowl.

Add liquid mixture and stir until dough is workable (when it's about ear-lobe consistency, not too wet/sticky or too dry). Add more flour or water as necessary, but only a tablespoon at a time.

Turn dough onto floured board and knead 10 minutes. Place dough in bowl oiled with olive oil, turning once to oil top, cover with damp cloth and put bowl in warm place until dough rises to double in bulk. Then punch down and let rise until double in bulk again. (For finer texture, dough may be punched down and left to rise a third time.)

Divide dough into two equal halves, knead each a few times to get bubbles out and form into loaves. Place in standard-size, oiled bread pans, turning once to oil top of dough. Cover and put in warm place until dough rises slightly above pan. Slash tops with knife and bake at 350° for about 35 minutes, or until bottoms sound hollow when tapped. Turn out onto wire rack to cool.

***Variation:** For less crumbly bread, halve the amount of sesame seeds and millet and increase the whole wheat flour by the same amount.*

Flax Seed Bread

The essential fatty acids in flax seeds are needed by every cell in the body to achieve optimal health. Flax seeds also provide dietary fiber and make your bread look very gourmet. To give your bread that professional look, cut the tops of the loaves with a sharp knife before you put them into the oven to allow them to open in the heat.

Makes 2 loaves   *Bake at 400°*

6 cups whole wheat bread flour
2 tablespoons baking yeast
1 tablespoon salt
1 tablespoon honey, maple or
   rice syrup
4 tablespoons olive oil

2 cups hot water
½ cup flax seeds
olive oil for greasing bowl for
   rising
flax seeds to garnish

Place 4 cups of flour into mixing bowl and add yeast, salt and sweetener. Using the dough hook, stir until well blended. Pour in oil, hot water and flax seeds and beat for a few minutes. Add remaining flour, ½ cup at a time, and knead with mixer for about 5 minutes. Dough will become smooth and elastic.

If you want to use a food processor, place ½ the flour in the work bowl with yeast, salt and sweetener. Turn on and off a few times to mix. Add oil, water and flax seeds and pulse again. Add remaining flour in 2-cup batches, pulsing after each addition. Dough will form ball and clean the work bowl in about a minute.

Pour a spoonful of olive oil in a large bowl and coat sides. Place dough in bowl. Turn to coat, cover with plastic wrap and let dough rise until double in bulk, about 20 minutes.

Punch down dough and turn out onto floured work surface. Cut in half. Shape each half into a round or oblong loaf. Place loaves onto baking sheet and cover. Let rise again until doubled in bulk.

Slash an X on the top of each loaf with a knife, brush loaves with water and sprinkle loaves with flax seeds to garnish.

Place baking sheet into cold oven and turn on to 400°. Bake for 45 minutes, or until loaves are deep golden brown. Turn loaves out onto cooling racks.

Variation: Add ½ cup onion flakes to dough and use more as garnish together with flax seeds. Or throw in some poppy seeds.

Note: Best eaten fresh or used for toast. Bread freezes well.

Soda Bread with Walnuts and Apricots

Drying fruit intensifies some of its nutritional attributes. Dried apricots, for instance, have more vitamin A than fresh apricots. In addition, dried apricots have the highest protein content of all dried fruit.

Makes 2 loaves   *Bake at 350°*

2 cups hot water
2 cups chopped dried apricots
1 tablespoon baking soda
1 cup honey
¼ cup olive oil

½ teaspoon salt
4 cups whole grain flour like
whole wheat pastry, spelt or
rye
1 cup chopped walnuts

Pour hot water over apricots in a large bowl. Add baking soda and stir. Cover with plastic wrap and let sit overnight.

Preheat oven to 350°. Grease two standard bread loaf pans.

Add rest of ingredients to bowl of apricots and any remaining water and stir to blend. The batter will be too thick to pour and not kneadable. Spoon into baking pans so they are ⅔ full. Using a wooden spoon or rubber spatula, push batter down to get rid of any air pockets.

Place pans in oven and bake for about an hour, or until loaves are nicely browned. Remove pans from oven and allow loaves to sit in pans on cooling rack for about 10 minutes before turning out.

Note: *If you store this bread in air-tight containers in the fridge once it's thoroughly cooled, it will keep for about a month.*

Desserts

I only make and serve desserts when I've company or at holidays. Then I love to make a dessert buffet. I prepare one dessert that is fruit and fat-free like raspberries, one that is chocolate—decadent and rich—and two or three others that provide contrast in textures, tastes and sizes. That way there's something for everyone, and dinner is a success. *It's the desserts everyone always remembers!*

Make desserts with whole grain flours and sweeteners like honey, maple syrup and Sucanat. You don't need white flour and white sugar to wow people.

If you buy baked goods, keep in mind that white flour products may have as many as 16 chemical additives just to keep them fresh. Though Americans are consuming less sugar, we're eating more refined sugars with names like corn syrup. Sugar intake now stands at 134 pounds per person per year. That is the highest amount ever recorded! In addition to many other unhealthy factors, refined sugars reduce the body's ability to destroy bacteria.

Whole grain flours can be varied. Whole wheat pastry flour is the one I use most. It's made from soft winter or spring berries and is lighter and has less gluten than whole wheat bread flour. You can substitute other flours for wheat. Spelt is a dream to work with and can be substituted one for one. Other flours like millet, rice, buckwheat and rye are different, and you'll have to experiment with quantities. Adding tapioca flour seems to work in many recipes when you use alternate flours.

Keep your flours, nuts, seeds and grains, too, for that matter, in the freezer for maximum freshness. They will remain loose. Flours should be brought to room temperature for baking.

Greasing with lecithin: Whole grain products stick to the pan more. Dilute ½ cup liquid soy lecithin with ½ cup canola oil. Mix in a jar and use this liquid to grease with. A thin film applied with a pastry brush works great. Alternately, you can dip your fingers in the mixture and grease. Keep a jar of lecithin and oil in the cupboard to use as needed.

Almond Clusters

From my mother, Beatrice Stark. This was always one of my favorites, and the whole almonds really make it! Almonds are a good source of mono-unsaturated fats, which are acceptable in the diets of those with cholesterol problems.

Carob powder is ground from carob beans found in the large pods of the carob tree. In Florida, when I was growing up, farmers fed the pods to cows. Carob has calcium and phosphorus, no caffeine and a low fat content. It's higher in B vitamins than cocoa.

Makes 24   *Bake at 350°*

2 cups whole almonds, toasted
¼ cup canola oil
½ cup honey
1 egg
1 tablespoon vanilla extract (less

vanilla and add ½ teaspoon
almond extract)
½ cup carob powder
½ cup whole wheat pastry flour
¼ teaspoon salt, *optional*

Toast almonds by placing on a cookie sheet in a 300° oven for 20 minutes. Remove from oven and allow to cool.

Grease two cookie sheets and preheat oven to 350°.

Using the steel blade of a food processor, blend oil and honey until creamy. Add egg, flavorings and carob powder. Mix in with quick on/off turns. Mix in flour and optional salt in the same way.

Spoon batter into a bowl and stir in almonds. Drop by rounded teaspoonfuls onto cookie sheets. Bake 10–12 minutes. (Flavor is lost if overbaked. So be careful.) Cool cookies on rack.

Brownie Pie

This brownie pie puffs up and then sinks in the middle, perfect for luscious scoops of ice cream. Brownie a la mode! Kids of all ages will love spooning hot fudge on top!

Serves 8   *Bake at 325°*

4 ounces bittersweet chocolate
1 stick sweet, unsalted butter,
** room temperature**
¾ cup Sucanat, honey or maple
** syrup**
3 eggs

3 teaspoons vanilla extract
½ cup whole wheat pastry
** flour**
2 tablespoons unsweetened
** cocoa powder**
½ teaspoon baking powder

Preheat oven to 325° and grease a 9-inch pie plate. Gently melt the chocolate in a double boiler over 1 inch of hot water. Set aside.

Using the steel blade of a food processor, mix butter and Sucanat together until fluffy. Add eggs and vanilla and incorporate by turning on machine for another minute. Batter will be light.

Add dry ingredients and melted chocolate to work bowl and incorporate with several quick on/off turns of the machine. Using a rubber spatula, spoon batter into pie plate and spread to edges.

Bake for 35 minutes, or until a knife inserted in the center of the pie comes out clean. Do not overbake. Pie should be moist. Remove pie plate to a cooling rack. When completely cool, cut into wedges and serve with a scoop of ice cream. Top with sauce.

Variations: *This pie can be made with dairy-free chocolate and vegetable oil in place of butter. You can top your pie with nondairy ice cream. There are also some wonderful dairy-free hot fudge toppings available in natural food stores. And if you're a carob lover like my Mom, feel free to substitute carob in this recipe.*

Note: *You can make brownie pie ahead of time, even the day before. Just cover with plastic wrap and leave at room temperature. Or freeze for a later date. Once again, allow to come to room temperature before filling with ice cream.*

Macadamia Nut Brownies

Macadamia nuts are native to Australia but are now grown in Hawaii, too. Because they have a high fat content, store them in the freezer to keep them fresh.

Makes 12 squares   *Bake at 325°*

1 cup honey or maple syrup
1 cup butter or canola oil
4 eggs
2 teaspoons vanilla
¾ cup carob or cocoa powder
¾ cup whole wheat pastry flour

¼ cup wheat germ
1 teaspoon allspice
1½ teaspoons baking powder
1 cup chopped macadamias
** (walnuts or pecans)**
1 cup chocolate or carob chips

Preheat oven to 325° and grease a 9 x 9 x 2-inch pan.

Using the steel blade of a food processor, combine liquid ingredients and carob powder. Add flour, wheat germ, allspice, baking powder and nuts to processor. Mix in with several quick on/off turns just so flour is incorporated and nuts are coarsely chopped. Add chocolate chips.

Using a rubber spatula, spoon batter into pan. Spread evenly and bake for 40 minutes, or just until surface is firm to touch.

Remove pan from oven and place on cooling rack. Let stand for 10 minutes and then cut into squares.

Buckwheat Brownies

Buckwheat brownies are great if you can't have wheat or gluten. But we've discovered that everyone loves them and the recipe doubles easily! Combining buckwheat flour with millet or rice flour increases the protein content of these cookies, too.

Sucanat is organically grown sugar cane which is pressed and the juice is sun-dried. So although it's a sugar, it's unrefined. Nothing removed, no processing. It doesn't seem to give one a sugar-jag like its refined counterpart.

Makes about 16   *Bake at 350°*

1 cup Sucanat	**½ cup rice or millet flour**
½ cup canola oil	**1 teaspoon baking powder**
2 eggs	**½ teaspoon salt**
1 teaspoon vanilla	**3 tablespoons carob powder**
¾ cups light buckwheat flour	**½ cup chopped walnuts**

Preheat oven to 350°. Grease an 8- or 9-inch square baking pan with a mixture of half liquid lecithin and half vegetable oil. (An almost invisible film of this mixture is all you need. Spread with a pastry brush or use your fingers!)

Using the steel blade of a food processor, blend together Sucanat, oil, eggs and vanilla.

With a few quick on/off turns, add flours, baking powder, salt and carob powder. Add ¼ cup walnuts and pulse in with two quick on/off turns of the processor.

Using a rubber spatula, spoon batter into baking pan. Sprinkle with remaining walnuts and bake 30 minutes, or until a knife blade inserted into the center comes out clean. Cut into bars while slightly warm.

Ginger Pecan Brownies

Both fresh and dried ginger have therapeutic properties. Dried ginger is said to work more on the lower extremities like stomach, kidneys, legs. Whatever, these cookies are chewy and rich-tasting!

Makes 12 squares   *Bake at 350°*

1 cup Sucanat   **½ cup whole wheat pastry flour**
1 egg   **¼ teaspoon salt**
2 teaspoons vanilla   **1 tablespoon cocoa powder**
1 tablespoon dried ginger   **1 cup chopped pecans**

Preheat oven to 350°. Grease an 8-inch square pan.

In a large mixing bowl, mix Sucanat, egg, vanilla and ginger with a wooden spoon until liquidy. Beat in flour, salt and cocoa powder. Add nuts and mix well. Batter will be stiff and hard to stir.

Spoon batter into pan. Wet your hands and pat out to corners. Bake 30 minutes. Cool 10 minutes and then cut into squares.

Ginger Cookies

These are the cookies Lise Stern, cookbook reviewer and columnist for *The Boston Globe*, loves to eat when she comes into our store. You'll love them, too! (You can use spelt flour in lieu of whole wheat pastry or rye flour.)

Anyone who's talked to me has heard me mention molasses. A half a cup contains 733 mg of usable calcium and lots of iron. Try a tablespoonful daily to cure what ails you.

Makes 24 cookies   *Bake at 325°*

1 cup canola oil
1 cup blackstrap molasses
2 eggs
1¾ cups Sucanat
3½ cups rye or whole wheat
  pastry flour
1 cup rolled rye or oats

1½ teaspoons baking soda
5 teaspoons ground ginger
½ teaspoon cinnamon
¼ teaspoon cloves
extra oats or candied ginger to
  garnish, *optional*

Preheat oven to 325° and grease two or three cookie sheets.

Using the steel blade of a food processor or a wire whisk, beat wet ingredients and Sucanat together until liquidy. In a second large bowl, combine dry ingredients.

Add wet to dry and mix just until combined. Place 2-inch balls of cookie dough onto greased sheets, leaving 2 inches between cookies and around sides of pan. Flatten balls slightly. If you wish, garnish each cookie with some oats sprinkled on top or a piece of candied ginger.

Bake for 15 minutes, or until cookies are somewhat firm when pressed gently. Remove cookie sheets from oven and place on cooling racks. Let cookies sit on sheets until cool.

Serving Suggestions: *Serve with a cup of tea, glass of milk or a fruit salad.*

Granola Cookies

Of course, our favorite granola to use in this recipe is our award-winning maple almond, reprinted below from our first cookbook. Our granola (with a modification or two) is sold in natural food stores everywhere under the name "Stark Sisters' Granola."

Makes 18   *Bake at 350°*

12 tablespoons almond butter
½ cup honey
1 teaspoon cinnamon

½ cup carob or chocolate
chips
1½ cups granola

Preheat oven to 350°. Grease several cookie sheets.

Blend almond butter, honey and cinnamon together using a wooden spoon. Add carob chips and granola. Batter will be heavy and hard to mix.

Using about ¼-cup batter, drop batter a good 2 inches apart on cookie sheets because these cookies spread.

Bake about 15 minutes. Remove from oven when cookies begin to brown lightly. Place cookie sheets on cooling rack for about 10 minutes. Then remove cookies with metal spatula to cooling rack.

Debra's Granola

3 cups sliced almonds
2 cups rolled oats
1 cup wheat flakes
1 cup rye flakes
1 cup barley flakes

1 cup maple syrup
¼ cup canola or safflower oil
1 teaspoon vanilla extract
¼ teaspoon salt, *optional*

Preheat oven to 275°.

Mix dry ingredients in a large bowl. (If you don't have a large enough bowl, divide dry ingredients equally between two.) Combine wet ingredients and salt, if desired, and pour over dry, mixing well using your hands or a rubber spatula. Make sure all the grains are well coated.

Spread granola in shallow baking pans and bake until roasted and dry, about 2 hours. Stir every 15–20 minutes.

When granola is dry and golden brown, remove from oven and stir. Let granola cool completely before storing in air-tight containers.

Note: *Makes a goodly amount!*

Hermits

Here's another wheat-free recipe. (Once again, feel free to substitute whole wheat pastry, spelt or rye flour for the alternate flours.) These cookies are softer and more crumbly with millet and tapioca or barley flour. It's nice to add variety to one's diet—even if you don't have to be wheat-free.

Makes 24 cookies   *Bake at 350°*

3 cups millet or rice flour
1 cup tapioca or barley flour
2 teaspoons cinnamon
1 teaspoon nutmeg
1 teaspoon cloves
½ teaspoon salt
4 teaspoons baking powder

4 eggs
1 cup canola oil
2 cups Sucanat
½ cup molasses
2 cups chopped walnuts or
   cashews
2 cups raisins or currants

Combine all ingredients and let batter sit for an hour.

Preheat oven to 350° and grease two cookie sheets.

Drop cookies by tablespoonful onto sheets, leaving a good 2 inches between cookies and around the sides of the pans. These cookies spread. Whoa, Nellie!

Bake for about 15 minutes, or until cookies feel slightly firm when gently pressed with fingertips. Remove cookie sheets from oven. Place on cooling racks. When cookies are completely cool, remove with a metal spatula to racks.

Note: Hermits tend to get better with age because the spices permeate and deepen in flavor. Don't try to stack; the alternative flours make them too tender.

Lemon Date Bars

You can always substitute whole wheat pastry, spelt or rye flour for barley and buckwheat. However, it's not as easy to substitute alternate flours for wheat because they have little or no gluten. And it's gluten that makes baked goods rise and stick together.

Makes an 11 x 17-inch pan of about 15 bars   *Bake at 350°*

**4 cups date pieces rolled in oat
   flour**
⅔ cup lemon juice
grated zest from 1 or 2 lemons
1 cup water
2 cups Sucanat
**7 cups barley and buckwheat
   flour**

1 teaspoon salt
2 teaspoons baking soda
**4 cups rolled oats, slightly
   blended**
1½ cups canola oil

Preheat oven to 350° and grease 11 x 17-inch pan.

Combine dates, lemon juice, zest and water. Over low heat, simmer mixture, covered, for about 20 minutes, or until dates are soft.

In the meantime, using the steel blade of a food processor and quick on/off turns, combine dry ingredients. Add canola oil and give another few quick on/off turns.

Press two-thirds of dough into prepared pan. Set aside remaining third in a little bowl. Using the same work bowl, blend date mixture and spoon over batter in pan. Crumble remaining dough on top.

Bake 30 minutes, or until slightly firm to touch. Cool 20 minutes before cutting.

Linzer Torte Cookies

Scrumptious and healthy! One fifth of an almond's weight is protein, and its oil is among the most nutritious of all nut oils. For instance, almonds are rich in the antioxidant vitamin E.

Makes about 16 cookies   *Bake at 350°*

2 cups ground almonds   **1 cup canola oil**
2 cups rolled oats   **1 cup maple syrup**
2 cups spelt or barley flour   **2 tablespoons vanilla**
½ teaspoon cinnamon   **1 teaspoon almond extract**
⅛ teaspoon salt   **½ cup raspberry jam**

Preheat oven to 350° and grease cookie sheets.

Using the steel blade of a food processor, pulse dry ingredients so oats are coarsely ground. Don't overprocess or will make paste!

In a large bowl, combine wet ingredients except jam. Spoon in the dry and mix well. Form dough into balls that fill a ¼-cup measure. Place cookies on sheets and flatten slightly, making an indentation in the center with your thumb.

Fill each center with ½-teaspoon raspberry jam.

Bake for 20–25 minutes, or until cookies are lightly browned around the edges.

Remove the baking sheet from oven and place on cooling rack. Allow cookies to cool and remove to serve.

Pfeffernusse

Pfeffernusse translates from the German as "pepper nuts"—anise-flavored cookies. Here are those pesky alternate flours again. You have to admit it makes cooking more interesting to vary flours and not always use wheat. Baking with alternative flours is certainly more challenging!

Makes 24 1-inch cookies   *Bake at 350°*

¾ cup rice flour   1 teaspoon almond extract
¼ cup oat or barley flour   ¼ cup honey
¼ teaspoon black pepper   ½ teaspoon anise extract
¼ cup poppy seeds   ½ teaspoon vanilla
⅛ teaspoon salt   oat flour for rolling
¼ cup canola oil   poppy seeds for rolling

Preheat oven to 350° and grease baking sheet.

Combine all ingredients in a bowl except extra oat flour and poppy seeds. Shape into 1-inch balls. Roll balls in oat flour, then poppy seeds. Place on baking sheet. Flatten each cookie slightly with a fork so the tines make a design.

Bake for 15 minutes. Remove cookie sheet from oven. When cookies are cool, pop in mouth!

Note: *Store poppy seeds in freezer to keep them from becoming rancid.*

Poppy Lemon Snaps

If you love poppy seeds and lemon, you'll love these snaps. Tapioca is a starch made from cassava roots. It's used as a thickener and holds crumbly flours together pretty well. It's almost entirely carbohydrate.

Makes about 24   *Bake at 375°*

1 cup tapioca flour
1 cup oat or barley flour (any
    other alternate flour)
½ cup poppy seeds
½ teaspoon baking soda
¼ teaspoon salt
¼ cup lemon juice

1 cup Sucanat
½ cup melted butter
4 teaspoons grated lemon peel
1 egg
2 teaspoons vanilla
1 egg white
2 tablespoons water

Preheat oven to 375° and grease cookie sheets.

Mix dry ingredients. Add wet except egg white and water.

Shape dough into 2-inch balls. Place a good inch apart on baking sheet and flatten with fork in both directions. Mix egg white with water and brush cookies using a pastry brush (or use your fingers).

Bake about 10 minutes, or until the edges of the cookies brown. Remove cookie sheets from oven and place on cooling racks. After about 5 minutes, remove cookies from sheets and let cool completely on racks. Store in air-tight containers.

Pumpkin Seed Date Cookies

Lots of oats in these cookies add good fiber to your diet. Tired of me saying that you can use whole wheat pastry or spelt flour in lieu of the flours listed below? Just think how hard it must be for those who need to be wheat- and/or gluten-free who pick up books that only call for wheat!

Men will benefit from a handful of pumpkin seeds daily because they're high in zinc, help prevent prostate problems and promote virility.

Makes about 36 cookies   *Bake at 350°*

1 cup canola oil
1 cup honey
1 cup soy milk
2 cups unsweetened shredded coconut
2 cups date pieces in oat flour
1 cup pumpkin seeds

⅛ teaspoon salt
1 cup quinoa or rice flour
1 cup barley or oat flour
2 tablespoons tapioca flour
3 cups rolled oats
4 teaspoons vanilla
1 teaspoon allspice

Preheat oven to 350° and grease cookie sheet.

Combine all ingredients and mix well. Drop by ¼ cupfuls onto cookie sheet. These cookies do not spread. Pat down batter with a wet hand.

Bake 15 minutes. Cool on a rack.

Variation: *Dried cranberries make a dramatic substitution for dates.*

Sesame Sables

What is halvah? It's a Middle Eastern and Eastern European confection originally made with crushed sesame seeds and honey. The real thing is hard to come by. We have a great halvah in our store which is made in Canada. If you can't find halvah, try using sesame tahini with a few spoonfuls of honey. Sesame seeds contain calcium that is more easily used by our bodies than the calcium in milk. And a half cup of sesame seeds contains 1,125 mg of calcium, compared with 590 mg per pint of milk!

Makes 24   *Bake at 325°*

**2½ cups whole wheat pastry
   flour**
1¾ cups Sucanat
½ teaspoon salt
¼ teaspoon baking powder
½ cup oil
¾ cup diced halvah

¼ cup sesame seeds
2 eggs
4 teaspoons lemon juice
1 tablespoon vanilla
2 tablespoons sesame oil
**1 ¼ cups sesame seeds for
   rolling**

Preheat oven to 325°. Grease several cookie sheets.

Using the steel blade of a food processor and several on/off turns, mix the flour, Sucanat, salt and baking powder. Cut in oil and halvah, again using several quick on/off turns of the processor. Stop twice to scrape down the sides of the work bowl with a rubber spatula.

Add sesame seeds and wet ingredients to processor, and using quick on/off turns, incorporate until the dough cleans the sides of the work bowl. Should be just a few seconds.

Place remaining 1¼ cups sesame seeds into a shallow bowl. Measuring about ⅛-cup batter per cookie, roll in your hands and then flatten slightly to about a 2-inch round. Press both sides of the cookie into the sesame seeds. Place on cookie sheets about 1 inch apart.

Bake until fragrant and lightly golden, about 25 minutes. Remove cookie sheets from the oven and place on cooling racks for 10 minutes. Remove cookies from sheets and finish cooling on racks—if you can keep yours hands off them that long! These are great.

Rice Crispy Squares

This wonderful recipe has been widely adapted from the cookbook *How Sweet It Is* by Janet Gilroy. It's one of the few recipes we like with rice syrup, which is a sweetener that's okay for diabetics. Rice syrup is not absorbed by the body like sugar or honey. Because it has to be digested, it takes longer to metabolize and doesn't give a sugar rush.

Makes 12 squares, or enough to fill a 9 x 13-inch cake pan

1½ cups rice syrup
6 tablespoons almond butter
⅓ teaspoon salt or 1 teaspoon white miso
½ teaspoon cinnamon
¼ teaspoon nutmeg
1 cup chopped dried apricots

1½ cups chopped almonds, roasted
2 tablespoons vanilla
8 cups crispy brown rice cereal or puffed rice and millet combined

Combine first 5 ingredients in a saucepan. Heat gently until mixture simmers. Add apricots and almonds and simmer 5 minutes more. Remove pan from heat. Stir in vanilla and crispy cereal. Mix thoroughly.

Spoon mixture into greased 9 x 13-inch pan and press firmly. Refrigerate until firm, about 45 minutes. Cut into 2-inch squares and serve.

Variations: If you don't have roasted almonds on hand, you can roast your own. Heat small pot or skillet. Add almonds and stir until lightly browned, about 5 minutes. Alternately, place almonds on cookie sheet in 300° oven and roast for 10–15 minutes. In either case, make sure almonds are cool before using in recipe. You want moisture to have a chance to evaporate so your squares won't be soggy.

Yankee Cranberry Clippers

Finally, there are dried cranberries from The New England Cranberry Company that are sweetened with apple and pear juice. No junk! They're chewy and sweet-tart. Cranberries are said to have antiviral activity.

Makes 16   *Bake at 350°*

½ cup canola oil
½ cup Sucanat
½ cup Barbados or sorghum
   molasses
1 egg
1 tablespoon vanilla
2 teaspoons apple cider vinegar
2 cups whole wheat pastry flour
1 ¼ teaspoons allspice

1½ teaspoons cinnamon
¼ teaspoon cardamom
½ teaspoon salt
½ teaspoon baking soda
¼ teaspoon baking powder
½ teaspoon black pepper
1½ cups dried cranberries
   (raisins, currants or dried
   apricots)

Preheat oven to 350° and grease cookie sheets.

Using the steel blade of a food processor, cream oil, Sucanat and molasses until fluffy. Add egg, vanilla, vinegar and all remaining ingredients except cranberries. Mix in with on/off turns of processor.

Spoon batter into bowl. Mix in all but ½ cup of the cranberries.

Measuring about ¼-cup batter per cookie, drop onto cookie sheets about 2½ inches apart. These cookies spread! Using moistened fingertips, press cookies down a little and top with reserved cranberries.

Bake about 15 minutes. Remove cookie sheets from oven and place on cooling rack about 5 minutes. When cookies are still slightly warm, remove from sheets and place on racks to cool completely.

Apple Chocolate Cupcakes

Of course, you can frost these, but it's not necessary. They're easy to pop into lunch boxes. Without frosting, they don't make a mess.

Makes 12   *Bake at 400°*

**2 apples, halved, cored
and grated
1½ cups honey
½ cup canola oil
2 eggs
2 teaspoons vanilla
½ cup milk or soy or rice milk**

**1½ cups whole wheat pastry
flour
½ cup cocoa or carob powder
1 teaspoon cinnamon
1 teaspoon nutmeg
1 teaspoon baking soda**

Preheat oven to 400° and grease muffin tins using half liquid lecithin and half canola oil.

Grate apples and place in a large mixing bowl. Set aside.

Using the steel blade of a food processor, blend honey, oil, eggs, vanilla and milk.

Using quick on-off turns of processor, blend in dry ingredients. Do not overmix.

Spoon batter into apples and mix just enough so apples are incorporated. Spoon into muffin wells so ⅔ full. Bake about 25 minutes, or until toothpick inserted into center of cupcake comes out clean.

Fresh Apple Cake

This cake is good enough to stand on its own, but, of course, it is delicious served à la mode or with whipped cream. Who ever said natural has to be dull and tasteless?!?

Apples, like soy products, are said to have estrogenic activity. They are also high in fiber and keep you from getting ravenous quickly.

Makes a 9 x 13-inch pan   *Bake at 350°*

3 cups whole wheat pastry flour   **½ teaspoon salt**
1 teaspoon baking soda   **1½ cups canola oil**
1 teaspoon baking powder   **4 eggs**
¼ teaspoon cardamom   **2 tablespoons vanilla**
1 teaspoon cinnamon   **3 cups peeled, halved, cored and**
2 cups Sucanat   **diced apples**

Preheat oven to 350° and grease 9 x 13-inch pan.

Using a wire whisk, mix dry ingredients together in a large bowl. In a separate bowl, whisk wet ingredients together. Add wet to dry and fold in apples. Spoon batter into prepared pan.

Bake for about an hour, or until the cake begins to pull away from the sides of the pan and a knife inserted in the center comes out clean.

Note: *You can also make this cake in a bundt pan, two 9-inch round pans or muffin tins if you wish. It makes a great tea cake or cupcakes.*

Blueberry Banana Crumb Cake

Blueberries bubbling up through a cake make me want to sit down with a spoon and eat the whole thing. Blueberries, like cranberries, contain a substance that blocks the attachment of bacteria that cause urinary tract infections.

Serves 12   *Bake at 350°*

Crumb topping:

¾ cup wheat germ
⅓ cup Sucanat
1 teaspoon cinnamon

⅛ teaspoon salt
4 tablespoons cold unsalted
   butter, cut into ½-inch pieces

Using the steel blade of a food processor, combine dry ingredients with several quick on/off turns. Cut in butter with several quick on/off turns, until mixture is crumbly when rubbed between fingers. Don't overmix.

Cake:

1½ cups blueberries
¼ cup honey
⅓ cup water
2 tablespoons lemon juice
2 teaspoons arrowroot
1 large ripe banana
1 egg
½ cup milk

1 teaspoon vanilla
2 cups whole wheat pastry
   flour
⅓ cup Sucanat
2 teaspoons baking powder
½ teaspoon salt
6 tablespoons cold unsalted
   butter, cut into ½-inch pieces

Preheat oven to 350° and grease 9 x 13-inch pan.

In a small stainless steel saucepan, combine blueberries with honey and water. Bring to a boil over low heat. Stir in lemon juice and arrowroot and boil, stirring, for 1 minute. Remove saucepan from heat and let mixture cool.

Again, using the steel blade of the food processor (don't bother to wash it), puree banana with egg. Add milk and vanilla and process until blended.

Add rest of ingredients and incorporate with several quick on/off turns of processor. Dough will just come together. Don't overmix.

Spoon dough into pan. Press evenly with a rubber spatula or wooden spoon. Using a fork, prick dough about 12 times and pour blueberry topping over it, smoothing surface with spatula. Sprinkle crumb topping over berries as evenly as you can.

Bake about 35 minutes, or until topping is lightly browned. Cool for 10 minutes.

Serving Suggestion: *Serve with ice cream, whipped cream or vanilla yogurt. This cake makes a fun, special breakfast with a cup of herbal tea.*

Carrot Pecan Cake

A great picnic traveler. This cake can sit out overnight at room temperature. Wonderful with a dollop of whipped cream or fresh raspberries!

Cooking carrots does not destroy their beta carotene. It's actually supposed to make it easier for the body to utilize.

Makes a bundt cake   *Bake at 350°*

5 medium carrots, grated   **1½ cups whole wheat pastry flour**
1 cup honey   **2 teaspoons baking powder**
1 tablespoon vanilla   **2 teaspoons cinnamon**
4 eggs   **1 teaspoon baking soda**
1 cup canola oil   **½ teaspoon salt**
½ cup wheat germ   **1 cup pecans**

Preheat oven to 350° and grease a 12-cup bundt pan.

Grate carrots into large mixing bowl and set aside.

Using the steel blade of a food processor, blend honey, vanilla, eggs and oil. Add all ingredients except pecans and blend in with several quick on/off turns of the processor. Do not overmix. Add pecans and chop into batter with 3–4 on/off turns of the processor.

Spoon batter into carrots and mix together using a rubber spatula. Batter will be thick. Spoon batter into prepared pan.

Bake about an hour, until cake begins to pull away from sides of pan and a knife inserted into the center comes out clean.

Cool cake in pan on rack for 20 minutes. Invert pan onto cooling rack and cool cake completely before serving.

Note: *A cream cheese frosting would be nice and pretty but caloric. It's not a necessity. This also makes a nice breakfast with herbal tea.*

Organic Chocolate Cake

Almost fat-free. Substitute carob powder for organic cocoa, if you'd prefer even less fat. This cake has no eggs. The cider vinegar activates the baking powder and makes the cake rise.

People will eat this cake up right away. We made zillions of these cakes for our store's birthday party one year and had none left. Someone even licked the crumbs out of the pans!

Makes an 8-inch square   *Bake at 375°*

1½ cups whole wheat pastry
  flour
⅓ cup organic cocoa powder
1 teaspoon baking soda
½ teaspoon salt
1 cup Sucanat

½ cup Wonderslim*
1 cup water
2 teaspoons vanilla
2 tablespoons cider vinegar
1 organic nondairy chocolate
  bar

Preheat oven to 375°. Grease 8-inch square pan with mixture of half lecithin and half canola oil.

Place dry ingredients in a large bowl. Mix using a rubber spatula or wire whisk. In a second bowl, mix wet ingredients, except vinegar. Add wet to dry. Mix well so there are no clumps of cocoa powder. When smooth, add vinegar and stir quickly.

Pour batter into pan. Bake for 30 minutes, or until a knife inserted into the center comes out clean.

Take cake out of oven. (This is where we add fat.) Break up the chocolate bar (with good sweeteners only, of course) and place on top of hot cake still in pan. Let soften and then spread over cake with a flat metal spatula. Cut cake into squares once it is cooled.

*If you want to make your own Wonderslim (a brand name product) simmer 1 cup pitted prunes in 1 cup water until soft and most water is absorbed. Blend with a food processor until smooth. Incorporate 2 tablespoons liquid lecithin, ½ cup water and 1 tablespoon vitamin C crystals. Store in a glass jar in the fridge. This makes a good fat substitute in baking.

Pumpkin Maple Cake

Call this sweet potato cake and you won't have many takers. Call it pumpkin maple cake and it'll be everyone's favorite. Go figure! Not only are sweet potatoes higher in nutrients than pumpkin, they are much easier to use. One-half mashed sweet potato contains about 23,000 international units of beta carotene, according to U.S. Dept. of Agriculture figures.

Makes a bundt or 9 x 12-inch cake   *Bake at 350°*

1½ cups cubed sweet potatoes,   **3¾ cups whole wheat pastry or**
**   steamed in jackets**   **spelt flour**
4 eggs   **1 tablespoon baking powder**
1½ cups maple syrup   **2½ teaspoons cinnamon**
1½ cups Sucanat   **½ teaspoon cloves**
1½ cups canola oil   **1 teaspoon baking soda**
1 tablespoon vanilla   **½ teaspoon salt**
1 teaspoon lemon juice

Preheat oven to 350°. Grease a bundt cake pan or 9 x 12-inch pan.

Using the steel blade of a food processor, blend sweet potatoes. (Don't worry if flecks of peel show. They won't in the cake!) Add eggs, sweeteners, oil, vanilla and lemon juice. Blend with quick on/off turns.

Combine dry ingredients in a large bowl. Add sweet potato batter and mix using a rubber spatula.

Spoon batter into pan and place in oven. Bake for about 45 minutes, or until a knife inserted in the center comes out clean. Remove pan from oven and place on cooling rack. When cool, turn cake out of pan. If you made cake in the lasagna pan, cut into squares and serve.

Variations: *To make a fancier cake, sprinkle greased bundt pan with sliced almonds, which will make a pretty pattern when the cake is unmolded. If you are using a lasagna pan, put almonds on top. We have even frosted this cake with a sweet potato frosting. Simply blend 2 cups steamed sweet potatoes with 1 pound of soft tofu or cream cheese and sweeten to taste with maple syrup.*

Tofu and Cheese Cheesecake

My mother often serves this cake to my father for breakfast with a fruit plate. He loves it and doesn't realize he's getting tofu, which is as important to men's health as it is to women's. If a sweeter taste is preferred, add up to ⅔ cup honey.

Makes 12 servings   *Bake at 325°*

Crust: 1 pound soft tofu
¼ cup wheat germ   1 pound farmer's cheese
¼ cup oat bran   6 large eggs
1 teaspoon Sucanat   ½ cup mild honey (clover)
¼ teaspoon cinnamon   1 tablespoon lemon juice
                                        1 tablespoon vanilla

Preheat oven to 325°. With unsalted butter, grease bottom and part way up sides of an 8- or 9-inch springform pan.

Mix crust ingredients and distribute over bottom and sides of pan, rolling pan around to spread evenly.

Using the steel blade of a food processor, blend tofu and cheese until completely smooth. Add eggs, one at a time, running processor about 5 seconds after each addition. With machine running after last egg, drizzle in rest of ingredients. Carefully spoon mixture into springform pan.

Bake on middle rack of oven for an hour. *Don't* open oven while baking. Turn off oven and let cake sit for another hour with door closed.

Remove from oven and place on rack until completely cooled. Refrigerate cake for several hours, or better yet overnight, to give flavors a chance to marry.

To serve, run butter knife around sides of pan, carefully open springform and remove. Place cheesecake, still on bottom of pan, on large plate.

Variation: To make a nondairy cheesecake, we love substituting 8 ounces soy sour cream or 8 ounces soy cream cheese for farmer's cheese.

Serving Suggestion: To make a scrumptious topping, mix 4 cups fruit like blueberries or raspberries with 8 ounces all-fruit jam in a pot over low heat until jam melts. Cool and top cake.

Mom's Apple Pie

This is the apple pie my brothers, David and Daniel, love. According to my Mother, it's never quite right, but David claims it's always the best he's ever eaten.

Makes a 9-inch pie   *Bake at 450°*

Crust:
1 cup plus 1 teaspoon whole wheat pastry flour
¼ cup oat bran (can omit and increase flour to 1⅓ cups)
¼ cup unhulled sesame seeds

1 tablespoon Sucanat
⅓ cup cold canola oil
3 tablespoons cold apple juice, orange juice or milk
pinch of cinnamon, *optional*

Preheat oven to 450°.

Sift flour into a large mixing bowl. Add oat bran, sesame seeds and Sucanat and mix. Add cinnamon, if desired. Into a measuring cup, pour, but do not stir, oil and juice.

Pour liquid all at once into flour mixture and stir lightly with a fork until mixed.

Round up dough until it forms a ball. Place on a 12-inch square of wax paper, which has been placed on a pastry cloth or a dampened surface to prevent slipping. (I use a clean formica countertop.)

Flatten slightly with hands and place another square of wax paper on top. Roll out gently into a circle until dough reaches the edges of the paper. Let rest while preparing filling.

Filling:
½ cup mild honey
1 tablespoon lemon juice
1 teaspoon cinnamon or cardamom

pinch of nutmeg, *optional*
6 large baking apples (Granny Smith or Macintosh)

Into unwashed bowl in which crust was mixed, pour honey and lemon juice. Add cinnamon and stir together.

Peel, core and slice apples into ½-inch pieces directly into bowl, stirring with fork to coat as you go along, until all apples are sliced and mixed. (I even wipe out the measuring cup with some of the slices before adding to bowl so as not to waste any residue of the oil mixture.)

Arrange apples in 9-inch pie plate, piling them slightly higher in center.

Carefully strip top layer of wax paper off crust. If cracks develop, push them together with your fingers (do not use water, just dry hands) or patch with a scrap of pastry.

Lift paper by corners and place pastry on top of apples, wax paper side up. Carefully peel off paper and build up a fluted edge to help keep juices from running out.

Prick crust all over with a fork, or make slashes with a knife, to prevent puffing and allow steam to escape.

Bake in oven for 10 minutes. Then reduce heat to 350° and bake another 30 minutes. Remove from oven and cool on rack.

Date Pecan Spice Cake

In Egypt, it was thought that hysteria could be cured by taking a mixture of cinnamon, cardamom and cloves mixed with honey. This mixture is said to tone the system. And the cake is wheat-free. Dates are also said to be high in natural aspirin.

Makes 1 9-inch tube cake   *Bake at 350°*

1 cup oat or barley flour   **1 teaspoon cinnamon**
1 cup rice or millet flour   **½ teaspoon cloves**
1 cup date pieces in oat flour   **½ teaspoon cardamom**
1 cup chopped pecans   **½ cup canola oil**
½ teaspoon baking soda   **1 cup honey**
½ teaspoon baking powder   **1 egg**
½ teaspoon salt   **2 apples, peaches or pears, diced**

Preheat oven to 350°. Grease 9-inch tube pan.

Mix all the dry ingredients together in a large mixing bowl. Using the steel blade of a food processor, combine all wet ingredients, except fruit, until thick and creamy. Add wet to dry. Add diced fruit. Mix with a rubber spatula just until everything is moistened.

Spoon into pan and bake for 40–45 minutes, or until toothpick inserted in the center comes out clean. Slice thinly to serve.

Baked Plum & Peach Crustless Pie

Simple to make, beautiful to behold, not too heavy after a meal. Not only do plums behave like prunes, but they are antibacterial and antiviral as well. Italian prune plums are especially easy to work with and they halve quickly.

Serves 6   *Bake at 350°*

2½ pounds plums (Italian prune plums work well), halved, pitted and cut into ½-inch wedges
6 peaches, peeled, pitted and cut into ½-inch wedges
½ cup honey or all-fruit jam

1 teaspoon almond extract
2 tablespoons tapioca flour
1 teaspoon lemon or orange juice
1 teaspoon cinnamon or allspice
pinch salt

Mix all ingredients together in a bowl. Let stand at least 30 minutes, or up to 1 hour. Stir occasionally.

Preheat oven to 350°. Spoon filling into glass or ceramic baking dish or 2 9-inch pie plates. Bake until fruit is tender, about 45 minutes.

Serving Suggestion: *Spoon warm into bowls or pretty wine glasses. Serve with dollop of whipped cream or scoop of ice cream if you feel decadent.*

Carob Icebox Cake

Carob is the roasted and ground pod of an evergreen tree. One advantage of carob is it has no caffeine, as does chocolate. Don't think of carob as a substitute for chocolate. Think of carob as its own taste sensation. Then you'll enjoy it.

In our kitchen, half of us love this with walnuts and half of us like the creamy texture without walnuts. The arguments have reached heated levels usually reserved for politics, religion and sex!

Serves 12–15

8 cups carob soy milk
1 cup arrowroot
2 teaspoons vanilla extract
1 drop almond extract
2 cups carob chips

½ cup maple syrup or other
   liquid sweetener
1 cup walnuts, toasted and
   coarsely chopped, *optional*
1 box whole wheat graham
   crackers*

Bring 6 cups milk to a boil in a saucepan. (Watch carefully as it boils over easily.) Turn down to a simmer. Dissolve arrowroot in remaining 2 cups milk with a wire whisk, and add to heated milk.

Cook mixture until thick, stirring constantly. This doesn't take long! Stir in extracts, carob chips, maple syrup and ½ cup walnuts (if using them). Remove pudding from flame.

In a 13 x 9-inch pan, spoon ⅓ of pudding. Cover with a single layer of graham crackers. (You can buy whole grain varieties in natural food stores.)

Continue with another layer of pudding and another layer of grahams. Finish with pudding. Garnish with reserved ½ cup walnuts and refrigerate until serving.

You may use less than a whole box.

Cherry Almond or Pecan Pudding

This pudding is a snap to prepare. A good combination with a dollop of whipped cream, frozen yogurt or ice cream. Yes, you can substitute nectarines or peaches. Slice and arrange on the bottom of the pie plate.

Rich in iron, cherries and cherry juice are often used to improve the blood and treat anemia. A handful of dried cherries in the afternoon is a healthy snack and good pick-me-up.

Serves 6   *Bake at 400°*

4 tablespoons canola oil
1 cup Sucanat
1 cup almonds or pecans
¼ teaspoon salt
1 teaspoon cinnamon

½ teaspoon nutmeg
1 teaspoon almond extract
4 cups pitted cherries
1 cup cherry juice

Preheat oven to 400°.

In a food processor, using the steel blade and quick on/off turns, combine all ingredients except the cherries and juice.

In an 8-inch pie pan, place cherries. Pour juice over them, just so bottom of pan is covered. Top with crumb mixture and bake for 20 minutes.

Remove from oven, cool and serve cut into wedges.

Note: *For convenience, you can use canned cherries. There are some wonderful canned organic cherries in natural food stores everywhere.*

Chocolate Chestnut Torte

Chestnut puree provides a rich, moist texture and a sweet, chestnut flavor. Chestnuts are high in protein and have virtually *no fat!* This for those of you who are appalled at the liberal use of nuts and seeds in many recipes in this book!

Makes 10 servings   *Bake at 350°*

1 cup peeled chestnuts (see Note)
1 cup boiling water
¾ cup honey
½ cup boiling water
½ cup organic cocoa
4 egg yolks
1 tablespoon amaretto or rum
1 teaspoon vanilla extract

4 egg whites
¼ teaspoon cream of tartar
¼ cup whole wheat pastry
  flour

Topping:
1 pint raspberries
1 cup all-fruit raspberry jam

Preheat oven to 350° and lightly brush an 8- or 9-inch springform pan with a mixture of half liquid lecithin and half canola oil.

Simmer chestnuts in 1 cup boiling water about 20 minutes, or until easily pierced with a fork. Drain.

In a food processor, combine honey, ½ cup boiling water, cocoa and chestnuts. Process about 30 seconds until mixture is smooth. Add egg yolks, amaretto and vanilla and blend again. Set aside.

Using an electric mixer, beat whites until they are foamy. Add cream of tartar and beat until peaks form and whites are stiff.

Pour batter from processor into a large mixing bowl. Whisk flour into mixture and then fold in egg whites. Scrape batter into prepared pan and gently smooth the top.

Bake for about 30 minutes, or until a cake tester inserted in the center comes out with a few moist crumbs. Transfer pan to a rack and let torte cool completely. Cake will sink and top will crack.

To serve, run a thin, sharp knife around the edge of the pan to loosen torte. Loosen springform and remove. Loosen bottom by running a long metal spatula underneath and transfer torte to a cake plate. To make topping, melt jam, combine with raspberries and spoon over cake before serving.

Note: *When I can, I use frozen, peeled, ready-to-use organic chestnuts which don't require simmering. But these are hard to come by, so you most probably will have to use dried chestnuts, which need to be boiled about 20 minutes until they are fork tender. You may need to add more water as they cook. We use dried chestnuts in many types of dishes year-round at our store and stock them on our shelves as well.*

Ice Cream Pie

Luscious, easy to make, always a hit! Prepare ahead of time. Variations that make this suitable for everyone are endless. What health attributes come to mind? Ice cream soothes the savage beast! Just make it ice cream without artificial this and artificial that! A dense ice cream without extra air and a higher butter fat content works best.

Serves 10

1 cup granola, cookie crumbs or chopped nuts (be creative!)
1 quart dense ice cream, softened
1 pint dense second flavor ice cream, softened

½ cup jam, maple syrup or chocolate or carob sauce, *optional*
½ cup granola, cookie crumbs or chopped nuts

Place granola in an 8- or 9-inch pie plate. Carefully spread first softened ice cream evenly over crust. Then dab second flavor in spoonfuls on top. Take a butter knife and swirl in second flavor to make a marble effect. Smooth top. Pour melted jam over top for another flavor sensation. (You could also marble topping in with ice cream.) Top with granola.

Freeze 20 minutes. Remove and cover with plastic wrap. Store in freezer until ready to use. Soften about 5 minutes. Cut into wedges and serve.

Variation: Substitute nondairy ice creams. There are ice creams made from rice milk and some from soy milk.

Suggestion: To make things even easier, purchase 3 pints of ice cream which are already several flavors in one. There's an organic ice cream I love which is vanilla, chocolate and toffee.

Mincemeat Pie Filling

This mixture keeps fresh for weeks and also makes an excellent strudel filling. Dates contain the highest sugar content of any fruit and are rich in vitamins A, B1, magnesium and phosphorus.

Enough for 2–3 pies

½ pound raisins
¼ pound prunes
¼ pound dates in oat flour
½ pound currants
2 tablespoons candied ginger
½ pound apricots
½ teaspoon nutmeg
½ teaspoon cinnamon

½ teaspoon allspice
½ teaspoon salt
¼ cup cognac or fruit juice
2 tablespoons lemon juice
½ pound honey
3 Granny Smith apples, chopped
½ pound walnut nuggets

Chop dried fruit in a food processor in several batches using a steel blade and on/off turns. Alternately, chop by hand. (Depending on how moist the fruit is, sometimes it's a lot easier to chop by hand with a cleaver.)

Combine all ingredients in a large bowl. Mix well.

Fill prebaked tartlet or pie shell with mincemeat.

Serving Suggestion: *This, too, can be topped with a dollop of whipped cream. Enjoy!*

Note: *Honey is a wonderful, natural preservative. It also keeps recipes nice and moist.*

Panforte

This Italian sweet is typically eaten at holidays and makes a wonderful gift. It keeps a long time at room temperature, which is good because a sliver goes a long way. Panforte is rich and satisfying.

Cinnamon is said to stimulate insulin activity, which is helpful for those with Type II diabetes.

Serves 16   *Bake at 300°*

½ cup whole wheat pastry flour
2 tablespoons carob or cocoa
  powder
1 teaspoon cinnamon
¼ teaspoon coriander
¼ teaspoon nutmeg
¼ teaspoon cloves

1½ cups coarsely chopped walnuts
1½ cups coarsely chopped dried
  apricots
½ cup coarsely chopped dried
  cranberries
½ cup dried currants
1 cup honey

Preheat oven to 300°. Grease the inside of a 9-inch springform pan.

Combine all ingredients except honey. Make sure there are no lumps of flour or carob.

Heat honey in a small saucepan over low heat until it reaches about 245° on a candy thermometer, or until it forms a firm ball when dropped in cold water.

Pour honey immediately into mixture and stir rapidly. Spoon batter into prepared pan. Press into an even layer with a wet rubber spatula. Bake for 45 minutes.

Let cake cool and firm in the pan on a rack. Run butter knife around sides of springform, release springform and remove. Invert cake onto serving dish. Serve in thin slivers with tea.

Plum Galette

A galette is a thin-crusted pastry. Top it with fruit to make an open-faced fruit tart. Feel free to use whatever fruit is in season—peaches, cherries, apricots, apples, pears or even grapes.

Serves 8   *Bake at 375°*

Pastry:
1½ cups whole wheat pastry
  flour
¼ cup Sucanat
1½ sticks unsalted butter, cold,
  cut into ½-inch pieces
¼ teaspoon salt
⅓ cup ice water

Filling:
½ cup toasted ground pecans
2 tablespoons whole wheat pastry flour
¾ cup Sucanat
20 prune plums, quartered
  lengthwise and pitted
1 teaspoon almond extract
1 cup plum preserves

Preheat oven to 375°.

Using the steel blade of a food processor and quick on/off turns, quickly combine pastry ingredients. Bits of butter remain visible in the finished dough. Roll out into a large oval onto an ungreased baking sheet.

Combine ground pecans, flour and ¼ cup Sucanat. Spread over the dough. (These dry ingredients will help absorb the juices that are released during baking.)

Toss plums with remaining Sucanat and almond extract and arrange on top of dough. Turn up a 2-inch rim of dough over fruit to enclose it and create a border. Bake galette for about an hour, or until fruit is tender and crust is crisp.

Remove from oven and brush fruit with preserves. (This gives the fruit a beautiful, shiny appearance and makes it look as if you bought it at a bakery.) Best served at room temperature, cut into wedges like pizza.

Miscellaneous

Forgive the mishmash and indulge me! You may think this section is loony and I'm nuts. But I love making food for my skin and creams to give to friends as gifts. We've had so much fun at Debra's Natural Gourmet learning about odd-ball foods like seaweeds that you won't find in the neighborhood hamburger joint and then passing that info on to our customers in newsletters that I couldn't resist including a little bit of that in this section. Enjoy reading and try something you haven't tried before. It might inspire you.

Homemade Marinated Sun-Dried Tomatoes

Use sun-dried tomatoes on French bread as an appetizer or jazz up pasta, rice or bean dishes.

Makes 3 cups

6 oz. sun-dried tomatoes
1½ cups apple cider vinegar
1⅓ cups olive oil
18 cloves garlic, sliced
12 whole black peppercorns
2 teaspoons dried basil

1 teaspoon dried oregano
½ teaspoon dried tarragon
½ teaspoon dried thyme
½ teaspoon dried marjoram
1 teaspoon dried parsley

Place tomatoes in a nonplastic or nonaluminum bowl. Heat vinegar in a stainless steel pot. Pour over tomatoes and let sit 1 hour, stirring occasionally.

Drain tomatoes (save vinegar for use in another recipe).

Combine remaining ingredients in a large glass jar. Add tomatoes, stir and cover. Let tomatoes marinate for at least 24 hours.

Marinated tomatoes keep for several months. They may be stored for a longer period in the refrigerator, but bring to room temperature before serving.

Red Curry Sauce

A great sauce on rice, tofu, chicken or shrimp and a wonderful dipping sauce for fresh vegetables. The natural sour flavor of tamarind, or garcinia, helps promote digestion, increases metabolism and suppresses the appetite. Research shows tamarind shifts calories from fat to glycogen, which we use for energy.

Makes 1½ cups

1–2 dried red chiles (arbol or cayenne)
⅓ cup chopped peanuts or walnuts

1½ cups unsweetened coconut or soy milk
1 teaspoon tamarind paste
2 tablespoons tamari or fish sauce

In a small skillet, toast chiles over high heat until fragrant, about 30 seconds per side. Cool. Finely chop with some of the seeds.

Using the same skillet, roast nuts, stirring over medium high heat until aromatic and lightly browned, about 5 minutes. Set aside to cool.

In a small saucepan, combine roasted chiles and coconut milk and bring to a boil over low heat. Stir in tamarind paste and tamari sauce and cook for 1 minute. Remove from heat and stir in peanuts.

Note: *The sauce is thin but very tasty. It's even good with a baked potato!*

Miso Sauce

Miso, made by fermenting soybeans, rice, salt, water and koji (a live culture which breaks down soybeans), is a great source of protein. Miso contains all eight essential amino acids and nine nonessential aminos. Fermentation makes it easy to digest and supplies beneficial microflora. Miso is high in B vitamins, too. However, miso is high in sodium. If you are on a salt-free diet, it's not for you.

Stir a spoonful of miso into soups or sauces as an excellent flavor booster or bouillon base. Miso, aged from several months to several years, is light or dark. The darker and redder varieties are aged longer and are stronger and saltier. Here's a simple miso sauce to serve over vegetables or grains.

Makes about a cup

1 tablespoon miso soybean paste
5 tablespoons tahini
1 cup water

1 teaspoon grated orange peel,
optional

Mix together miso, tahini and water in a small saucepan. Stir over low heat for 15 minutes. Remove from heat and stir in orange peel, if desired.

Variation: *Adding garlic to the sauce is always good!*

Apple Butter

You can make peach or nectarine butter the same way—just choose a different juice and use allspice instead of cinnamon. To make pear butter, substitute nutmeg for cinnamon.

Makes about 2 cups

1 orange
1 lemon
1 pound apples, unpeeled, halved, cored and chopped

1 cup apple cider or juice
1 tablespoon honey
¼ teaspoon cinnamon

Juice orange and lemon. Combine with rest of ingredients in a large saucepan. Bring to a near-boil, lower heat, cover pot and simmer for 15 minutes.

Uncover pot and continue to simmer over low heat until mixture is thick and most of the liquid has evaporated. This takes a good half hour. Stir occasionally during the last 15 minutes to prevent mixture from sticking to the pot and burning.

Remove pot from heat and let cool. Using the steel blade of a food processor or blender, puree sauce. If you prefer your apple butter a little chunky, only use a few quick on/off turns of the processor.

Cool and store in fridge.

Note: *Apple butter will keep for about a week, but if you want to make a big batch, you may freeze it and have it on hand.*

Apricot Cranberry Compote

This compote is spiced with ginger, which contains a substance called gingerol said to help prevent strokes. No matter that they say all sweeteners are alike—honey is a healer. It can be used to heal wounds and sore throats, and germs don't grow in honey.

Makes about 3 cups

1 cup dried apricots	½ cup apple or apricot juice
1 cup cranberries	½ cup honey
1 apple, unpeeled, halved, cored and diced	2 teaspoons minced fresh ginger
	pinch cinnamon, *optional*

Using a cleaver or the steel blade of a food processor, coarsely chop apricots, cranberries and apple. Transfer to a saucepan. Add juice, honey and ginger. Bring mixture to a near-boil. Turn down heat and simmer compote until slightly thick, about 10 minutes.

Remove pot from heat and transfer compote to a bowl. Add cinnamon, if you like, and refrigerate until cold at least an hour, or preferably overnight.

Use over pancakes, yogurt, ice cream or with a baked yam or winter squash.

Cranberry Applesauce

Cranberries add a tart flavor to applesauce that I love, and they make it more colorful. In addition, they're high in vitamin C and help prevent bladder infections.

Makes about 4 cups

2½ pounds tart apples, peeled, cored and sliced
1½ cups cranberries, washed
¼ cup unsweetened apple juice
¼ to ½ cup orange blossom or clover honey (depending on sweetness of apples)
1 teaspoon cinnamon

Combine all ingredients in a 2-quart saucepan and bring to a boil over medium heat. Stir, cover pot and simmer for 15 minutes.

Remove pot from heat and stir with a wooden spoon until desired consistency. If you like your applesauce really smooth, blend it using the steel blade of a food processor or a blender.

Return applesauce to pot and simmer over medium-low heat, uncovered, until mixture thickens, about 5 minutes.

Taste and add more honey, if desired.

Variations: Use orange juice or pineapple juice. Or add finely cut pineapple. Change quantities of cranberries or apples to suit taste. More cranberries make a darker, tarter sauce.

Note: When you can get your hands on organic cranberries, freeze them whole and unwashed. Then you can chop while still frozen for muffins, breads, pancakes—whatever.

Debra's Famous Cold Remedy

Honey coats the throat, cayenne warms and soothes and horseradish gets things moving! (Cayenne pepper is rich in vitamin C—higher even than orange juice.) So stop laughing and mix some up today when you're feeling healthy. When you're sick, you won't feel like doing anything.

Readers of my first cookbook will testify to the effectiveness of this home remedy for sore, scratchy throats and nasal congestion. So if you missed it the first time, here it is again!

Makes enough for the whole family

1 cup raw honey
1–2 tablespoons cayenne pepper

1–2 tablespoons prepared horse-radish with vinegar

Place honey in a glass jar. Add pepper and horseradish. Stir well until liquidy.

Store in refrigerator until you feel something coming on or have a sore throat. Take a 1/16-teaspoon dose, or just a tiny dot, as needed.

Variation: Add 1 tablespoon or more grated fresh ginger.

Inner Cleansing

Fasting is one of the oldest therapeutic methods known to humanity, and many cultures use fasting to improve health. It takes energy to process what we eat, so when we don't eat, the body is able to concentrate on dealing with food allergies or fighting illness. Fasting gives our most overworked and overtaxed organ, the liver, a chance to rest and do its job better.

The liver's health largely determines the health of the whole body because it's the liver, our protector, that filters and rids the bloodstream of toxins and bacterial wastes. The liver helps form red blood cells and is the major organ of metabolism for proteins, fats and carbohydrates. It has a harder job these days because we eat more calories, fats, sugars and alcohol than ever before, and we are exposed to an ever-increasing amount of environmental toxins, all of which the liver has to process. Naturopathic physicians believe low energy, poor digestion, allergies, constipation, age spots, headaches or hair problems can all be attributed to slight liver damage.

Although fasting is a great way to detox, it's hard to do while you work and have families to take care of. Fasting with a support group led by a naturopath is always a good idea. If you have time to slow down and fast, you might want to try the following for 3 days only:

1. **On rising:** Take 2 tablespoons cider vinegar in water with 1 teaspoon honey or 2 tablespoons fresh lemon juice in water. (A good lifetime habit, by the way.)
2. **Breakfast:** Potassium broth such as Bragg's Liquid Aminos in water, glass of freshly juiced carrot/beet/cucumber juice or organic apple juice.
3. **Midmorning:** Green drink with water. (Examples are chlorella, spirulina, liquid chlorophyll or freshly made juice like cucumber/parsley/celery/alfalfa.
4. **Lunch:** Glass of organic apple juice and/or fresh carrot juice.
5. **Midafternoon:** Cup of peppermint tea and/or green drink.
6. **Dinner:** Glass of organic apple juice and/or another potassium broth.
7. **Before bed:** Take 2 tablespoons lemon juice or cider vinegar in water with 1 teaspoon honey or royal jelly.

Drink 6–8 glasses of bottled or distilled water daily and get plenty of rest and sleep. Since this is an intense 3-day cleanse, you may experience headaches or unwellness if your system is full of toxins.

I find this fast too severe, so when I am stressed and want to make things easier for myself, I do the following once or twice a week: Start the morning with fresh lemon juice in water. Have as much of one kind of fruit as I want—4 apples, 3 bananas, 2 mangoes. For lunch, eat a big bowl of steamed brown rice with steamed vegetables on which I've squeezed the juice of a lemon and added a tablespoon or two of olive or flax seed oil. Optional, but recommended: sprinkle on seaweed and brewer's yeast. Repeat for dinner.

This modified fast allows me to eat, which I love, keeps my energy up, is easy on digestion and detoxes. I also drink herbal teas like ginger, "detox" or pau d'arco.

When you fast, the trick is not to return to eating ice cream every night! And don't ever break a fast with heavy or sweet food. Eat lightly for a few days—whole grains and vegetables—like the modified fast above. You might have a cup of miso soup and/or a hard-boiled egg or cup of yogurt as part of your daily routine. In the spring, greens make good liver tonics. Try alfalfa, dandelion, parsley, watercress or mesclun (a mix of baby bitter greens).

Again, don't try a fast of longer than a day or two if you are inexperienced. Don't fast if you are pregnant, nursing or in a weak or debilitated state.

Luscious Face and Body Cream

This makes a rich, wonderful face and body cream. But a little goes a long way. Although the cream seems oily, it soaks in within minutes and makes you feel silky soft! This is terrific food for your bod.

Makes about 2 cups

Group 1
¾ **cup apricot, almond, avocado**
  or grapeseed oil
⅓ **cup coconut oil or cocoa**
  butter
1 teaspoon liquid lanolin
½ **ounce beeswax**

Group 2
⅔ **cup boiled water, cooled**
⅓ **cup aloe vera gel**
few drops of essential oil of
  choice
few drops vitamin E oil

Melt group 1 over low heat in a double boiler. Pour into a measuring cup and cool slightly; you want mixture to be of pouring consistency. Oils become thick, creamy and solid at room temperature.

Place group 2 in a blender and blend at highest speed for 10 seconds. Then drizzle (just like making mayonnaise) group 1 into center vortex. Keep pouring slowly until the blender makes a spluttering or coughing sound. Like magic, you'll have a beautiful thick cream that looks just like the most expensive department store offerings.

Using a rubber spatula, scoop out into small glass jars. Refrigerate all but one, which can be stored in your medicine cabinet.

The blender will be tough to clean. Use your hands and lavish the cream over every portion of your face and body.

Strawberry Toning Mask

Here are some more fun natural beauty treats for your skin.

Makes less than a cup

**½ cup freshly squeezed straw-
berry juice**

**1 soupspoon liquid lanolin
1 soupspoon oatmeal flour**

To make the strawberry juice, use about a cup of freshly picked strawberries. Wash carefully and shake off excess water. Crush berries through cheesecloth into a cup.

Heat the lanolin in a small glass or enamel saucepan placed in a pan of hot water or double boiler over a low flame. When the lanolin melts, add the oatmeal flour. (You can buy oatmeal flour or just blend some oatmeal. Not only are the oats nourishing, they exfoliate the skin as well.) Stir until dissolved and well-blended.

Mix in the strawberry juice and beat with a fork or whisk until creamy before removing from the heat. Cool and store in a clean jar with a lid. Refrigerate if not used in a few days.

Apply gently to clean skin. Leave on for 30 minutes or so. Rinse off with warm water. Refrigerate when not in use.

Note: *Liquid lanolin is wonderful to use and can be found in natural food stores. One brand is Home Health.*

Apricot Cleansing Cream

**4 tablespoons apricot oil
2 tablespoons melted sweet butter**

**2 tablespoons sesame seed oil
1 tablespoon purified water**

Beat all the ingredients with an egg beater until completely blended. Pour into a lidded jar and use nightly as a cleansing cream. It helps soften and maintain the skin.

Milk Facial

Our skin is often blemished due to pollution, chemicalized cosmetics or many other factors. A milk facial will help clear blemishes. Just make sure your milk is the "real" thing—no synthetic bovine growth hormone—and make sure you use a good raw honey.

either 1 egg yolk, beaten (for dry
   skin)
or 1 egg white, beaten (for oily
   skin)

1 tablespoon milk
1 tablespoon honey

Blend ingredients. Apply the concoction to your face. Rub in gently but thoroughly. Then lie down for 30 minutes. Rinse off with tepid water. Does the rosy glow come from the 30-minute rest or the cream?!

Cocoa Butter Cream for the Throat

An excellent cream for a dry, crepey throat. Best results come when you wash the throat area and quickly apply a thin coating of the cream while the skin is still moist.

2 tablespoons cocoa butter
2 tablespoons liquid lanolin

4 tablespoons safflower oil

Measure all ingredients into a nonmetallic pot and heat over boiling water to a liquid state, or about a minute. Stir thoroughly to blend and pour into a small jar to keep.

Top Twelve Roundup

Here from our December 1995 store newsletter are a list of our 12 favorite foods for keeping healthy, wealthy and wise! Brew yourself a cup of green tea, pull up a chair and read.

1. **Almonds:** An Australian study found men with normal cholesterol who ate 3 ounces of almonds a day for 3 weeks cut their total cholesterol by 7 percent and bad/LDL cholesterol by 10 percent. Cancer clinics around the world recommend 10 almonds per day. One fifth of an almond's weight is protein, and its oil is among the most nutritious of all nut oils. Almonds are also rich in antioxidant vitamin E.
2. **Bee pollen and royal jelly:** Bee products are a complete protein because they have all the amino acids we need. Athletes count on bee foods for endurance and stamina. They contain hydroxydescanoic acid which kills *E. coli* and salmonella bacteria, they exert a radioprotective effect, and raw honey can be used topically to help heal wounds and minimize wrinkles. Royal jelly refreshes the skin, delays aging, slows the deterioration of collagen and contributes to quicker thinking and better memory by stimulating the circulatory system.
3. **Blackstrap molasses:** Anyone who's talked to me has heard me mention molasses. A half a cup contains 733 mg of usable calcium and lots of iron! Try a tablespoonful daily to cure what ails you.
4. **Green tea:** This tea contains polyphenol catechins, an antioxidant which protects us against the effects of radiation. Drinking green tea is said to lower cholesterol, reduce blood pressure and blood platelet stickiness, thus inhibiting arteriosclerosis. As an antiviral agent, green tea extract is being used to fight HIV. Try it to help fight the flu.
5. **Hot peppers:** Hot peppers contain capsaicin, which prevents carcinogens from binding to DNA. Perhaps, raw oysters and clams are always offered with hot sauce because hot peppers kill harmful bacteria! Putting hot sauce on food also speeds up metabolism and improves digestion. Peppers do not harm stomach lining or promote ulcers. Capsaicin compounds are now used in cream products that treat pain associated with postherpetic neuralgia and herpes zoster, an affliction of the nervous system.
6. **Kale:** The Center for Science in the Public Interest rated kale number one among vegetables in terms of total nutrients. Kale is called

"The King of Calcium" and, like other members of the cruciferous family, helps prevent cancer. It also contains phytonutrients which help regulate estrogen.

7. **Garlic:** While garlic was used in ancient Egypt to build strength, today we know garlic lowers serum cholesterol and blood pressure and helps prevent heart attacks and strokes. It appears to lift mood and is a good cold medication.

8. **Seaweed like kelp and dulse:** Seaweeds are nutrient-rich, yet low in calories, rich in iodine and high in protein. Dulse contains all 43 trace minerals. All sea vegetables are important for skin and hair. Researchers have found that sea vegetables remove radiation from the body and act as decontaminators. They are used in Japan to fight against leukemia and breast cancer. Kelp also kills the herpes virus. Toss into soups, stews and casseroles.

9. **Shiitake mushrooms:** Rated number one on an ancient Chinese list of superior medicines and touted as a substance that promotes eternal youth and longevity, shiitakes contain a virus that produces interferon, which fights cancer. They are used to treat hepatitis B and cirrhosis and work particularly well at healing the liver.

10. **Soy foods:** Breast and prostate cancer are low among the Japanese. Studies say soy products are the reason. Tests show soy products also lower blood cholesterol and seem to deter and help dissolve kidney stones. You can get varying amounts of the benefits of soy from soy milk, tofu, tempeh, miso, soy grits, soy oil, tamari and soy flour.

11. **Sweet potatoes and yams:** "If you want a good jolt of beta carotene, the substance that seems to protect against heart disease and cancer, simply eat sweet potatoes," says Jean Carper in *Food: Your Miracle Medicine.* They're also number two on the Center for Science in the Public Interest's "best veggie" list. They provide lots of fiber and are easy for the body to digest when you're stressed. Try a couple of baked sweets for breakfast!

12. **Tahini and sesame seeds:** Sesame products are eaten in some cultures in place of dairy products because of their high calcium content. In fact, calcium from sesame seeds is more easily used by our bodies than calcium from milk. And a higher percentage of the calcium contained in sesame seeds actually works for us. Eaten for thousands of years, sesame seeds were believed to possess magical properties and they contain sesamol, which fights rancidity. A powerhouse of nutrition!

Of course, there are lots of other great foods we love and foods that we all know need to be a part of our diets. We hope the above list reminds you of a food you've meant to try or to introduce into your diet on a more regular basis.

Index